Can I Bring
My Own Gun?

For Linda & Alex

Can I Bring My Own Gun?

Seth Freedman

Five Leaves

Can I Bring My Own Gun?
by Seth Freedman

Published in 2009 by Five Leaves,
PO Box 8786, Nottingham NG1 9AW
www.fiveleaves.co.uk
ISBN: 978 1 905512 64 5
Copyright © Seth Freedman, 2009
Cover photograph © Seth Freedman

This book is published in association with Guardian Books. Guardian
Books is an imprint of Guardian News & Media Limited. The
Guardian is a registered trademark of Guardian Media Group plc.

guardianbooks

Five Leaves acknowledges financial support
from Arts Council England

Five Leaves is a member of Inpress
(www.inpressbooks.co.uk),
representing independent publishers
Cover design: Darius Hinks
Typesetting and design: Four Sheets
Printed in Great Britain

Foreword

Former IDF Soldier: 'Occupation Breeds Terror' screamed the headline. My eyes scanned the article, an increasing sense of bewilderment enveloping me the further down the page I got. "I continually wonder at the clear-eyed, urgent, incisive and powerfully argued [articles] that Seth Freedman writes for the *Guardian*," it read. "Today, he's published another called Occupation Breeds Terror. Seth brings the perspective of a former IDF[1] soldier who now realizes the futility of his service and the futility of Occupation. He is a British Jew who made *aliya*[2] and served out of a sense of duty to his adopted country. Gradually, it has dawned on him that new thinking will be required from both sides to achieve real peace. We need more of Seth's humanity and decency."

Seeing my articles dissected by readers and disseminated around the world was nothing new; this was late November 2007, almost a year since I had begun writing for the *Guardian*. From the off, my pieces had attracted praise and criticism in equal measure, gushing forth in a never-ending stream of back-slapping or indignant anger, and this latest response was no different.

I was continually drawn back to the short, sharp headline at the top of the page, which – in six carefully chosen words – delivered me the bluntest notice yet as to how far I'd journeyed from the man I was when I first moved to Israel three years earlier. *Former IDF Soldier: 'Occupation Breeds Terror.'* I read it over and over, a half-smile, half-grimace spreading across my face as I considered the implications of what it said about me and my relationship to my adopted country.

A decade earlier, I'd have been baying for the blood of any Israeli soldier who'd performed such an abrupt *volte*

5

face in public and questioned the actions of the IDF's high command. A decade earlier, I'd have mocked and scorned any commentator, Israeli or otherwise, who advocated taking Israel's foot off the Palestinians' neck and giving them the chance to prove that they could talk a language other than terror. A decade earlier, the best solution I could come up with in my school's sixth form magazine was light years away from the thinking of my seasoned, post-army self:

"...For every terrorist attack, retribution must occur in the form of 'an eye for an eye, a tooth for a tooth', as it is written in the Torah. Execution of known terrorists would soon have the Arabs where they belong – begging the Israelis for compassion, not demanding land so [that] they stop killing Jews..."

A week is a long time in politics; ten years is an eternity in the life of a wide-eyed immigrant to the Holy Land. From the bars and clubs of the West End to the checkpoints and settlements of the West Bank, the journey I have made since arriving in Israel has been an intense one of discovery, of myself and of my new country. At the same time, thanks to my platform in the *Guardian*, it has also been a public voyage, in which my every emotional reaction and stage of political maturity has been pored over and analysed by my army of readers.

Inspired by their criticism as much as by their support, I have forced myself into the most uncomfortable of situations, confronting the ugly and brutal side of the Israeli Occupation that I once was proud to assist in during my time in uniform. From the neglected Bedouin tribes of the Negev, to the oppressed Palestinian villagers of the Hebron Hills and beyond, I have chronicled hundreds of stories from the conflict, as well as my own reaction to them as a fully-fledged Israeli citizen. In doing so, I have found that my views, beliefs and prejudices have shifted significantly.

The politics I support today are far removed from those that drove me to migrate to Israel in 2004, and the reasons I have modified my stance so dramatically can be

6

found in the diaries and articles I have written through-out the past three years. My status as a holder of both British and Israeli passports means that I have had unfettered access to both sides of the divide, gaining access to Israeli settlements and outposts just as easily as I cross into cities under PA (Palestinian Authority) rule, which Israelis are banned from entering.

As such, I have had my eyes opened to the horrific con-ditions of the refugee camps of Jenin and Bethlehem, and have also been exposed to the extreme right wing rhetoric of hilltop settlers who spoke to me as a fellow Jew, hold-ing nothing back as they spouted their messages of hate. All of this has had a profound impact on me, and has left me a much-changed man from the one I was when I first set out for Israel.

At the same time, I am by no means alone amongst my generation of *olim* (immigrants) to Israel. Many of my peers have gone through similar processes of self-realisa-tion concerning the country they have chosen to call home, and this is greatly to Israel's benefit in terms of those who can have an impact on the future of this fledg-ling country. By exposing ourselves to the raw reality of the conflict, through first-hand experiences – whether in military or civilian frameworks – we better understand the complexities of the region, and are better armed to approach the precarious situation.

***

If you spend a summer traversing South America in the blazing sunshine, chances are that by the time autumn comes around, you'll be sporting a tan several shades darker than when you began your trip. However, since the bronzing of your skin occurs gradually over a period of time, you might well not notice how brown you've become until it's pointed out by a shocked friend upon your return home from your travels. So it is too with undertaking the kind of political journey upon which I've embarked. On a day to day basis, it barely occurred to me how far I'd come from the rhetoric and rationale that I employed when I first moved to Israel to serve in the army. It took moments such as reading *Former IDF Soldier: 'Occupation Breeds Terror'* to show me how my 'tan' appeared from the outside.

Hence the half-smile, half-grimace. The grimace, because I couldn't help but think what my former self would have made of it all; the smile, for essentially the same reason. I served, I saw, I conquered my prejudices – and my political evolution was the result. Almost two hundred articles in, I have been nothing if not honest in my continual reassessment of my position, and when a respected political commentator writes: "We need more of Seth's humanity and decency", it's worth a thousand sneering accusations of being a "Self-hating Jew".

In this book, I hope to shed light on the way in which a British-born, observant Jew can set foot in Israel, starry-eyed and believing that the best way to assist his country is to enlist in the IDF, and then – upon coming out the other side of fifteen months in combat – realise that he couldn't have been more wrong. What began as a tentative dipping of a toe into the choppy waters of the Middle East has become a three-year long headfirst dive into the political whirlpool that engulfs the region, and this book chronicles every stroke and kick that has led me to this point – from the inauspicious beginnings in the lower echelons of the IDF:

> *Yael and I sensibly curtailed our afternoon drinking on the beach, as it would have been pretty poor form to turn up drunk to my first* Mahal *meeting. We walked back to the hotel, got changed, and then took a taxi to Avi Naor's office near Arlozorov in time for five o'clock.*
>
> *Walking through the doors and into reception, I practiced my thuggish scowl. I'd wet-shaved my head an hour earlier, and my Bulgari sunglasses provided the perfect cover for me to scope out my fellow recruits. Yael walked alongside me, holding onto my arm to show any competi-*

tion that I was already taken. She needn't have bothered, since all but two of those present were boys, and the lone pair of girls looked tougher than most of the males present – which made sense, I supposed. The only girls likely to volunteer for combat wouldn't be of the painted-nails-and-stiletto-heels variety.

We sat down, and I began talking to the boy next to me. American (naturally), he seemed a bit preppy compared to what I'd expected of my co-volunteers, but then I supposed that, sans shaved head, I wasn't that different either. None of us were going to be Navy Seal types, else we'd have enlisted in our home countries the minute we turned eighteen, and we must have all come from well-off backgrounds to have been able to afford to take the time out to serve for the next fifteen months. He was brimming with questions about the army, whereas for my part I was happy to sit back, let the others do the talking, and let it all wash over me. After all, what could I possibly need to know? I expected the army to provide for my every need, tell me exactly where to be and when, and to not have to think for myself till at least 2006.

Once the meeting started, Avi was peppered with questions shot at Gatling-gun speed. "How much will we earn?", "How much time off do we get?", "Can our friends visit us on base?" – and so it went on, for a good hour and a half. Yael was paying far more attention than me, even taking notes, and I slouched lower and lower in my chair as the Americans droned on and on. Just as it looked as though the session would run over into Happy Hour at the beach bars, Avi decided it was time to wind up proceedings. "OK, that's probably all we have time for," he announced. "Does anyone have one last question for me, before we go?"

A silence descended over the room. Who was going to take on the responsibility of asking the "final question", which had better be good, since it was the last one that was going to be asked before we turned up at base in a couple of weeks' time? Slowly, a hand was raised by one of the boys off to the side of the group. When Avi nodded his assent, he stood up, revealing himself to be a pudgy-looking stoner-type, clad in backward-baseball cap and baggy football shirt. Speaking in a slow, Texas drawl, he began with a disclaimer. "I know this may sound like a bit of a stupid question, y'all," he apologised, before turning to Avi, "but can I bring my own gun...?"

9

The place erupted, except for our dazed friend who'd asked the question, who still looked expectantly at Avi for an answer. For my part, it dawned on me what a bunch of chancers we all were. None of us had the slightest clue what we were letting ourselves in for, nor did we have any older siblings who'd served to guide us through it – for heaven's sake, we were even stuck with a boy who thought he could bring his own weapons from home... Avi gently explained that no, the army preferred to provide the machine guns themselves, but his voice was drowned out by the peals of laughter still ringing out. As for me, I took it as my cue to depart. Yael and I slipped out of the building and back into the warm Tel Aviv night. We headed straight for the beach, where the festivities resumed in earnest, safe in the knowledge that however clueless I might be about the army, at least I was in good company. And, for better or worse, these same people would be the ones I entrusted with my life for the next year and three months. Lucky I'd written a will already, really...

---

[1] Israeli Defense Forces

[2] Literally "ascent" – immigration to Israel

Introduction

Night fell over the village, though it made no difference to us lying slumped against the walls of the nagmash (APC – armoured personnel carrier). Ten of us crammed into a space not much bigger than a double bed, paying for Shai's poor driving by getting flung around the interior every time we hit a boulder in the road. We shared the space with the remains of our lunch, as well as tomorrow's breakfast, but – in the heat – we'd have been lucky if it hadn't decomposed by the time we got round to eating it. The sweat pouring off our heads and down our faces was black with dirt, and everyone's shirts were stuck fast to their backs. A wet t-shirt contest, but without the girls – and Gabe looked like being the winner. He resembled a melting snowman, and only the fact that he moaned quietly from time to time stopped me thinking he'd passed out in the back.

Occasionally, I'd muster the energy to stand up and crane my neck towards the small panes of bulletproof glass at the top of the nagmash, so I could get my bearings – but it was a waste of time. The windows were far too thick to see anything clearly, and what I could see appeared to be yet more and more winding country lanes. We'd been through the town centre once, and now seemed to be circling the deserted backstreets over and over.

The sun might have gone down, but it was still as hot as an oven. The roar of the engine showed no sign of abating. Having been stuck in this cauldron for fifteen hours, I couldn't have cared less by this point whether we caught the terrorists or not – I was up for calling it a draw, and arranging a replay for two weeks' time.

11

Not so our beloved Mem-Mem (platoon commander). He stood up at the front of the nagmash, like the figurehead at the bow of a ship, urging Shai to drive ever onwards towards God knew what. The Mem-Mem manned the Mag machine gun mounted on the roof, swiveling it in the direction of any unfortunate who was sharing the cobbled roads with our mini-tank. Eventually, we noticed that we were slowing down. It sounded as though we were now driving off-road, which was usually a sign that we were looking for a place to park up and rest.

Perking up momentarily, we debated whether this was a five minute leg-stretching pit stop or the couple of hours sleep we'd been promised. It turned out to be the latter – and we piled out of the back door and surveyed our surroundings. We seemed to be in the back garden of a mansion-sized house on a residential backstreet – and the owner's family was peering at us from the porch with a mixture of bemusement and disgust.

We took positions – everyone covering one another, guns locked and loaded, as we edged forward towards the house on the orders of the Mem-Mem. The squad from the other nagmash were also here, approaching from the other side of the garden, and we were now twenty-strong as we descended on the impromptu-hotel we were going to commandeer for the night.

The Mem-Mem delivered curt instructions in Arabic to the various family members sitting on chairs on the veranda. From the way they shot out of their seats, it was plain he hadn't gone overboard on the charm. Taking Matan with him, he disappeared inside the house and set about locking the family in the basement, before letting the remainder of us in to search the rest of the building. Once we'd declared it clear, we all gathered in the lounge to receive our orders. We were to guard in pairs, everyone doing twenty minute shifts over the next four hours while the others slept. We stripped off our shirts, rolled them up as pillows, and crashed out on the tiled floor of the living room.

We were under strict orders not to touch anything in the house; not even to use the bathrooms to wash up in. The place was a proper palace, compared with some of the shacks we'd been used to searching – it turned out that we always take over big houses, in order to avoid embarrassing poorer folk who would be ashamed of their meagre possessions. Either way, it still felt like we were taking liberties, half-naked and sprawled out all over the floor of this family's lounge.

But, as they always told us, business is business. I could hardly argue; this was a round-the-clock mission, and we could hardly drive all the way back to our side of the border every time we needed to sleep. Also, we couldn't sleep in the nagmashim, as it would make us sitting targets to any RPG-toting enemies who might fancy their chances. However, the fact that we kept the family locked in the house with us – rather than sending them to neighbours – was a bit suspect. It smacked of human shields, if you asked me – but, then again, no one was seeking my opinion. So I just passed out and went to sleep.

During my shift, I quizzed Yaron as to the family's whereabouts. "They're down there," he grunted, using his M16 to point at the locked door of the basement. Which was pretty sobering – an entire family, herded into their own cellar so that their enemy's troops could grab a few hours' sleep. I knew what I'd have thought if a group of squaddies had pulled that one on my family. Necessary or not, there was no way we were winning the peace with this particular clan – but we weren't here to make friends, I supposed. Either way, for the proud father of the household to have to kowtow to a gang of eighteen year old IDF soldiers must have left a lasting impression on his offspring. And no doubt fuelled the next generation of hatred and resentment.

***

As I watched the second *Intifada* unfold on the television news from the comfort of my London home, I felt the piercing stare of an Israeli Lord Kitchener penetrate the veneer of contentment behind which I dwelt. My country needed me, I knew, and with every bus that exploded in Jerusalem and Tel Aviv, the feeling that I should be playing my part in defending my people from the murderous militants who strove to destroy them grew stronger.

I had always had a natural affinity for Israel, born out of both religious affiliation to the land of my forefathers and a more personal attachment to the modern-day Jewish state. Twice-yearly childhood holidays and a hedonistic gap-year spent travelling the country had cemented Israel firmly in my heart, and watching impotently from the sidelines as the country went up in flames during 2002 was not an option I could bear much longer.

I'd been at school with plenty of ex-pat Israelis, many of whose elder siblings had already done their three years national service. I had cousins in Israel too, including one whose husband was an air-force colonel and came from a distinguished military family. I'd always been envious of those who had the chance to don uniform in defence of the country, whilst the best we could do back home was send the BBC angry emails attacking their reporting on the Middle East.

Watching "The Jenin Diaries" in the cinema – a shot-on-location film of an IDF unit during Operation Defensive Shield – I began to formulate a plan. A bit of research on the internet revealed that the Israeli army took foreign volunteers into their combat regiments, which left me with mixed feelings. I'd always hated guns and violence, thanks to my upbringing in a CND-activist, liberal household, and I had no real desire to go through the rigours of basic training for eight months. However, I was propelled past those reservations by the feeling that I too could 'do something' for my people, linking me historically to the warriors of King David's army and all who came in between.

And so it was that, in November 2004, I found myself in a barracks on the outskirts of Tel Aviv, struggling to pull on eight-holed combat boots and staring wide-eyed at my olive-clad reflection in the mirror of a spartan army changing-room. Within a matter of months, I would be on my first tour of duty in the heart of the West Bank, just another foot-soldier in the regiments of Israeli infantry, doing my damnedest to convince myself that this was the only way to ensure the survival of the Jewish people in their minuscule Mediterranean refuge.

***

Speaking in the wake of the London bombings in 2005, Ken Livingstone declared:

> If a young Jewish boy in this country goes and joins the Israeli army, and ends up killing many Palestinians, that is wholly legitimate. But for a young Muslim boy in this country, who might think 'I want to defend my Palestinian brothers and sisters' and gets involved, he is branded as a terrorist.

At that point, I was a fully-fledged combat soldier, having completed eight gruelling months of basic and advanced training in the heat of the Negev desert. I'd been almost a year out of London, by which time London had been as good as taken out of the boy. I was as at home with my M16 slung over my shoulder as I ever had been with my laptop case swinging behind me as I strolled through the streets of Hampstead Garden Suburb. Watching the aftermath of the 7/7 carnage in my former home, I couldn't help but wonder if this was the wake-up call Londoners needed to see why Israelis behaved as they did in their own existential war on terror that they'd been embroiled in for decades.

However, whilst on the surface I was still happy to believe my commanders that the only way to defeat the militants who surrounded Israel was via a strategy of war and offence, the longer I spent on active duty, the more the cracks started to appear in that line of argument. During training, all of the indoctrination went unchallenged by us rookies since it was merely theoretical; shooting cardboard terrorists and staging raids on mock-up Palestinian houses was akin to carrying out controlled experiments in secondary school chemistry laboratories. But when it came to manning checkpoints in Bethlehem, or bursting into family homes in villages on the outskirts of Tulkarm, suddenly there was a far deeper, far more real element thrown into the fray: that of the Palestinians themselves.

Our first placement after graduating training was guarding Rachel's Tomb, a site of pilgrimage for Jews, situated on the edge of the Al-Aida refugee camp in Bethlehem. At that point, the Bethlehem stretch of the security wall was still unfinished, which meant extra troops were required to provide protection to the thousands of visitors who thronged daily to the site. We rode the bullet-proof buses from the checkpoint to the Tomb, as much to calm the nerves of the tourists as to provide any practical assistance. Rock-throwing youths dispersed long before we could dismount the buses and give chase, and the shatterproof glass in the windows was sufficient to repel the sporadic attacks.

We were required, however, to carry out regular patrols of the Muslim cemetery behind the Tomb, as well as the narrow alleys of the refugee camp, where our presence did nothing to abate the tension that was palpable on every street corner. Decked out in full combat gear, with words of encouragement from the pilgrims ringing in our ears as we left the Tomb, we would march towards Al-Aida and straight into a scene from CNN. A teeming refugee camp, piles of rubble everywhere, Arab men lounging on half-built walls, and us: six heavily armed Israeli soldiers.

On one, roasting hot, summer's day during a routine patrol the inevitable happened – a group of youths, screaming "Allahu Akhbar", greeted us with a hail of stones, and we took cover behind a nearby building. The *Samal* (sergeant) explained that he and his partner Shtricks would hide behind a wall while the other four of us walked in a snake-like formation in view of the youths. The aim was to draw another barrage of rocks, at which point the *Samal* would arrest one or two; it was too easy, and on the second time of our walking, their throwing, our retreating, the *Samal* leapt out and slammed one boy up against the wall, grabbing him by the neck. A typical, scruffily dressed, sullen boy of maybe fourteen; the *Samal* asked us if he'd been one of the stone throwers. I said yes, without being one hundred percent sure – it hardly mattered, since the objective was to make a point to his friends.

We marched him up to our base, with one dodgy moment as a group of 25-year old men ran shouting towards us; we trained our guns on them and made them back off. With the boy made to walk between Shtricks and the *Samal*, we delivered him to the *Samech Mem Pay* (vice-squadron commander). It was our first unplanned arrest (i.e. not on a raid) so everyone swarmed around the kid like he was a rare butterfly we'd netted. The boy was made to sit in the sun against a wall, and threw the cup of water he was offered all over the *Samech Mem Pay*, as he cursed and shouted.

During his time in detention, another soldier asked me if we'd beaten him – "no" – and the *Samal* was off on a roll. He was acting unnecessarily proud – strutting around and beaming gleefully – considering he'd only nabbed a teenager, with five armed soldiers behind him as back up. He staged a graphic demonstration of how he'd grabbed the boy for all who hadn't been there, all in full view of his captive. After about twenty minutes we marched him out to hand him over to his parents, who had been summoned to meet us at the end of the closed zone.

We met the parents for the handover, the father had to lift his shirt to prove he wasn't wearing a bomb belt before

17

we allowed him near us. That done, we returned inside – grudgingly, but the patrol was over. The debriefing was very interesting though; we sat in exactly the same positions back in the *Samal's* room – only one hour on, but older and wiser in the same sense as someone after their first sexual experience or first time experimenting with drugs. Yet here we were, dissecting the experience as though it was only another part of training – not as though we'd been in a very real, very dangerous situation that nearly became a riot when the men had descended on us from all directions after word of the arrest spread.

I peppered the *Samal* with questions: Was this really the best way to keep the peace and calm the tension? Did he think the kid would learn from this for good or bad? We disagreed completely. He maintained that the boy would learn his lesson for the good; I said that was wishful thinking – he was plainly a hero amongst his friends now. I stated that I felt the *Samal* was too proud of what we'd done; unsettlingly so, but he may have been trying to act that way because it was our first experience, and he wanted us to take pride in how we'd done.

Once the debriefing was over, we discussed what had happened amongst ourselves. Why did our being merely on patrol, not beating someone or damaging property, cause such violent reaction? Why did little kids who, until we went on patrol, had been playing with kites and footballs in the street, suddenly become mini-terrorists and invoke Allah's name as they tried to wound us? As we mulled over the cause and effect, it was clear that several of us weren't comfortable with our seemingly over-the-top and counterproductive reaction to the stone-throwing. The David-and-Goliath overtones of the situation were clear – and if they were obvious to us, we who were supposed to act like unquestioning automatons in the service of our country, then those on the other side of the divide would no doubt see it even clearer.

As the weeks wore on, and we spent more and more time dealing with the locals through the sights of our guns, it became increasingly apparent that we were never going to win over hearts and minds as long as our only contact with them came in a tense and violent atmosphere. Did we really have to bark curt instructions in Arabic to "stop or I'll shoot" at women approaching us on the checkpoint? Did we really have to drag a man out of his car at gunpoint with his son watching on, drinking in the whole sorry scene and indelibly imprinting it on his young mind? Was there another way; a way to engage with the Palestinians which wouldn't compromise our security, but at the same time wouldn't increase the animosity that they felt towards us – the faceless oppressors in helmets and flak jackets?

The final straw happened in two back-to-back stages, as far as my commitment to our methods of soldiering was concerned. The first was raiding the house near Tulkarm, which, in the context of war, was perfectly acceptable practice as far as our commanders were concerned. But not to me, when I saw the wide eyes of the families' children as we screamed at their father – their hero, their protector – and wrested from him the reins of power inside his own house. That was when it started to dawn on me just what kind of effect our actions were having on the next generation, who were guaranteed to end up hating us when all they saw was us herding them like cattle and imposing our will on them from a position of untouchable, untrammelled power.

A few days later, our unit was called upon to bolster the forces massed in Homesh, a West Bank settlement scheduled for evacuation during the "Disengagement" from Gaza and four West Bank settlements. Despite the threats of the settlers that they would fight to defend their homes from eviction, our commanders decided that we would ignore their incendiary words and deal with them without our weapons to protect us. This was, they said, in order to pour water on the fires of tension between the two camps, and was a far cry from the way we dealt with Palestinians who made similar threats to

19

our safety. I took this up with the *Mem-Mem*, asking whether, if this softly-softly approach was the best way to reduce the tension with one group of 'enemies', could it not be similarly useful in calming hostilities when dealing with the local Palestinians?

Of course, he was deaf to any protest on my part, assuring me that the Palestinians were different entirely, kid-glove treatment would be out of the question. In the event, settlers attacked and wounded dozens of soldiers, but the incidents were brushed under the carpet by the authorities, who were keen to paint the settlers as 'peaceful protestors' in comparison with their ever-violent, ever-aggressive Palestinian counterparts.

And so it continued: when posted to Bet Jalla, we would take part in raids on local schools, breaking up playground football matches to arrest teenage 'suspects' at gunpoint; when on the Lebanese border, we responded to news of 'infiltrators' by roaring up in convoys of Hummers in a show of force. There was only one way to deal with the Palestinians, the Lebanese, or any other non-Israelis – and that was by fighting fire with our own, vastly-superior, infernos.

By the time I was demobbed, I was convinced that by means of the occupation, and by means of the tacit support we provided the illegal settlement enterprise, we were never going to make any progress in convincing the Palestinians that we had even the merest shred of interest in peace. When in uniform, I was powerless to otherwise convince the Palestinians that I met, since they only saw the shrapnel-proof helmet, the loaded semi-automatic, and the grenades hanging from my combat vest. Similarly, I had no way of discovering for myself what they were like as people, rather than as potential security threats – which was the way the commanders wanted it, in order to prevent their charges 'going soft' in their defence of the state.

However, when I stole into Palestinian Authority territory for the first time – on an illegal foray into Bethlehem when on weekend furlough from the army – I finally saw life in the refugee camps and Palestinian towns for what it was: mundane, civil, and outwardly no different to life on the Israeli side of the border. Granted, there was clearly an undercurrent of support for the resistance, as was evident from the martyrs' posters that graced the walls and windows of countless backstreets, but was that really any different from the way in which we Israelis lionised and beatified our own valiant war heroes?

By virtue of a valid British passport, as well as a healthy dose of chutzpah, I could go where Israeli angels feared to tread, and the experience proved invaluable in terms of shedding the blinkers the army forced me to wear. "You can only oppress people if you've been conditioned to dehumanise them," a friend had told me at the start of my service, and he was right. The army couldn't have held such a grip on its soldiers, and by extension the Palestinians, if it allowed us to meet the men and women behind the stereotype. So, once I'd put my prejudices aside and gone to see the reality for myself, the blinkers were off; I could no longer pretend that everyone behind the wall was hell-bent on destroying Israel and all who dwelt within her borders.

The realisation was abrupt; the reaction violent. Upon leaving the bosom of the army, I set about seeing for myself what life was like on the other side of the security barrier. Jenin, Ramallah, Hebron, Nablus; I went wherever I could in search of the truth behind the propaganda, and what I saw chilled me. Everywhere I went, I saw suffering and humiliation, rage and fury that resulted from the subjugation under which the residents lived – in which, until a few months earlier, I had been willing to participate.

Nevertheless, the prism through which I viewed their plight and heard their words was still smeared with the bias of a lifetime of pro-Israel education; from my school-teachers, from my youth club leaders, from my army commanders, and from my peers with whom I socialised in West Jerusalem. However, through writing about my experiences for the *Guardian*, and reading the reaction of those reading my articles, I was exposed to the other side of the coin. The activists, aid workers, peaceniks and other individuals who I'd for so long dismissively scorned, played a huge part in the cathartic process which I underwent.

Upon re-reading Ken Livingstone's post-7/7 words, I was struck by the truth of his statement. Of course, in theory, choosing to take up arms in defence of Israel was a far cry from strapping on explosives and seeking to murder as many Israeli civilians as possible, but was there really such a difference? Not all IDF missions were motivated by peaceful intentions; similarly not all Palestinian resistance involved wanton slaughter of civilians. Israelis, and supporters of Israel, glorified those fighting for their interests, therefore it was hypocritical to demand that the Palestinians didn't similarly fête their own resistance fighters.

The more I banged my anti-occupation drum, the more I was confronted with the accusation that 'you don't know what you're talking about; you haven't been in the country long enough to realise how much they hate us'. But fifteen months in a combat unit more than qualified me to counter that claim. Rightly or wrongly, in order to be taken seriously in Israel, right- and left-wingers alike had to jump through certain hoops to prove they not only knew what they were talking about, but also that they were prepared to do their bit for the society in which they live. Despite my own reservations about where and how I served in the army, I was convinced that I was far better equipped to face my critics precisely because I had enlisted.

But that didn't mean having to don combat boots and maraud across the West Bank making the Palestinians' lives a misery, and that was a view shared by ever-increasing numbers of ex-combat soldiers in Israel. A study by Haifa University concluded that: "Over the course of their military service, combat soldiers become less right wing, adopt more dovish political views and are more open to compromise on security matters". Whilst it was easy for the armchair-warriors to urge Israel on to ever more combative lengths in their pursuit of regional dominance, for those who experienced first-hand the unpleasantness of occupation it was often a different story.

Three and a half-years after pulling on my boots and nervously handling my chrome-plated M16 for the first time, I still could not divorce myself entirely from the soldier I once had been. Whilst I abhorred the route down which Israel had gone in its drive to subjugate the Palestinians and maintain its military superiority, I was still convinced that serving in the army was the right thing to do, if only to prove my commitment to my adopted society. If I had had my time again, I would not have served over the Green Line, especially if it meant protecting the illegal and immoral rash of settlements in the area, but I would still have served within 'Israel proper', or else have done another form of voluntary national service.

Whilst foreign volunteers continued to flock to Israel to enlist, fight, and prolong the occupation under the guise of 'helping Israel', then – sadly – Ken Livingstone was right. The double standards applied were shocking; preaching a path of war on either side should have been condemned outright by all involved. Only then would those engaged in more peaceful efforts to resolve the conflict have been able to make their voices heard above the maelstrom. Only then would there be another way in which wannabe-soldiers, like myself, could fulfil their desire to 'do something' to protect 'their' country. And only then would there be a reason to believe that there was a viable alternative to another sixty years of war and aggression.

Of course, there was no denying that the Palestinians bore at least some share of responsibility for the

23

prolongation of the conflict. However – as became clearer and clearer, the more time I spent researching the situation for myself – to pretend that the hostilities were merely a case of mutual misunderstanding was untrue, and counterproductive. Regardless of the traumas suffered by the Jewish people throughout history, subjugating the Palestinians was unacceptable – and the Palestinians' reaction was understandable. Anyone who denied the validity of their pain and anguish was, in effect, denying the pain and anguish of downtrodden victims the world over – including, of course, that of the Jewish people themselves.

The longer the status quo is allowed to persist, the more Israelis are conditioned to believe that their government's oppressive policies are somehow acceptable, and the more Palestinians realise that the entire Zionist state apparatus would never take its foot off their collective windpipe. Whilst the key issues are merely skirted around by Israel and her supporters, rather than seriously addressed, the chances of peaceful resolution were slim to none. This much is clear to all observers, as was witnessed in the months after I left the army, with Hamas' ascent to power in the Occupied Territories, and the outbreak of war in the north.

Chapter One

"We're quite enjoying this... [the fact that] Jerusalem is the safest place to be in Israel at the moment. My cousins called from Haifa to say that they were planning to leave their home and come and stay with us for a while..."

Upon overhearing those words on the bus home, it occurred to me just how bizarre my world had become over the last week. The eye of the storm was indeed the calmest place to be, if the situation inside Jerusalem was anything to go by as tensions escalated on the northern border. To the outsider, Israel appeared to be a hotbed of tension and alarm, a sliver of land where worry and fear was etched onto the face of every civilian, every mother and father of a soldier, every veteran of past battles won and lost. However, in Jerusalem at least, it was anything but. I was feeling pretty blasé about the whole affair: the World Cup had captured my attention for the month of June, the Premiership wasn't due to restart until August, and so it seemed wonderfully timely that the anticipated July-long lull got filled by the latest Middle East war.

Because, truth be told, that was about as far as the current hostilities had impacted on my sun-bleached, palm-tree-shaded world. Of course I cared. Of course I followed the developments. Of course I mulled over events with my friends every time we talked, speculating on the whys and wherefores till the cows came home. But, of course, that was exactly how the armchair supporter watched football too. It was all a film. It was all entertainment. It was all so near, but yet so far.

Jerusalem, for once, was – as the woman on the bus so bluntly put it – not in the firing line, and that was hugely significant in terms of how I related to the unfolding war.

For all the Katyusha barrages, for all the dead and wounded up north, here in the capital the mood was no different today than it was a week ago. All it would take would be one bomb in a Ben Yehuda cafe, and the whole of the capital would be paralysed with fear – but, thank God, that hadn't happened. Yet. Thus, in my part of town, life went on as normal. We got up, went to work, played football in the park, drank in the bars, stumbled home and passed out, and did it all again the next day.

I watched the news round the clock – but then again I always did – whilst my disinterested and soap-addicted flatmate Nurit pouted and asked me to change the channel, which was pretty standard behaviour for the generation of Israeli youth with whom I mixed. They had all served in combat units for three years; they were all tired of living under constant threat; they all dreamt of Goa and Laos as the bombs fell.

Of course, I'd also served; I only got out in January, and my last tour was three months of serving on the same base that had been attacked by Hezbollah at the start of this battle. I'd watched soldiers cross into Lebanon via the same gates that we used to use when out on patrol. But it was still like a film to me. Unless I got called back up. Which could have happened, but I wasn't holding my breath. For a start, I was in regular infantry, and my only specialty was being part of a four-man 50-calibre machine gun team. Whereas Nurit was an APC driver; a skill far more useful and far more necessary for the present conflict.

So, call up aside, life went on. My circle of friends and I were too young to remember the wars of '67 and '73, so we didn't have anything with which to compare this latest battle. It was like the first time I ever abseiled: I wasn't scared at all, whereas the second time was far worse, since I had the memories, and therefore was more cautious and apprehensive about the dangers involved. Along with this naivety, I was also lazily complacent about our chances of "winning". I'd been brought up to believe that the Israelites always won really; from the days of the Romans all the way to the present wars with our Arab neighbours.

On top of all this, Jerusalem was the best place to be due to the "chessboard effect". As in a game of chess, where the first aim of defence is to surround the king with a few pawns and a rook, the security wall and the ring of soldiers around the capital had achieved the same thing. The conflict had by and large been pushed out to the edge of the board: down south (Sderot) and up north (Nahariya, Kiryat Shmona). That said, the fact that Haifa was now within range (and Tel Aviv too, according to some reports) was an alarming development – which was why left and right wingers alike were delighted with Israel's iron fist reaction to Hezbollah. All of which I saw via the prism of Sky News – it felt like watching Operation Desert Storm all over again; something to talk about, for sure, but nothing really to worry about.

Ten days later, and I found myself feeling somewhat more sombre, somewhat more morose, and somewhat less lackadaisical than I had been in my original reaction to the hostilities. A story was breaking about the shelling of a houseful of women and children in Qana. Initial reports were claiming dozens of wounded Lebanese and, as with any unfolding tragedy, the numbers rose steadily over the next few hours. By the time I'd had breakfast and was ready to leave the house, nearly thirty bodies had been brought out of the razed building, with the inevitable assertion being made by politicians around the world, that Israel had carried out a massacre of the innocents.

I was on my way to the *miluim* office, seeking to over-turn the reserve duty exemption granted to me and all of the foreign soldiers in my unit, because I felt like I should be volunteering now as I had done two years earlier. The last place that I wanted to be was in Lebanon, but I also felt it my duty to offer myself in the stead of another reservist with more commitments than me, such as a wife and family. Plus, with all the Israelis around me getting called up in droves, I felt like a kid in the school playground who was always last to be picked when the captains were choosing sides: "I wanna play too," I heard myself whine – but, in truth, I didn't really.

All weekend, I watched Nurit in tears as she said goodbye to her paratrooper friends, who had been called up for two days of training before heading straight across the border into South Lebanon. This was the start of the war encroaching into my world. Young Israelis who were regularly round at our house, suddenly called up to fight, leaving Nurit convinced she would likely not see all of them again. Which was heavy, heavy stuff – especially when I saw the tears in the boys' eyes, the real and raw fear, the rush of emotions as they spent their last hours of freedom trying to relax and pretend it wasn't happening.

I spoke to some of the boys with whom I served, and who were still in their three-year stint, and found that they were due to leave the relative safety of Jenin later in the week, heading off to the border to bolster the ground operations taking place. The chances were that not all of them would make it back. The chances were that I would be donning my green beret again at a military cemetery sometime soon. The chances were that this war could run and run.

The longer it went on, the worse it got for Israel. If Israel went after Hezbollah from the air, more Qanas would happen; more innocents would die. But If they didn't take aerial action, Hezbollah would keep shelling Israeli cities, keep killing civilians, and think that through violence, they could overcome Israel.

The killing in Qana brought out the worst in some people. The reaction from the EU's Javier Solana – that "there can be absolutely no excuse" for what happened – was reminiscent of Kofi Annan's shocking accusation that Israel intentionally targeted UN peacekeepers the week before. In both cases, the speed of the reaction and the unequivocal finger pointing did nothing to convince Israel that the EU and UN were in any way neutral in their dealings. How could Solana possibly know that nothing could or would justify the air strike? Israel later released footage showing Katyushas being launched from Qana, suggesting that Hezbollah deserved the blame for using civilians as human shields, but of course Solana needed something to say then and there – and chose to condemn, rather than weigh up the facts as they emerged. The lame-duck Lebanese prime minister also had strong words for the attack – "heinous crimes of the Israelis" – but the strength of his words had never been matched by his actions in reining in Hezbollah, so Israel owed him little.

I was concerned that it was only my connection to this country that had prevented me condemning some of our actions of late. If I had heard that Russian forces had blown up a building in Chechnya, killing twenty-eight people, I was sure that my first reaction would have been to blame the Russians rather than the Chechen separatists, so I could grudgingly accept why non-Israelis might have been quick to jump all over the IDF for the Qana assault.

Another interesting point about Qana was the absence of men amongst the dead and wounded. I heard it intimated on Sky News that the lack of men meant that their men were all Hezbollah fighters and those killed were their wives and children. Whilst what a child's father did for a living certainly did not permit the child being killed, it suggested that they were left there rather than evacuated from the town because of their cynical fathers, whose cause would be bolstered by a catastrophe such as this. All speculation, all presumption – but worthy of consideration nonetheless.

Another thought that stayed in my mind was that when the scale of the death and destruction became clear, the first reaction on the Lebanese street was to smash into and ransack the UN offices in Beirut. When cartoons offended the Muslim world earlier in the year, violent and deadly protests swept the Arab world. When Palestinian fighters were taken to be buried in Gaza, Kalashnikovs were fired into the air and curses rained down on Israel. All of which were depressing ways to deal with loss or upset, especially when contrasted with the tears and anguish, yet lack of violence and threats of revenge, at the average Israeli funeral. Were we really the hotheads; were we really the antagonists? I honestly didn't know, but I did know that we controlled our primal rage in ways of which the militants from Gaza to Ramallah to Tyre should have taken note and repeated, if they wanted us to believe that they were potential partners for peace.

At the same time, the continual obsession with keeping a scorecard of the numbers of dead and wounded on each side did no one any favours, and avoided the real issues at stake. Israel protected its citizens with bomb shelters[3] and air raid sirens, thus Israel had less casualties of war. Hezbollah appeared to use their fellow citizens as human shields, in the full knowledge that when a Qana happened, it played into their hands around the world. Dead babies sold newspapers; a few cars on fire in Nahariya didn't.

But Hezbollah started this war, and that was the crux of the matter. If Lebanon couldn't rein them in, then it fell on Israel to do so. And that's what it seemed to be doing, but at a huge cost to both sides. Not just in terms of the numbers of dead and injured, but also the fact that yet another generation would, during their formative years, see the physical and mental scars on their communities and act accordingly. The tears over the weekend in my flat and in Qana appeared to have been shed in vain – especially when pitted against the kind of rhetoric being spouted in the building next door to mine.

"Repeat after me – *Aravi tov...*"

"No – I don't want to"

"Say it, just say it – *Aravi tov...*"

I shrugged and acceded to his demand, "*Aravi tov...*"

"*...Aravi met*". And with that, a broad smile spread

across his face, as he beamed with paternal benevolence, having taught me one of the most important axioms by which to live my life. Namely, that "A good Arab is a dead Arab". Welcome to Israel in wartime.

This was the effect that the war was having on those around me, both in Jerusalem and back in the Motherland. Previously moderate friends had turned into nationalist bigots; previously meek and mild acquaintances now spouted bloodthirsty rhetoric when urging on "our boys" in Lebanon; previously unacceptable racism was now dropped into conversation as casually as the weather forecast or the football results.

So it was with my fifty-year-old neighbour, Yossi, who taught me all I needed to know about the world's billion or so Arabs in one easy-to-remember phrase. I was sitting on my garden wall, enjoying the last rays of the Friday sun, drinking a can of Coke, and bothering no one. Yossi came downstairs to throw out his rubbish, spied me, and before I could make a run for it, approached me and clamped a bear-like hand on my shoulder.

We exchanged pleasantries, before he launched into his daily diatribe about how the Muslims were out to kill us all. He knew that I didn't agree with him – in fact, I thought his views repugnant – yet still he persisted with his mission to "educate" me. Whenever I argued back, along the lines of "But not all of them want to kill us...", he smiled wryly and said "You're a young boy – you don't understand. Come and talk to me in twenty years, and then we'll see if you say 'Yossi – you were right.'"

It was a waste of time arguing the toss with him. His logic was easily deconstructed – his generalisation and prejudices for a start – but the fifty-year-old hatred behind it was harder to shift; it had calcified on his mind like plaque on teeth. All I could do, forcefully, was show him that his xenophobia did not rub off on me, no matter how many times he bombarded me with it. I was caught between having to show *derech eretz* (respect) to an elder, and wanting to deliver his smug face a right hook for his racism. As I told him, rewind sixty years, and the whole of Europe was using the exact same phrase as him, with only one minor adjustment: substituting Jew for Arab. But he smiled beatifically again: "Let's talk about it in twenty years, boy."

I played football twice a week with a crowd of ex-pat Brits and South Africans. Largely religious, largely well-educated, largely jumped-up little racists. Until the conflict started, I was happy to ignore the occasional anti-Arab remark that I heard as we warmed up; it wasn't the right arena to get in an argument, I decided – but then came the war. Now, as we got changed for the match, all those around me were full of violent declarations of defiance. "Let's napalm the whole country"; "We need to show the Arabs who's boss"; and, my favourite, "One soldier's life is worth more than ten of their villages" – straight out of the Kahane[4] guide to tolerance and morality.

I was neither an apologist for, nor a sympathiser with, the terrorists who attacked Israel non-stop. In fact, it was Homat Magen (Operation Defensive Shield in Jenin, 2002) that finally made up my mind to move to Israel and fight for the land of my forefathers. However, there was a difference between defending your country with decency and turning into a rabid Islamophobe the minute things started to heat up.

But it was hard to stand up to these "patriots" when there was a war raging. Inevitably, when I suggested to my footballing friends that perhaps napalm was going a bit far, I was asked "Well, what would you do? Invite them round for tea and give them some more land?" Obviously not, but that didn't mean I shouldn't rail against the casual comments that genocide was somehow acceptable in the current situation. Not because I really thought my fellow footballers had much influence outside the football pitch's fence, but because it filtered down into what they taught their children and others who looked up to them. One boy said that our friend Ari, who'd been called up and was off fighting in Lebanon, had "shot an

Arab – so we should let him play for free next game". And everyone laughed, and no one said a word in protest.

Then, on a larger scale, was the jingoistic attitude rife around the country. Early on in the war, Bank Leumi plastered billboards with adverts declaring "Israel be strong" and "We will triumph"; noble sentiments indeed, but I found something disturbing about the blurring of war and peace. Namely, that a company dedicated to profit margins and yields should suddenly be drawn into chanting nationalist slogans instead. Of course, the rationale behind it was to entice new business to this patriotic firm, but I'm not sure I'd have approved had it been Natwest screaming "Batter Baghdad" on a North London high street.

I had never felt entirely comfortable with the *Sun's* devotion to "Our Boys in Basra" when I lived in England, but now – having witnessed the same thing here – realised that this was the inevitable response of a nation at war. We had to get behind our troops, we had to support the war effort – but at what expense? Mainly at the expense of rational and balanced thought, it seemed.

"This war's turned me into such a racist," said a friend of mine in London as we discussed the hostilities over the phone. Her first reaction to the fighting had been one of extreme sadness and fear for Israel – perfectly understandable, though I didn't share the pessimistic outlook. However, as the war progressed and world opinion shifted against Israel, the siege mentality took over for her, and countless other British Jews. Fear bred defensiveness, which in turn manifested itself in ways such as hostility to outsiders – or, to give it another name, racism. There was no excuse that could be held up to logical inspection for this kind of xenophobia. If she was saddled with anti-Arab emotion, then "it's all because of the war" was no more acceptable than saying she was anti-Pakistani "because they come over here and take our jobs". Or that she hated Jews "because they run the world, innit?"

At the same time, the coverage of the war by the different news networks was telling. British Jewry, and no doubt other Jewish communities round the globe, liked to vent their frustrations at the perceived bias against Israel in the media. "The BBC are so anti-Israel"; "CNN just hate us" they complained. Fine – but had they ever seen Fox News? A hundred killed in Lebanon and they led with two wounded civilians and a burning car in Haifa. Not that there wasn't anti-Israel bias out there, but there was enough pro-Israel sentiment that it seemed more a case of horses for courses than a blanket hatred of the Jewish state by the world's media.

For all that I wanted our own house put in order, for all that I wanted to believe that we could make peace with our enemies and live happily ever after, an incident in England did nothing to assuage any doubts I might have had. The Muslim Council of Britain, the seemingly moderate voice of Islam in the UK, sent shivers up the collective spine of the British public with an open letter to Tony Blair. In it, they implied that Britain's foreign policy needed altering if the country wanted to prevent further terrorism on its soil or in its skies. This was a shocking declaration for them to make publicly, the idea that a Sword of Damocles – in the shape of bus and train bombings – hung over the government, and that only policy-change in favour of the terrorists would stop the sword from falling. A frightening image emerged of alienated Muslim youth in Britain who were ready to kill for the cause – but not only that; also that they had managed to convince their elders and betters that the only way they'd halt their murderous plans was if the government acceded to their demands.

That was a perfect example of what would happen in Israel if racist and xenophobic behaviour was not stopped. Left unchecked intolerance would spread, strangling even the moderates amongst us with its extreme views and threats of violence. We were not there yet; after all, the Kach party was banned and remains so –

but under the surface in Jerusalem, and over the counter in the *Shtachim* (the Territories), the throwaway comments of today seemed set to beget the Jewish terrorists of tomorrow.

***

Once the war was over and the dust had settled, things returned to normal – or as normal as they had ever been in this most turbulent of regions. Emboldened by my trip to Ramallah earlier in the year, I began venturing out more and more into the West Bank, alongside Alex, who by now had made *aliyah* and was living a few roads away from me in Jerusalem. A far more political animal than me, Alex had been forging links with various NGO workers and activists, and started taking trips to see the work they were doing in the field. Gradually I realised that, rather than glean my knowledge second-hand from his accounts of his visits, I'd do better to accompany him as he sought the stories behind the headlines – and our first joint port of call was a beleaguered Arab hamlet on the outskirts of Jerusalem.

As I sat on the ruins of yet another demolished house in the tragic village of Al-Nueman, I wondered why we Israelis thought we merited any kind of sympathy at all, let alone the kind of kid-glove treatment those on the Israeli right believed we deserved.

What we'd sown in Al-Nueman could only yield a harvest of more anger, more bitterness, more hate. And that was just from the residents – what the rest of the world would feel for the Zionist machine was another story altogether.

What had happened to Al-Nueman was nothing short of criminal. Twenty-two houses, home to a tight-knit community who had lived in the same hills for generations, it sat on land annexed by Israel during the '67 war. However, due to the villagers' clan chief living in a town located deeper in the West Bank, the Al-Nueman residents were registered under his address, and consequently denied Israeli status and IDs. This meant they could not enter Jerusalem, which – whilst far from ideal – had at least been tolerable until the plans for the security wall were finalised.

Al-Nueman was to be fenced off, like many other Palestinian hamlets and villages, but – and this was the Kafkaesque nightmare of Al-Nueman – they would be on the Israeli side of the wall once it was completed. West Bank residents who couldn't go to the West Bank. People living in Israel proper who couldn't go into Israel. Prisoners in their own homes? Precisely.

I wasn't one to bang a drum for peace, co-existence, or make-love-not-war. I left that to the Israeli girls with flowers in their hair; to the long-haired Israeli boys back from Goa with opium-infused fantasies. Reality told a far different story – the fact that there were PFLP[5] members amongst the town's residents didn't exactly make me want to rent a villa there in the summer months; the fact that our host wore a beaming smile and spoke perfect Ivrit (modern Hebrew) didn't convince me that he didn't harbour inimical thoughts towards Israeli Jews, but then that was mere conjecture. Whereas the hard facts were these: Israel had stitched up this village – which was in many ways a microscopic example of the Occupied Territories as a whole – and, furthermore, every tentacle of Israeli authority was complicit in the crime.

From the upper echelons of government which delayed reviewing the residents' pleas for Israeli citizenship, to the municipality which served demolition orders on the houses, to the border police *Magavniks* who hassled the locals on an hourly basis.

In late 2005, *Magav* thugs stopped two Al-Nueman residents, tried to arrest them both, only one of them cooperated and the second was found later tied to his mule and beaten unconscious. The forty-three year old never came round – he died, and so too did the chance of his eight children ever forgiving and forgetting what had taken place in the name of Israel's security.

After meeting on Hebron Road, we climbed into our cars and set off for the village. We turned right, past the imposing, fortress-like settlement of Har Homa, and down into the low land. Within seconds, the landscape became indistinguishable from the countryside in any of the Middle Eastern states. Dotted on the side of the golden, barren hills were stone houses, and down in the valleys were neatly planted rows of olive trees.

The roads we drove along were in such a state of disrepair that we were reduced to crawling pace – they were meant to be maintained by the Palestinian Authority but, as has been witnessed over the last decade of misrule, the coffers of the PA were rarely put to good use for its people.

As we approached the edge of Al-Nueman, up rocked a jeep full of *Magav*. The first display of their might was to blare on their horn to attract the attention of two passing youths. They checked their IDs perfunctorily, and to an outsider their behaviour was perfectly above board. At the same time, having spent a month doing exactly the same in Bet Jalla, I knew that it was this low-level form of assertion of power that kept the Palestinians constantly resentful of us – just as the black and Irish communities in London felt during the Stop-and-Search years and the Prevention of Terrorism Act.

We reached the house of Yusuf, a rotund, well-turned out resident and de facto head of the welcoming committee. He ushered us into a beautifully tended garden – lush grass, neat flowerbeds, rather at odds with the villagers' assertion that their water was routinely cut off for weeks at a time by the army. However, splitting hairs was not my aim, just as listening to the sadly-familiar recounting of IDF abuses by Yusuf was also not my top priority. Anyone could meticulously detail the complaints of the Palestinians, the rebuttals by the Israelis, and go mad.

Instead, I preferred to focus on my emotional reaction to the visit. Of the seven of us touring, two of the group were non-Jewish Europeans: one a human rights worker from Paris, the other a film-maker from Bosnia. Their presence sharpened my feeling of guilt and shame at what we were witnessing; had we been a homogenous group, all Israeli and all Jewish, then perhaps I wouldn't have felt that our dirty laundry was being aired in public. And this was one of my main concerns with Israel's policy toward its Palestinian neighbours.

I didn't claim to be a military expert, and I was sure that there were strategists who had an explanation for every little incident carried out by the army in the interests of national security (road blocks, ID checks, house demolitions), but this was beside the point. To the outsider, the treatment of the West Bank residents was nothing short of brutal and oppressive, and it was no wonder that organisations such as the BBC treated Israel with such disdain when the likes of the Bosnian filmmaker were exposed to situations like that of Al-Nueman. We could decry Hamas' policies all we liked; we could use suicide bombings as justification for the security wall, but – until our own house was put in order – we would never win over world opinion. Or be able to hold our heads up high.

Because Al-Nueman was a tragedy, plain and simple. There could be no possible humane explanation for the complete cutting off of this unassuming cluster of houses from the outside world. It was nothing short of malice – and it was being done in my name. The government continued with the expansion of settlements, continued to fight terror with Draconian measures, continued to rule with an iron fist, all the while doing nothing to attempt to win the hearts and minds of those over whom they ruled.

Almost no one cared enough about the plight of Al-Nueman to do a thing about it. The futility and hopelessness of this particular village was overwhelming; the area had been earmarked for the extension of Har Homa, and the government were doing their level best to bully the residents into upping sticks and leaving. Did the settlers know, or care, what their cheap housing meant in terms of Palestinian distress and disruption? Did anyone in *Magav* realise the enormity of killing a father of eight and leaving him tied to his donkey, yards from his family home? Did anyone in Israeli officialdom give a damn that we were displacing and dispossessing these people in exactly the same way as our enemies had been doing to us since Biblical times?

I doubted it. And, much as the shame should have been felt more by the main protagonists than the man on the street, we were all complicit in the crime by our ostrich-like refusal to acknowledge what was happening in our own back yard.

In the Book of Samuel, the prophet Nathan told King David a parable, during his rebuking of the king for his underhand pursuit of Bathsheba. He spoke of two neighbours – one man very rich, with a flock of a thousand sheep; the other dirt poor, with just one lamb in his possession which he loved as though it were his own child. When a guest came to visit the rich man, the wealthy farmer went next door and stole the other man's only sheep, which he slaughtered and served to his friend for a meal. A totally unnecessary theft, a totally heartless and selfish act – and, I was sorry to say, Israel was behaving like that rich farmer.

We appeared to be pursuing a policy of making the Palestinians' lives a misery just because we could. Leaving aside that overbearing anti-terror measures were actually counterproductive (how many of the dead man's eight children would grow up to be peaceniks?), what had happened to the collective Israeli sense of right and wrong? Where had all the good guys gone?

As we left the village, heading back for Jerusalem, Har Homa loomed above us, underneath thick evening clouds, atop its perch on the hill. For an instant, it appeared like a juggernaut thundering towards the West Bank, ready to crush anything in its way. Al-Nueman cowered below like a rabbit, frozen in the headlights, unable to run, unable to avoid its crushing under the wheels of the eighteen-wheeled settlement lorry. Only we, the voters and citizens of Israel, could put the handbrake on. Until we did, we had only ourselves to blame when the world pointed its finger at us.

Our visit to Al-Nueman was like a slap in the face left me questioning the truths I'd been led to believe about our policies towards the Palestinians. Of course, the penny had been dropping ever since my army days, but now that I was seeing the results of our actions up close and personal – meeting the victims and hearing their tales – the speed at which I recoiled from my previously held beliefs accelerated. I channelled my anger through my writing, penning a scathing attack on those who were perpetrating such crimes against the villagers and letting Alex publish it on his website, but still I found it hard to change all of my spots at once. However, the process had begun in earnest, and over the next couple of months, the more evidence I saw of how the occupation was crushing the Palestinians, the more the bile rose in my throat, and the harder I found it to stay silent in the face of such injustice.

My next major trip with Alex was a tour with Breaking the Silence, a group of penitent former combat soldiers who sought to expose the harsh realities of the IDF's subjugation of the Palestinians in the perennial flashpoint that was the city of Hebron.

We met the group in Jerusalem, boarded the coach, took our seats and sized up the other passengers. I could have described them with my eyes closed – a fairly predictable mix of the denizens of left-wing liberalism sat perched on the cushioned seats. Long haired, *kipa* (skullcap) wearing Israeli men; middle-aged Scandinavian women with accusing eyes; older, sager grandparents with weather-beaten faces; young girls with heavily pierced visages, dripping with beads and sequins. As I settled in my seat, the PA crackled into life and the grating tones of an Israeli speaking broken English bored its way into my eardrums. Yehuda, a founding member of Breaking the Silence, wasted no time in giving us a detailed history of the troubled city of Hebron. An ex-commander of a combat unit stationed in Hebron, Yehuda came across as a genial man, sporting a long ponytail, beard and *kipa*, and appeared to now be far from the type of combat commander so prevalent in the IDF. It was apparent that his current guise as apologist was a form of self-help for a soldier who'd seen and done too much, too young. His speech was akin to hearing a reformed wife-beater narrating a slide show of some of the more savage injuries he'd inflicted on his spouse.

As we traversed the countryside between Jerusalem and Hebron, we passed the checkpoint by Bet Jalla where I had spent a month during my own tour of duty. An over-eager peace protestor had daubed "Apartheid Wall of Shame" on an overhanging stretch of concrete alongside the road. Noble sentiments indeed – pity it was only a bus shelter that found itself on the receiving end of the confused vandal's wrath. A more sombre experience however, was watching Arab workers constructing the real security barrier as we got deeper into the West Bank.

Once through the settlement of Kiryat Arba and into Hebron proper, we alighted and spent the rest of the tour on foot. The sun blazed away in a cloudless sky, the border policemen gripped their semi-automatics tightly as they accompanied our group, and the settler zealots stared menacingly at us as we wove our way round the city. The place seemed like a ghost town, as usual; boarded up shops, demolished blocks of flats and not a car on the streets. The only other pedestrians were the mobs of settlers swaggering around with their ancient rifles like Orangemen in Drumcree, and the occasional couple of Palestinian residents sidling up the alleyways. Yehuda took the opportunity every thirty metres or so to halt our progress and recite another anecdote of Jew-on-Arab violence, interspersed with a few acknowledgments of Palestinian atrocities that had also taken place.

Yehuda's use of the word pogrom to describe the regular rampages of the settlers through the Arab market evoked uncomfortable images of pre-war Eastern Europe, though I supposed that was his point. However, I was more put out by the plain ignorance of our group – banal, glaringly obvious questions were normal, as well as an obsession for taking pictures of soldiers interrogating the local Palestinians. A picture may have told a thousand words, but the problem here was that the tour group had no idea what it was like to be a scared, young soldier confronted with potentially mortal danger every minute they were out on patrol. It was all too easy to take a photo of the paramilitary thug harassing the poor Palestinian and flaunt it as 'evidence' to all your friends back in Switzerland, but the soldier was only doing his job. The real issue was the blanket refusal by the government to rein in their expansionist plans for the settlements, which gave carte blanche to the right wing nationalists to continue their daily incitement of the other side. Not that the photo of the soldier wasn't linked to the government's West Bank policy, but I felt that people didn't see the whole picture if they concentrated too hard on the street-level imagery.

We wound up in the garden of a hospitable Palestinian family who were evidently old hands at recounting their plight to Breaking the Silence groups. Whilst taking their testimony with the required pinch of salt, I was dismayed to learn we wouldn't be meeting with their settler counterparts. In the name of balance, I felt it wrong that we only heard one side of the story, but perhaps it was for the best that we weren't forced to endure a religious fundamentalist launching a vitriolic verbal attack on his non-Jewish neighbours.

Yehuda then gave an eloquent final address, speaking of his own personal experience of defending the land of our forefathers. It was a moving testimony, and left us with plenty of food for thought, though the whole experience clearly threw up far more questions than it answered. Was there another way? Was there really no convincing the settlers that the needs of the many (the vastly overwhelming Palestinian population of the city) outweighed those of the few? And could the Israeli government really be taken seriously when it happily subjugated thousands of Hebron residents in order to provide a couple of hundred fanatic settlers with unfettered access to the entire town centre?

The same questions came to the surface a week later, when we joined a group of volunteers from Rabbis for Human Rights on a solidarity trip to a group of Palestinian farmers in Turmusiya, a Palestinian village near the settlement of Shiloh.

It was high season for the olive harvest to take place, but – thanks to the bullying tactics of the local settlers, coupled with the indifferent attitude of the army to the harassment – the farmers only felt comfortable going about their business with international volunteers alongside to deter the settlers from causing trouble.

Once there, we were herded onto the back of a pickup truck which drove us at breakneck speed along the rock-strewn dirt tracks towards the olive groves. As the morning progressed, the much-touted hordes of marauding settlers failed to materialise, causing me to wonder what all of the fuss was about. The army were doing their job, just as the then Defence Minister Amir Peretz had promised they would – sitting on a nearby hill, protecting us, ensuring the harvest could proceed unimpeded. We picked olives for two hours, quickly learning how to do it from the farmers, and then we were summoned to eat breakfast. The whole of the extended family who owned the crops sat down under a tree, where a feast had been laid out for us – or, for the men at least. The women were relegated to their own circle, with a distinctly less bountiful array of dishes to eat. The food, whilst plentiful, was pretty standard farmer fare – breads, salads, dips – but the cheese was something else. Deep fried and salted to perfection, I would gladly have handed over Jerusalem and its outer suburbs to the Palestinians in return for a couple of kilos of this manna from heaven. Which is why it was pretty lucky I wasn't involved in final-status negotiations on the Israeli people's behalf.

We worked and chatted with the Palestinians in equal measure until about one o'clock. The only worry was the threat of settler attack, which – whilst none occurred when we were there – clearly had taken place countless times before. We were taken to see evidence of hacked-down trees, plus the well that the farmers had dug and the settlers had apparently defiled soon after, tossing waste and poison into the water hole. However, it was preaching to the converted; we needed no convincing that those settlers who took the law into their own hands merited nothing but contempt. It was beyond me how seemingly religious people could justify the wanton destruction of other people's property in such a way – it went against all of our teachings and moral codes.

But, despite my incomprehension, that was what happened on a regular basis, hence we had all given up our time to come and aid the Palestinians in gathering their crops before the settlers could come to disrupt the harvest. What turned out to colour my day indelibly, however, was nothing to do with the settlers and their actions. Instead, a ten-year-old's t-shirt ended up being the focal point of the time I spent in the fields – and did nothing to convince me to come back and help out again.

As we took a break from picking olives, we found ourselves quickly surrounded by six of the family's children. The self-styled leader of the kids was a cocky, confident boy of ten, proudly sporting a Hamas t-shirt as he spoke of his admiration for Hassan Nasrallah, the leader of Hezbollah. He then boasted of how he threw stones at soldiers, before declaring that "all Jews are bad", though he found it hard to say to our faces. Out of the mouths of babes, indeed. For all the polish and slick presentation of the older generation of his clan, singing their desire for peace with us, calling us "brothers" and so on, the words of their offspring spoke volumes. As did the fact that the parents had decided to allow their son to wear such a provocative t-shirt, when they knew a truckload of Israelis were coming to give up their time and help them with their work. It would be akin to my parents letting me wear a BNP hoodie in front of a black family who'd come to help us clean for *Pesach* (Passover).

Whilst the actions, and lack of basic respect, of one particular family hardly represented Palestinians as a whole, that we were effectively working for the same people who voted in a party bent on our destruction left a bitter taste in our mouths. A *mitzvah* (good deed) was a *mitzvah*, but the recipients weren't looking so good in our eyes as we discussed our feelings later on.

Once we'd finished our work, we went to meet the other volunteers in a field a couple of miles away, where we got word that the third group were embroiled in a stand-off with a group of settlers who were accusing them of trespassing on settlement land. We rushed over in our bus to bolster the numbers, a frisson of excitement present that there could be imminent action, but the police had already intervened and defused the situation. Spitting blood, our comrades boarded our bus, recounting tales of gun-toting settlers swaggering around, harassing the farmers and making their lives a misery. I didn't doubt them for a minute, but when Josh told them the tale of the boy in the Hamas t-shirt, one of the more vocal women on the bus said "Well, if they'd seen the settlers' behaviour today, it would have turned anyone into a Hamas supporter."

This was too much for me. It was perfectly acceptable, to the casual observer, for kids to sport t-shirts of a party dedicated to Israel's destruction, on the back of an unfortunate verbal run-in with a couple of men from the settler side. It was all a bit too trite for my liking, a bit overly sympathetic, a bit over the top. But the settlers weren't my people, and neither were those on the radical left. I'd just come to have my eyes pried open even further to the daily turmoil that reigned in this part of the country, and in that respect I had had a successful day.

Where I was less successful was in contextualising what I'd seen; by allowing myself to focus merely on the boy's offending t-shirt, I was guilty of the same mistake for which I'd castigated my fellow visitors in Hebron. Just as their concentrating on taking photos of soldiers arresting Palestinians was counter-productive, so was my obsession with the t-shirt – though it would take several more trips, and a great deal more insight on my part, to overcome my own shortcomings.

I was still finding it hard to emancipate myself from the shackles of Israel-right-or-wrong bias, when I got invited to spend the day in Jenin's refugee camp, site of one of the more notorious battles of Operation Defensive Shield in 2002. We were guests of the local children's theatre, which relied heavily on overseas donations to continue to operate in the midst of such sprawling poverty. The most extraordinary event of the day took place next to the "Not to Forget" mural in the heart of the camp. Zacharia Zubeida, head of the West Bank wing of Al Aqsa Martyrs' Brigade and survivor of six IDF assassination attempts, also happened to have been involved in the theatre when he was a young schoolboy in the early nineties. Unseen by the locals for the last two months, he was understandably extremely careful to limit his public appearances to a minimum. However, having been told a sympathetic foursome had come to see his alma mater, he made a brief, impromptu appearance to address the group for five minutes. Good looking, young, charismatic and a keen self-publicist, it was easy to see why he had achieved such mythical status on both sides of the Green Line. At the same time, however, his hands were stained with the blood of scores of Jewish civilians – which was pretty sickening.

Once back inside the relative safety of Israel proper, I had mixed feelings about having met such an infamous figure as Zubeida. On the one hand, as a budding journalist, I couldn't deny feeling a visceral thrill upon being presented to him in the heart of the bandit country that was Jenin's refugee camp. However, looking into the eyes of a man who had devoted so much of his life to the slaughter of Israeli soldiers and civilians alike, I felt the bile rise in my throat as I imagined the joy he took in causing so much misery to others. I still looked at the situation through a superficial, linear prism in many respects; had I been more perceptive, I might well have given consideration to what drove a promising young actor to jettison his dreams and take on the mantle of freedom fighter/militant/terrorist (or however else he was described). I had spent years applying the same logic and insight into the actions of the Israelis – defending the settlers in my teenage years, defending the army during my build-up to *aliyah* – yet refused to do the same when it came to their Palestinian counterparts.

It was this that was to be the biggest catalyst in speeding up the process of revising my own political position – once, that is, I graduated from writing for Alex's cosy, parochial website to the international platform provided by the *Guardian*. No sooner was I thrust under the fierce spotlight shone by the *Guardian's* army of readers, than I was forced to swiftly address my own prejudices, preconceptions and predispositions in a public fashion – and I relished the challenge.

---

[3] Or at least its Jewish citizens, shelters were fewer on the ground in Israeli Arab areas.
[4] Meir Kahane, the late leader of the outlawed but still influential right-wing and anti-Arab party.
[5] Popular Front for the Liberation of Palestine, founded by George Habash.

Chapter Two

One of the abiding memories of my pre-*aliyah* trips to Israel was the first time I went to the Cave of Machpela in Hebron. Buried there were the three patriarchs and three of the four matriarchs of the Jewish and Muslim faiths. The site is of enormous spiritual importance to both religions. I travelled there during the relative lull between the first and second Intifadas, and the journey from Jerusalem was a far simpler exercise than the average tourist now faced.

As I prayed at one of the tombs with my father I glanced through a metal grille over to the other side of the chamber, where Palestinian worshippers were praying with equal fervour. So near, yet so far; a shared ancient history, indeed, yet a recent past that had divided the two sides almost irreconcilably, to the point that they could not even pray together in peace.

And what a difference an Intifada made. The security wall, the equally notorious maze of checkpoints, the tortuous inquisitions as you tried to get from A to B, had all but destroyed the tourism industry in the West Bank, as well as slammed the brakes on any interaction between the natives on either side of the divide. Hebron, as the more moderate Israelis and Palestinians loved to reminisce, used to be one of several meeting points between the two peoples. Israelis on weekend trips would throng the bustling markets over the Green Line, buying up Palestinian goods and interacting with their neighbours in a way that seemed almost incomprehensible to today's battle-hardened generation.

Kipling's famous phrase – "Oh, East is East, and West is West, and never the twain shall meet" – sounded apt for a region oft described as the fault line between the

Arab world and the West, yet it didn't quite tell the whole story.

As Marina Benjamin vividly described in her book *Last Days in Babylon* (Bloomsbury, 2007), Judaeo-Arab relations in the pre-'48 Levant were more often than not the epitome of successful integration. She painted a halcyon picture of Baghdad's Jewish community thriving amongst its Sunni, Shia and Christian neighbours; all of which stopped once the Jewish State was established and relations between Arabs and Jews immediately soured.

With all this in mind, I set off again for where Israelis feared to tread – this time to Bethlehem. My friend and I headed to Checkpoint 300, less than two miles from my front door. The cabbie gazed at us inquisitively in his mirror as I told him our destination in perfect Hebrew. Israelis were strictly banned from entering Area A, which included Bethlehem, but my British passport, my friend's American ID, and a healthy dose of chutzpah meant that we could circumvent the rules for the purposes of our trip.

Upon brandishing our Western papers, we were waved through cursorily by the border guards, who had bigger (and more Palestinian) fish to fry. Once through, we made our way along the deserted streets that characterised this side of Bethlehem. Strangled by the wall, choked by the non-stop incursions, the once-thriving tourist trap had now been reduced to a ghost town, devoid of any life save for the desperate crowd of taxi drivers vying for business.

We were headed for the refugee camp of Al-Aida, and were painfully aware of the massive shift in living standards of those unlucky enough to be the wrong side of the fence. Of the nearly five thousand residents, unemployment had surged from 30% before the Intifada to nearly 70% now – and it showed.

If some of Jerusalem's buildings were crumbling and worn, they looked like mansions compared with the homes in Al Aida. The presence of the army hung over the town like a rain cloud that threatened to burst at any moment. Youths and adults alike gathered aimlessly on street corners, all eyes trained on the well-dressed boy and girl sauntering past in the afternoon sun.

It was a place with no hope. And, whether or not the residents of Al Aida or Hebron could ever have been won round to trust their Israeli counterparts as they once seemed to have done, whilst the walls – both physical and mental – stood defiantly between the two sides, the chances of resolution grew slimmer by the day.

So how could the rapprochement begin? It had to start from the ground up: "get them while they're young". What little opportunity arose had to be seized upon, whether joint demonstrations, sporting events between peers from both sides, or weekends away for families of neighbouring communities. I was not alone in believing this, as a resident of nearby Sur Baher showed when I met him a week later.

The man I met would, as he assured me and I didn't doubt in the slightest, one day "lead not only my own village, but all of my people from the region". And what made his story so inspiring, so compelling was that six years earlier he had nearly strapped on a belt and become a suicide bomber...

Fouad Abu Hamed was born and raised in the East Jerusalem village of Sur Baher, where his family used to own 40,000 dunams of land "before it was stolen from us". As a consequence of the seizure of their property, he grew up in abject poverty and in a fiercely anti-Israel atmosphere. But, amongst all the rage and hostility that swirled around him in his village, Fouad realised early on that cutting himself off from the occupiers was not going to get his community out of their situation.

Aged seven, he announced to his family that he wanted to learn Hebrew, and by the ninth grade of school he was already volunteering for Magen David Adom (Israeli version of the Red Cross). Upon finishing school, he took up a coveted place at the Hebrew University, but his parents' lack of funds meant that he had to leave almost immediately and transfer to the less salubrious, but free, Qalandiya Community College.

Once there, he studied land surveying – "but I hated it. I just did it so that I'd have a degree." He ditched surveying at the first opportunity, taking up a job at the Israeli human rights group B'Tselem. He worked with them for six years, taking advantage of the Hebrew he'd learned to befriend his Israeli colleagues and establish himself as an Israeli Arab "they could trust".

After a lengthy spell at B'Tselem, he decided to put the immense knowledge of the Israeli system that he had gained to good use for his community. When his first daughter was born, he decided to enter into protracted legal action with the Jerusalem municipality, who had taken the decision not to spend money building a school for Sorbher's female students.

"I looked at my daughter and thought hold on – I pay my taxes, I've got Israeli citizenship, so how can they deny my child the elementary right of education?" He said. "I decided to fight the system" – and, six years later, he won. In the midst of his battle with the authorities, it occurred to him that he could do far more to improve his village, and came up with a plan that was to propel him to legendary status in his hometown.

He approached the Kupat Cholim (state health authority) and asked them to grant him a loan with which to build a clinic in Sur Baher, assuring them that there would be thousands of residents who would join. Reluctant at first – worried that they'd never recoup the money they lent – the Kupat Cholim bosses stipulated that he needed to guarantee a starting thousand potential clients before they would release the funds to him.

A couple of years on, and nearly ten thousand people had been served by the two clinics he had opened – one in the centre of Sur Baher, the other a few miles away in Bet Tzafafa. The clinics turned Fouad into a rich man, as well as earned him the adoration of his grateful community.

Driving through the village in his plush car, it was clear that Fouad had developed something of a messianic complex – but who could blame him? "What a shame to drive such a beautiful car on such smashed-up streets," he remarked – at once bemoaning the plight of his town and ramming home how far he'd come. Gangs of youths staring sullenly at his approaching car suddenly burst into smiles of greeting when they realised who was driving; old women coming out of the grocers were similarly delighted to see him roaring by – and he lapped it up.

"They love me because I love them," said Fouad with an expansive sweep of his hand. "I could easily move my family to West Jerusalem, or to live with the other rich Palestinians out in the country, but I'll never leave Sur Baher. What kind of example would that set for the young ones here?" He talked of "young ones", yet he was only thirty-five himself, with years of philanthropy ahead of him.

But, as we sat in his lavishly decorated office in the Sur Baher clinic, he told a story of how it was nearly all so different. He had mentioned earlier how his Jericho-born wife lost her father to an IDF bullet in 2001, and now he used the aftermath as proof of how close he came to giving in to the hate himself.

"My wife was eight months pregnant when her father was shot, and we travelled to Jericho to be with her family as soon as we heard the news. At the checkpoint, the soldiers told us firmly that we weren't crossing, so I used my Hebrew to explain the story and appealed to them to let us through to comfort her relatives. The soldiers got angry, and one of them threw my wife to the ground – a woman about to give birth, yet they treated her like an animal."

At this point, Fouad's eyes flashed with the six-year-old anger that, whilst he'd masked it well, still burned away in his mind. "I'd never been so angry, and I decided to become a bomber myself to avenge the treatment she and her father had received."

One way or another, he was talked out of the decision, and channelled the anger into assuming the mantle of saviour of his village. The clinics, the charity work, the project for young Arab businesswomen (which was where I met him), all stemmed from the decision to choose life, rather than slaughter himself and a busload of innocent Israelis.

He was the first to admit that there was a great deal wrong with Palestinian society and its leaders; "sold up the river" would be the best way to translate his attack on those in power on the other side of the wall. But he refused to give in, nor to let those around him do likewise. It was all about empowerment for Fouad, and he was not looking for help from the lacklustre and reticent Israeli authorities either.

Which was lucky, since the Jerusalem municipality was notoriously ambivalent when it came to improving the lives of the Arab residents who fell under their remit. "I don't have time to wait around for the politicians," said Fouad. "I want a better future for my children, not just for their children, or their children's children".

Considering the amount he had achieved by the age of thirty-five, it was not hard to believe him when he spoke of garnering more power and influence over the coming years. He spoke with the calm yet compelling style of Mustafa Barghouti, whose failed leadership bid for the Palestinian Authority was mourned by many, and whose moderate views were light years away from the murderous rhetoric preached by his cousin Marwan.

The most striking aspect of Fouad's ascent was the way he refused to constantly attack the Israelis, recognising the futility in those who wallowed in their misery whilst doing nothing constructive to better their lot. Of course he blamed Israel for his people's plight – "I want to inspire our youth to improve their community by themselves, because the Israelis couldn't care less about us" – but he had better things to do than sit around and complain.

Fouad's recent achievements, and his plans for the future, should be an inspiration to not just his own people, but to those on my side of the divide too. His charitable intentions, and his willingness to befriend Jewish Israelis are a portent of hope in terms of the future. Whether he will go all the way to the top and end up leading his people remains to be seen, but he's already done an incredible amount more for their cause than he ever would have had he strapped on that belt.

***

The 59th anniversary of Israel's independence was to be celebrated throughout the country later in the week, and the hype was reaching fever pitch in the days before the party began. However, nestled amongst the jubilant articles in the Israeli press, came news that sales of Israeli flags had fallen at an even more pronounced rate than last year, a decline attributed to "angry settlers", according to one manufacturer.

These were the same angry settlers who were planning an incendiary march to Homesh on Tuesday, the very settlement that my unit was involved with clearing during the Disengagement two years ago. Homesh was thus of special interest to me, since I took great pride in having been part of the operation, and I had watched with remorse as the pressure mounted for the settlement to be reoccupied by those we thought we'd evicted for good.

My diary, which I kept during my army service, reminded me of the rage that built up inside me as we prepared for the Disengagement. As we trained for the violent resistance which the settlers had threatened, we learned that we would be going in minus guns, helmets or ceramic vests – which was incomprehensible, to me at least:

> *"...It's born out of political chicanery rather than soldiers' welfare – when I complain about the rude and nervous*

manner with which we deal with Palestinians, I get told safety of the soldiers is paramount, and only after that is there a place for politeness, etc. Here it's the exact opposite..."

And for what? It was hardly as though we were renowned for our kid glove treatment of those on the other side of the wall who we deemed a threat to national security. So why did we show such restraint when dealing with the fifth columnists who, nearly two years later, were still sulking petulantly about not getting their own way?

There was something sinister about the continued sporting of orange ribbons by disgruntled settler supporters, as though they believed that their star would begin its ascent again, and they wanted to show the rest of the country that they were not finished yet. It was not as though orange was their colour before the Disengagement – they adopted the symbol purely to show their resistance to the decree, and should have had the good grace to grin and bear it once the deed was done.

By all accounts, their resurgence was gathering pace again. Homesh had been the site of several 'reoccupation' marches in recent weeks, and one would have been forgiven for thinking that the tacit complicity of the security forces in not preventing the gatherings was a sign of the double standards that existed amongst the army's top brass.

After witnessing the way that the border police dealt with the weekly protests at Bil'in by the Israeli left, it was inconceivable that – as the Israeli daily paper *Haaretz* reported a month earlier* – "the IDF knows the chances of completely blocking all the participants from reaching Homesh are slim". This was the same army that had no problems making sure that thousands of Palestinians had to navigate a labyrinth of checkpoints just to get from one

---

http://www.haaretz.com/hasen/spages/841465

village to another every day, yet bleated that it couldn't possibly deal with a few hundred right-wingers hell bent on reaching their old stamping ground.

From a government, that only last year had its heart set on ceding even more land in an attempt to advance the peace process, it sent quite a telling message to the world. It refused to stand firm against those unable to accept the finality of the last withdrawal.

What was going on here, that allowed such a sensitive piece of land, in such a sensitive region of the world, to be the scene of yet more antagonistic and unruly behaviour? Inevitably, the last gathering at Homesh in March ended with violent clashes between the settlers and the Palestinian youths who came to watch the demonstration take place, after "some 15-20 right-wing activists approached the group and threw rocks at them" according to *Haaretz*.

It wasn't as though these protestors didn't have previous. They were notoriously adept at bringing the country to its knees when they didn't get their own way. Their attempts to prevent the Disengagement ranged from burning tyres at intersections to opening fire on Palestinian workers, in a vain bid to derail the political process that was taking place.

For my part, I was dubbed a Nazi and a traitor by the rabid teens who I dragged away from the perimeter fence, but I laughed it off, considering just who the insults were emanating from. The only treason taking place was by those resisting legitimate Knesset orders, and the only fascism on display appeared to be from those determined to continue their illegal repression and subjugation of their Palestinian neighbours.

My diary entry from the next day summed up my feelings:

> "...As we left Homesh's grounds for the last time, I spat unceremoniously on the grass from the window of the bus. Fuck this place, and all who lived here – no one has done more to endanger me and my people than the

*antagonistic settlers who've spent so long winding up the
real natives of the West Bank..."*

I stood by that now, as I watched with anger the bending
over backwards of the army and politicians to appease
the latest batch of subversive protestors. As two commentators pointed out in *Yediot Aharonot* earlier in the
month, the fear was that "this is the first phase in which
they are testing the response of the IDF and Israeli society". That they chose to use Independence Day to launch
such a high-profile second phase of their campaign was a
sign that their confidence was high, and that they would
bask in the spotlight as they went about their quest.

For a country so proud of its nearly sixty years of independence, it was quite something when it allowed its
celebrations to be overshadowed by a group of extreme
dissidents sticking two fingers up at their government.
The protests at Bil'in and Homesh weren't a world apart
in terms of violence; it was only the response that
smacked of duplicity on the part of the Israeli authorities.

The build-up to Independence Day ends with Yom
Hazikaron, in honour of the fallen soldiers who died
defending their country. It is always darkest before the
dawn, according to the saying – and so it is with Israel's
national holidays. Twenty-four hours before the
Independence Day celebrations begin, the country enter
into a day-long period of sombre reflection, remembering
those who gave their lives in service of the state.

At a pre-arranged time, air raid sirens across the land
sound their mournful wail, and every single Jewish
Israeli, and some of their Arab counterparts, down tools,
stand stock still, and respect the memory of the dead with
the utmost reverence. After all, in a country so small, yet
caught up in so much conflict, there is almost no one
whose life had not been touched by the ravages of war at
some time or another.

Memorial services are arranged, and well attended, the
length and breadth of the country, be they at military

57

cemeteries, war memorials, or in synagogues and schools. Serving soldiers don their dress uniform, polish their M16s and Tavors, and stand alongside the veterans of Israel's many wars, paying tribute to those who hadn't made it along the way.

And, in a forest clearing in the middle of nowhere, stands a unique memorial. Erected in the days of the late Yitzhak Rabin, it bore testament to the hundreds of foreign volunteers, *Mahalists*, who gave their lives in defence of the country that may not have been their motherland, but that had meant more to them than life itself.

I was a *Mahalist*, but I was embarrassed to attend the remembrance service that day. After meeting some of the true heroes who stood shakily alongside me in the blazing April sun, how could I not have been? Within minutes of my friends and I arriving at the site, I was embroiled in a conversation with a Holocaust survivor, whose sacrifices and devotion to his people put any effort of my own to shame.

Gabriel Goldschmidt came to London from Hamburg on the Kindertransport in 1939, though most of his relatives were doomed to perish. He was raised by a Jewish family in Golders Green, then – when war broke out in Israel in 1948 – heeded the call to arms that his brethren in the Holy Land put out across the world.

"I arrived on a Thursday, and by Friday I was already in uniform," he told me. No training, no induction – nothing. He was a field medic, and treated the war's amputees until, as he put it, "I'd worked so much that I ruined my own back." "So many" of his comrades fell in battle, yet he was delighted to see that many of his fellow soldiers were still well enough to attend this year's memorial alongside him.

"But tell me about yourself," Gabriel urged me. What could I tell him? That I – the privileged stockbroker from Hampstead Garden Suburb – decided one day to jack it all in and swap the City for the sun? That, as a mere afterthought, I'd opted to don combat fatigues myself, seeing my integration into Israeli society as dependent on my willingness to bear arms?

I was answering no desperate plea from a country in distress; quite the opposite. I was using Israel to answer my own cry for direction. So I came, I fought, I conquered my selfishness – and had nothing but love for those who did it the far harder way, like Gabriel.

However, as I – and the fellow *Mahalistim* of my 2004 draft – milled about, sporting our berets with a certain swagger and pride, we came across the next set of recruits straight off the production line. As with our group of volunteers, the bulk of the group was American, with the usual liberal smattering of Brits, Europeans, South Africans and others.

We were immediately set upon by the wide-eyed rookies, who all demanded to know what we'd done in our time, whether we'd seen much action, and how hard it had been for us. My earlier humility dissipated along with the smoke from my cigarette, as I segued effortlessly into the battle-hardened *Nahal*[6] veteran that I liked to think I was.

But, and there was always a but, I also knew what was coming. As I described my unit's participation in the Disengagement, two of the American boys' faces switched from fascinated to crestfallen. "But," one of them cried, "that must have been awwww-ful, to have to do that to your own people," "Yeah," said his friend with the Mach3-shaved head, "Wouldn't you have rather been out dealing with some cocksucker *A*-rab?"

Here we go again, I thought. The same wanton disregard for the other side, the same rampant racism, the same inability to hear quite how distasteful the words coming out of their own mouths sounded. And, without wishing to sound as generalising as those I denigrated, it was always the Americans who spouted this rhetoric.

At least, that's how it was in the three batches of volunteers with whom I served. On our base, casual racism was bandied about from dawn till dusk by preppy boys from Manhattan who suddenly became tough guys once that coveted machine gun was thrust into their eager hands.

If the apple didn't fall far from the tree, then the attitudes of the American recruits proved the point. No wonder they flew to Israel all gung-ho and full to the brim of anti-Arab rhetoric, when their own government preached the same views at them from cradle to grave.

We were all screened for physical weakness when we signed up, but any ill-will and hostility to those on the eastern side of the wall wasn't, or couldn't have been, rooted out. Instead, a bunch of trigger-happy, fired-up set of gap-year soldiers were let loose in a war zone that they saw as no more than a 3-D version of a Playstation war game.

That wasn't to say that there weren't the same bad apples in the 1948 volunteer corps, but the problem with today's *Mahalistim* was that the programme had become just another extreme sport to some. The volunteering side of things was clearly superfluous to present-day Israel's requirements, with its vast manpower and military might, which was backed by a benevolent American government.

Thus *Mahal* attracted a mixture of potential Israeli citizens, like myself and my friends, and a clique of wannabe heroes who only served so that they got to impress the Brandeis girls with their heroic tales when they headed back home.

As I listened earnestly to Gabriel recount stories of true heroism from '48, I couldn't help but wonder whether the magic of *Mahal* would be the same in fifty years time. Would those who served then see me and my peers as representative of a golden age of selfless sacrifice, or just a perverse crew who served more for their own self-interest than for that of the state?

Whilst I pondered those questions, there was another side to the Israeli army which was even harder to swallow, in terms of who was serving and why. The "Gap Year Gunmen", as I called them, who served alongside me in the *Nahal* infantry brigade before flying back to continue their lives in the Diaspora, were indeed a source of concern to Israelis and foreign observers. However the whole issue paled in comparison when, a few days later, I went to the Western Wall for an army graduation ceremony in which my best friend's sister was participating. She was coming to the end of her time in *Marava*, the ten week programme designed for foreign, gap-year teenagers who were in Israel to experience as many facets of Israeli life as possible during their trip.

Whilst several of the participants of her year-off programme were volunteering for Magen David Adom, she and five others were taking part in *Marava's* version of the basic training that real soldiers went through at the beginning of their IDF service. On paper, *Marava* recruits were as "real" as any other soldier in the Israeli army. Were they to come back and live here, their ten-week service would be knocked off the amount of time they had to serve. They were officially accredited with the same points that Israeli conscripts amassed during their spell in training.

As I watched the tourists flock to the spectacle of fifty gun-toting youngsters standing to attention beneath an Israeli flag flying proudly in the wind, I was struck with the thought about how these kids would be perceived by those on the outside.

The pictures I took of my friend's sister and her fellow Londoners, with their M16s slung over their shoulder, were no different to the photos that caused such abject horror in Jews around the world, those of children at Hamas summer camps posing with similar weapons, in similar stances.

The participants of both the *Marava* and Hamas programmes were being manipulated by the same warlords with the same self-serving interests in perpetuating conflict. Granted, there was a huge distinction when it came to Hamas indoctrination of children, leading them to glorify, and seek to emulate, suicide bombers. The *Marava* scheme made no overt demands of its participants to murder Palestinian civilians indiscriminately, nor to beatify those who did so.

61

But, semantics aside, the idea that it was somehow an acceptable part of a year-in-Israel programme to undertake combat training in the IDF should not have been anywhere near as palatable to Diaspora Jewry as it was. The same parents who were struck with mortal fear at the idea that their little angels would be caught up in a terror attack didn't even bat an eyelid at the thought of them spending weeks on end learning to fire heavy machine guns and mortars under the gaze of IDF commanders.

On my "gap-year-in-Israel" I, too, spent a huge amount of time trying to get a feel of life for the average Israeli, travelling the length and breadth of the country, including spells on kibbutzim, at religious seminaries, volunteering at soup kitchens, and so on. However, my only contact with the army came whenever an olive-clad soldier strutted by on the street, attracting admiring gazes from my friends and me.

There was nothing wrong, in my mind, in lionising and feting those whose business was defending the State of Israel. But, by the same token, those who believed that Palestinians had the right to resist Israeli occupation with violence could similarly be excused for making heroes of the fighters of Hamas, Islamic Jihad, et al, who provided the same service for their people.

Encouraging teenagers to spend time working with paramedics, or volunteering in a development town, was all well and good, and a fine example of how altruism and desire to experience Israeli life could be successfully combined. But permitting them to dive head first into boot camp and the inherent brainwashing of life in the forces was a different matter. How could the same parents then demand that the Palestinian parents did as they said and not as they did?

Perhaps now was the time, in an age when the Israeli war effort relied far more on sophisticated weaponry than manpower itself, to call time on the system that allowed foreign recruits to flood in from abroad. If a young Jew had his heart set on making *aliyah* and staying in Israel for good, then he should have been made to serve in the army upon receipt of his citizenship – but not before. And for those who were looking for a slice of authentic Israeli life on their gap year, they should have been restricted to benign, non-violent, voluntary causes.

Because, if we are to ever get to the point where war is not synonymous with life in this troubled region, it is essential that we cease our glorification of the army to the starry-eyed youth flocking to Israel in their formative years. The Israeli army is a necessity, but it shouldn't have been elevated to a position of glamour and desire as well.

Having now come through the other side of my own spell in uniform, I was adamant that I was going to put as much distance as possible between myself and the type of soldier for whom serving was a chance to deal "cocksucking *A*-rabs" a lesson. The longer I wrote for the *Guardian*, the more I realised how out of kilter my views on Israel were in comparison with the left-wing politics I held when it came to conflicts and crises in any other area of the world. I found myself siding with readers over the I/P issue whose opinions, in any other arena, I would have done my damnedest to oppose.

As the mist lifted from around my eyes, I saw that either I was lying to myself about my left-wing credentials, or I was lying to myself over where I stood in the I/P debate. The more I saw, and the more I learned in my post-army phase, the more I realised it was my Israel-related stance that was totally askew. With every trip into the West Bank, the feeling grew stronger, and a trip to Bethlehem in May was just one such occasion.

"I remember when all this was just fields," I remarked to Erika as we crossed the border between Jerusalem and Bethlehem. I was only half-joking; when I'd served in the army, Checkpoint 300 had been a couple of border policemen lazing in the sun, a queue of pedestrians waiting under a corrugated iron shelter, and a line of cars stretching as far as the eye could see.

Now the labyrinthine network of walkways and steel bars had all but removed the human interaction from the process of traversing the line between the two cities. A camera watched all who entered, and a voice boomed out from a wall-mounted speaker, barking instructions to the travellers to display their documents. When it came to us, a cursory flash of our Western passports saw us waved swiftly through.

On the other side of the crossing was a posse of taxi drivers, all of whom descended on us, hopeful eyes belying the hopeless situation the cabbies had found themselves in ever since the erection of the security wall. When I'd first visited the city, in pre-Intifada days, this road had been bustling with Jewish and Christian tourists alike, snapping up souvenirs en route to visiting their respective holy sites.

Now it was like a ghost town. Rachel's Tomb, which I guarded during my army days, was now even more protected than before, and only Jewish tour buses could enter the demarcation zone that surrounded it on three sides. Behind the tomb was the Muslim cemetery in which we used to play cat-and-mouse with the youths throwing pipe bombs and rocks at us, and behind that lay Al-Aida.

It was there that we were heading, to talk to the head of the Al-Rowwad Cultural and Theatre Training Centre, which was located in the heart of the camp. When I'd called Abdel Abudsrour – the centre's director – earlier in the day, he'd offered to come and meet us outside the camp, believing we'd never find our way through the maze of narrow streets by ourselves. I told him we'd be fine, though didn't explain why I was so familiar with Al-Aida's backstreets, for obvious reasons.

As we strolled through the neighbourhood, curious heads turned in our direction to check out the Western visitors in their midst. For my part, I was remembering all the times we'd stormed the camp, locked and loaded, hurling tear gas canisters to disperse the crowds who'd gathered to take us on. The camp was a miserable place, with little for the young to do, save winding up the soldiers at the tomb and lobbing rocks at the Jewish buses.

However, there was an alternative – the Al-Rowwad Centre. "We don't want more martyrs," said Abdel. "Our aim is 'beautiful resistance' instead of violence". He was in charge of over two hundred children from the camp, who came to the centre every day after school, taking part in various artistic activities until six in the evening.

Two-thirds of the camp's residents were under eighteen, and Abdel had overseen the expansion of the centre from two rooms in his parents' house to the sprawling complex it occupied today. "There is no limit to the number of children we will take – all we ask is that the children have no political affiliation, that they behave properly and don't take part in violence against the soldiers."

This was easier said than done, as I knew from my own experience. I used to watch the kids at play from my guard tower, witnessing how a friendly kick around in the street would morph quickly into a stone-throwing frenzy whenever a patrol passed by. Keeping the kids indoors and off the streets removed the temptation, said Abdel, and also showed the army that the adults were taking responsibility for their youth.

"I believe in breaking the stereotype," he said. "I want to show that there's another side to these children other than just the violent impressions that are given in the media. The cameras only come to Al-Aida when there's trouble, so the world thinks we're all just savages. We're not."

When asked about the future, Abdel's face fell. "Everywhere else in the world, people look forward to the future, believing life will get better and brighter as time progresses. But in Al-Aida, the here and now is the best we can hope for – every day gets worse and more painful for us. It's been that way since Oslo."

The facts on the ground backed up his claim. Unemployment in the camp had soared. Incursions by the army were on the increase. And "kids are losing respect for their parents, as they watch them unable to do anything to better their families' lot," according to Abdel.

When I asked whether the children were ever exposed to their Jewish counterparts, Abdel pointed to the wall and shrugged. "Some of them have been on tour to Europe with the centre, where they met Jews, but they'll never meet Israelis." He said that he tried "to teach them to look at the other side as human, rather than through the prism of religion", but without projects like Centre for Creativity in Educational and Cultural Heritage (CCECH, see p.87), the chances of convincing his charges of that were slim.

And, truth be told, Abdel wasn't interested in working with Israelis. "On one of our trips to Europe, there was the opportunity to perform with a troupe of Israeli kids, but I refused. We're not monkeys in a zoo, shaking hands with the other side to make the audience feel good. When there is respect and equality from the Israeli side, only then will we work with them."

Abdel also claimed that the media was irredeemably biased against the Palestinians – mirroring the opposing claims constantly made by Israelis against the press. "We are stupid in how we deal with the media, whereas the Israelis are excellent," he said. "Plus, we are portrayed as masked gunmen, and the Israelis as the helpless victim. The Palestinian voice can't reach the Western media, so the West just thinks we're all violent terrorists."

Despite his dedication to his charitable work at the centre, it was Abdel's despondency and paranoia that left the most lasting impression. His assertion that the world's media was anti-Palestinian, his idea that life would only get worse for his people, his hostility towards anyone on the other side of the wall: an example of how even the most optimistic could lose heart.

After earning his masters degree in France, Abdel gave up the opportunity to live in the West for good, opting to come back to Al-Aida to "help my community overcome the occupation". Several years later, and he'd scaled back his dreams, and now seemed satisfied if he could just help his town tread water. If things kept getting worse, if he kept believing that the world just didn't care about his people, then how long Abdel would keep promoting his message of non-violence to his flock was anyone's guess. But, having seen during my tour of duty how the rage under the surface in Al-Aida could erupt at any moment, if the likes of Abdel lost hope, there would be no more fingers in the dam when it next threatened to burst.

To the south of the country, in Gaza, the dam had burst a long time ago, and the questions being asked on the Israeli street centred around how to put the "unruly" Gazans back in their place. With every Kassam rocket fired into Israel, the calls grew louder for a decisive hammer blow to be dealt to those living in Gaza to remind them who was boss – a return to the gung-ho rhetoric being spouted a year earlier during the war with Hezbollah.

There was a beautiful symmetry in a British trade union taking the decision to boycott Israeli academics in the same week that the former Chief Rabbi of Israel proclaimed that the army should "carpet bomb Gaza". Whilst I wholeheartedly abhorred the boycott for a myriad of reasons, the fact that lecturers voted the way they did was somewhat less surprising after considering the type of zealots, like the ex-Chief Rabbi, who publicly dragged Israel's name through the mud.

Citing various Biblical precedents, the firebrand Rabbi Eliyahu ruled that "there was absolutely no moral prohibition against the indiscriminate killing of civilians during a potential massive military offensive on Gaza aimed at stopping the rocket launchings", according to the *Jerusalem Post*.

The situation vis-à-vis rocket attacks on Sderot was, of course, leaving many Israelis feeling impotent and insecure; after all, the cross-border assaults had been going on for years, and no government had yet found an effective solution for dealing with the onslaught. The reason they had struggled to solve the problem was, largely, down to their reluctance to wantonly slaughter civilians in the process of taking out the missile launchers.

However, according to Rabbi Eliyahu, that was exactly what we should have been doing. Collective punishment? No problem. Because, in his eyes, "the entire populace is responsible because they do nothing to stop the firing of Kassam rockets". Leaving aside the fact that it would have been a task of Herculean bravery for unarmed civilians to try to rein in a mob of bloodthirsty militiamen, Eliyahu appeared to be setting a precedent that could have blown up in our own faces, both metaphorically and literally.

After all, he appeared to suggest that any illegal action by a group of Palestinians rendered all their fellow countrymen equally guilty. I wondered then what he would say about the frequent and flagrant violations of international law that Israel committed in the name of achieving their national aims. Would he have then agreed that all Israelis were fair game for Palestinian attacks just because the government continued to build illegal settlements in the West Bank, or tortured Palestinian prisoners in their jails?

I doubted it; no one in their right mind could have made such a preposterous claim. I might have been ashamed of some of my government's actions, but I refused to be held personally responsible when a coalition that I didn't vote for committed crimes in the name of the State. But, then again, I didn't consider all Palestinians responsible for the Kassam attacks against Sderot – whereas Eliyahu did. His double standards were made even more unconscionable when one considered his standing in the Jewish community.

The man was no fool. He must have known, when writing his 'open letter' to the then Prime Minister Olmert, that his words would be seized upon and devoured by Israel haters and anti-Semites the world over. Yet he still published his bile, and now we would all reap the consequences.

As if his words weren't incendiary enough, his son then chimed in with an even more graphic description of hate: "If they don't stop after we kill 100, then we must kill a thousand. And if they do not stop after 1,000 then we must kill 10,000. If they still don't stop we must kill 100,000, even a million. Whatever it takes to make them stop."

The rabid Eliyahus didn't speak in my name, nor those of my equally horrified friends who read their words with revulsion that morning. But our trying to distance ourselves from Eliyahu would have had little impact on the world at large. He was the big name, he was the Jewish spokesman – and he'd just guaranteed our pariah status in lecturers' unions and elsewhere for a long time to come.

Another example of religion being used to justify extremism on the Jewish right was the untrammelled racism and hostility espoused throughout a guided visit to Hebron which I took part in that summer. "No left winger would *dare* come on this tour," laughed Reuven, as the smug faces of his acolytes smiled in agreement. I stole a glance at Erika, who held her deadpan expression and gazed silently out of the window. We were two hours into the tour, and had so far played the part of potential settlers to perfection.

I had often been accused by some of the more wild-eyed readers of CIF of being a Mossad agent, but this trip was the closest I'd come to subterfuge. Having been alerted by Alex to the upcoming tour, Erika and I had decided to go in undercover, as it were, so as not to arouse any suspicion from our fellow attendees.

For me, that meant detaching the diamond stud from my ear, and donning a *kipa* and smarter clothes than I normally decked myself out in. For Erika, it meant long sleeves, a below-knee length skirt, and a demure

69

demeanour in the vein of good Jewish girls the world over. A hard act for us both to keep up.

The day out was organised by the shadowy Jerusalem Capital Development Fund (JCDF); a group, in its own words, "dedicated to reclaiming and strengthening the Jewish presence in eastern (historic) Jerusalem, greater Jerusalem and parts of Yesha". In simpler terms, they were the antithesis of rapprochement with our Palestinian neighbours, seeking instead to force them out of their towns and to conquer more and more of their land in the interest of the Jews.

We met in the plush lobby of the Inbal Hotel in West Jerusalem; I'd like to say we were an eclectic mix of Jews from all walks of life, but that was never going be the case. All-American, all religious, all secure in their conviction that the cause of the Jewish people trumped all other hands in the Middle East game of poker.

As we listened to Reuven's introduction, it became apparent that the JCDF and its supporters felt hard done by and marginalised by mainstream society, and Reuven's rhetoric reminded me of John Nichols' rants in the film *Bowling for Columbine.* "If you read the propaganda – I mean news – in Israel, you'll see how all our fearless leaders care about is giving away our land", he began, subtly working his audience into a mood of contempt for the powers that be.

Our first stop, once we boarded the bus, was at Rachel's Tomb in Bethlehem. "Does it make any sense at all that Rachel's Tomb is outside the Jerusalem city limits?" asked Reuven as we drove through the security wall encircling Bethlehem. Everyone shook their heads in sympathy with his message, clucking sadly as Reuven assured us that "Bethlehem gets less and less safe all the time".

JCDF owned the house adjoining the tomb, which we had used as our barracks when our platoon served there. The group aimed to get planning permission to turn it into an $8 million Batmitzvah centre, where girls could celebrate their coming of age ceremony in style. But it

70

was not altruistic motives that spurred them on; the centre's erection would serve the purpose of artificially inflating Jewish tourist numbers to the area, in a bid to convince the authorities to annex the Tomb to Jerusalem and eat into even more of the Palestinian territories.

As we drove to our next stop, the village of Abu-Tor, Reuven spoke of his grand plan for "solving the Arab problem". His use of phrases was already disturbingly close to the rhetoric of a certain group of Europeans in the 1930s, so when he advocated "putting all the Arabs on trains and sending them to Jordan", it was hard to keep my counsel and not flash him a mock *sieg hiel*.

One of the more astute passengers on the bus pointed out to Reuven that "we have to buy them out, surely. We can't just ship them out on trains, because that would be like the Shoah". No, said Reuven, "we'll tell them 'you're no longer welcome in this country', and then let Jordan or Egypt deal with them."

Erika, meanwhile, was struggling even more in her need to keep *shtum*. We'd joked about Stockholm syndrome when we realised we'd be out all day with the group, but there was precious little chance of that happening as we listened to the poison being spouted.

"How many Arabs are too many?" asked Reuven rhetorically. "Any that you can count are too many," he gleefully declared, his crisp white shirt and knitted *kipa* no giveaway as to the vitriol within. "If you need your car repaired," chortled Reuven as we drove through the Wadi Joz neighbourhood, "come here, because the exact part that was stolen from you can be bought back on the cheap here."

As I watched the faces of the others on the bus crease up with laughter, I wondered what they'd say if I hit them with a joke about cripples or queers. No doubt they'd all have been up in arms, telling me there was no need for that kind of prejudice – all the while blind to their own hatred that was somehow "acceptable" because it was only the Arabs they were talking about.

71

What made it worse was the "sinister grandma" angle, a phrase we coined in the army to describe the little old ladies who used to come to Rachel's Tomb and advocate all kinds of slaughter against our enemies when trying to show us soldiers their support. On the tour itself, the seemingly benign Christian couple from Tennessee who'd joined us out of "solidarity for God's people", were actually the worst of the lot.

As we stood on the Mount of Olives, listening to Reuven's tall tales about yet more Arab aggression, the wife of the Tennessee ex-marine whispered that "if you ever need any help blowing up that dome [the Dome of the Rock], ask my husband – he's worked with explosives and he'd love to help". My mouth was already gushing blood from the hole I'd bitten through my tongue, but I bit it yet again, resolving to let my pen do the talking instead.

I cornered the couple during a break in proceedings and, all the while keeping up my rightwing cover, gently asked them if they meant it when they said earlier that "we support the Jewish people, *whatever* they do". "Yes, of course," said the woman. "But what if Israel did something illegal or immoral?" I probed. "We-ell, I don't believe they ever would," she maintained. "OK, but let's say they did, then what?" I went on. Her face contorted in confusion, she replied that "Maybe I'd stop supporting them then but, like I said, that just won't happen."

The rest of the trip was spent listening to snide little digs about the Palestinians and barefaced lies about the political situation of the country, all the while touring the villages in which the JCDF hoped to purchase yet more property. My favourite assertion of Reuven's was that "Arabs just grab people's land and settle on it, flooding the place with their friends and family"; how he said that deadpan, given his day job, was beyond me.

He described wholly Arab villages as "not gentrified...yet", but assured us that a Jewish presence would help them embrace modernity and respectability. We were told that "some of the so-called refugee camps they reside in have nicer houses than we live in ourselves", and that "Arabs can always find money to outbid us [JCDF] for property when they need to".

Feeling physically sick when we alighted at the end of the marathon tour, Erika and I were in two minds whether we should have been stitching them up by writing about the day's events. However, every single one of the adoring passengers on the bus would have been returning to their own flock to preach Reuven's message of hate, and if our own forum was via the written word, then why shouldn't we have had our say too?

After all, to paraphrase Niemöller's famous poem, "first they came for the Palestinians, and I didn't speak out...". And, if the likes of the JCDF had their way, that analogy was as apt as it was horrifying.

The world's eyes were firmly focused on Israel that summer, and not just because of the hostility between the IDF and the Gaza militants. June saw the fortieth anniversary of the Six Day War, when Israel – as well as successfully repelling the multi-pronged attack on its borders from all sides – annexed the West Bank, Golan Heights, and the rest of Jerusalem that it didn't already control.

I was commissioned to contribute several pieces to the CIF debate about the war's ramifications, and I opened with a staunch defence of the army's capture of Jerusalem, barely realising how at odds my emotional judgment was with my new-found powers of rationalisation. As the words poured forth from my fingers, I let my heart rule my head, earning me the opprobrium of a vast swathe of my readers, many of whom couldn't understand how I could be so seemingly anti-Occupation one day, yet a fierce defender of certain aspects of it the next:

June 5th 2007 – The Jewish Mecca – Comment Is Free; The Guardian
> *From the very first time I came to Israel on holiday, so have I stuffed letters to G-d in the crevices of the Wailing*

73

Wall in Jerusalem. These days, you don't even have to be physically present at the Wall to have your supplications inserted into the cracks between the stones – faxed messages can be printed out and taken to the Wall on your behalf, or your message transcribed by phone and carried there by hand. A webcam transmits live images of the Wall round the clock via the internet – testament to the sheer magnitude and importance of the structure to World Jewry, and proof of one incontrovertibly positive outcome of the Six Day War.

Leaving politics aside – which, granted, is near impossible to do in relation to the Israel/Palestine conflict – the capture of the Old City in the war in 1967 was of immense religious and spiritual significance to the Jewish people. From the diehard secular to the ultra-orthodox, there is no place on Earth that embodies Judaism like the Wailing Wall.

In religious terms, it is by no means the holiest Jewish site in the world. That tribute belongs to a stone a few hundred metres away that lies under the Al Aqsa Mosque, and which was relinquished to Muslim control as part of the post-1967 settlement. For all its military might and prowess at the time, one notable part of Israel's conquest of the Old City was its refusal to expropriate the Temple Mount site, preferring instead to cede control to the Waqf religious authority.

This is in stark contrast to conquering armies the world over, who have – since time immemorial – waylaid the holy sites and structures of their defeated enemies and erected their own altars in their place. Even Judaism authorised such destruction in Bible times – when the land of Canaan was captured, the troops were commanded to "Destroy their altars, and smash their stones". This assertion of power has taken place ever since, all the way to the present day (witness the Taleban's destruction of the ancient Buddhas when they wrested control of Afghanistan).

However, the treatment meted out to the Wailing Wall – an outer wall of the long-destroyed Jewish Temple – in the years preceding its capture by Israel was nothing short of scandalous. Recognising the importance of the structure to the Jews, various groups tried to neutralise its power and destroy its potency for the Jewish people. Houses were built right up to the edge of the Wall itself, and it was impossible for a time for Jews to pray at the site.

74

Thus, when the Wall was recaptured in 1967, it is no wonder that the rabbis of the time proclaimed it a near-miracle, and an event of such importance in the Jewish people's history. For the part of those Israelis who were less religious, but no less proud of their victory, the conquest of the Old City necessitated a change in name for the Wailing Wall.

The Wall had been so named because it represented the tears that the Jews shed through their dark years in exile and now – having returned home – they were no longer out in the spiritual wilderness. Hence the decision was taken to rebrand the Wall as merely the Western Wall, recognising its position in the former Temple structure, and doing away with the negative connotations of its former name.

All of this, when taken in the context of the fortieth anniversary of the Six Day War, should indicate why any final settlement is bound to stall if it includes the provision of handing back the Old City. For someone like me – a Zionist raised in a religious home, albeit a left-wing one – the issue is far too complicated for a black and white answer.

On the one hand, I would have no problem with Israel withdrawing from the West Bank in general, even though sites of such historic and religious importance such as Hebron and Jericho would be handed over. I believe that it must be in the State's interest, and thus the interest of Jews worldwide, to trade land for peace (assuming it does mean peace), however attached we are to certain parts of it.

However, I cannot apply the same standards to the Western Wall. It is akin to asking the Muslims to hand over Al-Aqsa – there's just no way they would, and who can blame them? Thus, when combined with the location of the Western Wall – on the edge of Jewish West Jerusalem, and thus not difficult to annex to a final-status state – it seems justifiable to insist on its retention.

But this double standard on my part doesn't stand up to scrutiny, I am the first to admit. If I wouldn't cede control of the Wall to the other side, then how can I tell a Hebron settler that he must give up his claim to the Cave of Machpela?

All that I can think is that there are some sites which cause too much bloodshed, too much heartache, and too many wasted years of peace to justify keeping hold of. The

Western Wall is not one of them – it is, to all intents and purposes, the Jewish Mecca. It is, and always will remain, the focal point of World Jewry, and thus its recapture in 1967 must be the last time we are ever tasked with winning it back.

***

At that point, I was just beginning an eight week tour of West Bank settlements with my cousin and fellow *Guardian* writer, Josh Freedman Berthoud, in which we intended to gather research for a book about Jewish settlers. The longer we spent in their company, the more I realised how far I'd come in terms of jettisoning the selfish and superficial thinking that used to dominate my thoughts and still dominated theirs. However, all it took was a quick glance back at "The Jewish Mecca" to remind me that I was by no means completely 'cured' yet. That wouldn't happen for a good few months to come...

---

[6] *Nahal* was my regiment, *Mahal* is foreign volunteers in general.

Chapter Three

Linda Grant, author of *The People on the Street*[7], a frank and eye-opening account of everyday Israelis she met whilst living in Tel Aviv, came across some of my earlier offerings on Alex's site, and made contact with me in late 2006. After meeting me in London, she decided to introduce me to Georgina Henry, deputy editor of the *Guardian* and in charge of the paper's groundbreaking Comment Is Free (CIF) internet offshoot.

Since launching nine months earlier, the site had been a roaring success, teaming the talents of *Guardian* columnists and contributors with an ever-burgeoning legion of readers, who were encouraged to respond as robustly as they liked to every article published. They did so in droves – articles appeared on the site at hourly intervals, and elicited scores of responses, producing "threads" of discussion that resembled online sessions of a debating society. Comments poured in from every corner of the globe, often prompting the article writer to join in and defend his or her position, and as every month went by, the status and reputation of CIF grew exponentially.

Alex had already had three articles published on CIF, and it was clear that the readers had an appetite for anything related to Israel/Palestine (I/P). The *Guardian*, being one of the most prominent left-wing newspapers in the world, had always had something of a turbulent relationship with Israel – at least, that was how it had been presented to me throughout my formative years in Northwest London. I grew up in an unashamedly-*Guardian* reading household, yet outside my home's four walls, the chorus of derision aimed at the *Guardian* (as well as the BBC, amongst other media outlets) was deafening.

By virtue of taking a critical line towards the Israeli government's policies and the actions of the IDF, the *Guardian* had earned a place as the bete noire of the mainstream Zionist camp amongst English Jewry, who viewed any reproach of the Jewish state as tantamount to heresy. With all this in mind, and having penned a couple of non-I/P articles to open my account on CIF, I launched a pre-emptive strike aimed at the army of detractors who would no doubt pounce all over a Jewish *oleh* (immigrant) venting his frustration with the Israeli authorities via the channels of the *Guardian*. As expected, it provoked a storm of protest within minutes of appearing on the site, as well as its fair degree of praise from those in the opposite camp. With that debut, I found myself waist-deep in the mire of I/P debate, attacked from both right and left, called every name under the sun, threatened with physical assault and expulsion from Israel... and I loved every minute of it.

January 2nd, 2007 – Spare the Rod... – Comment Is Free; *The Guardian*

> When my parents used to catch me bunking class to go down to the snooker hall in Kentish Town, my plaintive cries of "but all of my mates were there too" cut no ice at all. "We're not talking about your friends – it's you we're concerned with," replied the united front that is my mum and dad. And the lesson stuck. Nowadays, when I watch the way that British Jewry refuses to criticise Israel for its oft-suspect policies, I can't help but apply the same logic that my parents used ten years ago. Who cares what the other "kids" are doing, in this case Hamas, Hezbollah, et al; it's our child we're concerned with. Our fifty year old teenager Israel, who needs a few life-lessons in order to mature into the adult we all hope it will become. Spare the rod, spoil the child.

> ***

> Sitting around my parents' Friday night table on a recent trip home, the subject of criticising Israel was served up

along with the hors d'oeuvres, and outlasted each course until it was time for the post-prandial whisky to be downed. Sparking the debate was the news that internecine war had broken out at a nearby synagogue, whose monthly magazine had been scheduled to include a critical piece on Israel until certain community stalwarts intervened. The ensuing furor culminated in two long-standing bastions of the synagogue resigning their membership in disgust, and the publication of the offending article caused no end of bitter splits in the communal camp.

As we went round the table expressing our opinions, it became clear that a generational divide was firmly in place. My grandparents had reservations about "any public criticism" of Israel – espousing rhetoric akin to that which counsels us not to air our dirty linen in public. One guest took this argument a step further, stating that "the only time when it's OK to criticise Israel is when Israel's image is good in the eyes of the world". He illustrated this point by saying that the last time that he had publicly censured Israel had been in 1998, when he was teaching at Berkeley. Israel had enjoyed a brief period of global approval at this pre-second-Intifada time – and apparently this was the only reason he had felt comfortable making disparaging remarks about the state. It was quickly pointed out to him that his reasoning flew in the face of logic – "So you're saying that the worse Israel behaves, the less you're allowed to criticise it?", to which he could only concur. Accepting that his stance was long on emotions and short on rationale, he shrugged as though to say "Yeah, but this is Israel we're talking about…" And that's the essence of the problem. The seemingly moral, rational and fair individuals who I've grown up around in the Jewish community suddenly suspend their quest for truth and reason when it comes to the Holy Land. And it'll blow up in our faces if we carry on this way.

For a start, we'll lose the trust of the international community if we continue trying to defend the indefensible. Instead of trying to turn the spotlight away from Israel and onto the enemies who surround us, it's time we acknowledged that Israel itself is far from blameless in the current conflict. It doesn't mean that we are being traitors, or playing into the hands of our foes – far from it. Instead, it would show that we are worthy partners

79

for a process of understanding and peace, since we are able to put rational arguments above emotional ones, and place truth on a higher level of importance than "loyalty".

I'm not comfortable with the argument that those loyal to Israel shouldn't criticise it, as I have been taught over and over during my formative years (though, fortunately, not at home). Loyalty does not mean turning a blind eye – the "spare the rod…" concept is central to my uneasiness. If we do not take the opportunity to educate Israel whilst it is growing up, we'll be left with a wild, unruly adult version in fifty years time, totally oblivious to critique or censure – which many would argue Israel already is today. Secondly, British Jews should open their eyes and see that plenty of Israelis have absolutely no problem slagging off their own government and military without a second thought. Homegrown Israelis don't hush up their doubts over policies just because they're scared that the world is watching. Quite the opposite, in fact. They know that a public show of opposition to, say, house demolitions by the army, or the construction of the security fence, are in fact a great opportunity to show the world that not all Israelis think and act the same.

Emboldened during the meal-time debate by a mixture of self-righteousness and Laphroaig, I made an impassioned speech to the table. "It is me – and other critics of Israel – who are the true Zionists, the true supporters of Israel. We help Israel to see its failings, rather than just lavishing praise upon it when times are good. We aren't fair-weather fans, who make a great fuss over the good deeds but then go quiet over the bad ones. Thus we are the ones who can hold our heads up to the world and say 'deal with us – we're playing with a straight bat'". And it's true – the one surefire way to lose the trust of the international community is to be faced with black and call it white. Lying, or at least burying our heads in the sand, won't win us any respect.

It was pointed out that it feels uncomfortable to be seen criticising "our own" – but that's not a good enough reason not to do it. Just as it pained my parents to punish me for skipping school and honing my snooker skills, they did it nonetheless, with an eye on the bigger picture. It was also mentioned by the older diners at our table that I didn't understand, because I didn't live through the war and creation of the state – thus didn't get what Israel

80

means to the Jewish people. "It is our bolt hole, our refuge
for when anti-Semitism rears its ugly head..." I was told.
But that's just it. It is our refuge, it is our country – fine.
That's a given – and the state's not gonna disappear just
because we criticise it when necessary. The opposite, in
fact – in order for it to survive, we must give it the tools it
needs to get on with its neighbours, to learn to play fair,
and to merit respect in the eyes of the world.

Later on in the conversation at dinner, my grandfather
asked me if he had as much right to comment on Israel as
an Israeli does. I replied that yes, he does – every Jew is a
citizen of Israel (due to the right of return) – though it's
each person's choice whether they take it up or not. Israel,
for good or bad, was given to each of the world's Jews in
1948 – and thus it is the responsibility of every one of us,
wherever we may be, to stand up and tell it where it is
going wrong, whenever the need arises.

***

The piece attracted over two hundred responses from the
readers which, set against the CIF average of around
thirty per piece, meant that I was immediately invited to
contribute articles on a regular basis. I soon was turning
out two or three a week, carving out a niche as the only
ex-pat, ex-soldier, ex-right-wing commentator who was
trying to find out the truth behind the propaganda he'd
been spoon fed throughout his Zionist-oriented life.

I had carte blanche to cover whichever topics under the
I/P umbrella I chose, which opened up a wealth of opportunity to travel the country and see the realities of the
situation up close and personal. I spent a day with the
embattled Bedouin who lived in the Negev desert and
were continually hounded by the authorities, who demolished their homes and accused them of squatting. I
visited the ever-expanding illegal settlements of Maaleh
Adumim with the Israeli Committee against House
Demolitions. I interviewed Palestinians in East Jerusalem about their lives under Israeli rule; I went to
right- and left-wing demonstrations and spoke to those

taking part – and all the while I told the readers what I thought of what I'd seen and heard, and they reciprocated in droves.

One such occasion was the weekly protest at Bi'lin, a Palestinian village in the West Bank that had become the focal point of the anti-security barrier protesters who demanded the authorities halt their construction of the so-called "apartheid wall". The demonstrations regularly ended in violent clashes between the army and the marchers, many of whom were Israeli peaceniks and international activists who joined the local Palestinians in their struggle. I wanted to see for myself what went on at Bi'lin, and headed to the site with Alex and my cousin Josh early one Friday morning.

Later, as we crouched on the hill watching the border police firing tear gas at the stone throwers, I opined that this had been the most depressing day I'd spent in this troubled country. What had begun as a peaceful protest had quickly descended into mayhem, with rubber bullets, stun grenades and rocks all fighting for airspace – and I was thoroughly fed up.

Reading the *Guardian's* report on the affair the next day, I realised that there was a positive side to what had taken place, namely that the protest had united Palestinians and Israelis in their quest to combat the perceived crimes of the Israeli government. That part of the spectacle was clearly a source of comfort, indicating that perhaps the two peoples weren't as polarised as one might have thought, and that they had put their differences to one side when it came to fighting injustice.

One thing I was sure of was that what was happening to Bil'in was utterly abhorrent. The security wall, whether one loved or hated it, should not have been snaking its way through the village of Bil'in. Israelis and Palestinians alike recognised this, hence the weekly protests at the site for the last two years.

This was my first visit to the area, having thus far been loath to participate in a protest that routinely ended in bloodshed and pandemonium. I had been on the other side of the fence. I had been the soldier firing tear gas canisters to disperse rock-throwing crowds. I had done the soul-searching afterwards, wondering if our response had been proportionate and justified, or whether we'd overstepped the mark whilst claiming self-defence.

But, after what I witnessed in Bil'in, that same soul-searching and introspection was clearly lacking in the organisers and participants of the protest. If you walked into a bar and someone starts a fight with you, you could put it down to them being the one with the problem. If you walk into ten bars, and ten people take you to task, then it was probably you with the problem, I thought. So it was with Bil'in. Countless protests had resulted in violent clashes, yet it happened week in, week out, and no one did a thing about it.

Of course, it was only a tiny percentage of protestors who took up arms. What had begun with a carnival atmosphere up in the village, turned into a peaceful, joyous procession through the fields and up to the fence. The crowd strolled along, singing songs of peace; Palestinian and Israeli flags vied for attention, waved enthusiastically by the bangle-swathed arms of the marchers. As we approached the gate, we could see the heavily-armed border police massed on the other side, ready and waiting for their arrival. The border police weren't renowned for their diplomacy and tact, and the crowd knew this and acted accordingly. At first.

Smiling broadly, and making no sudden moves, the front rows of protestors walked up to the soldiers and sang their songs with gusto. The soldiers smiled beatifically, watching events with expressions of benevolence and amusement. Veteran peace activist Uri Avnery took up a prominent position at the front, calmly delivering his message to the young soldiers a foot away from him. The press pack stood on the ridge above, filming and photographing the goings-on, and all seemed well with the world. The calm before the storm.

After quarter of an hour, a Palestinian man – egged-on by his peers – climbed up onto the gate and walked across it, tightrope style, to the cheers of the onlookers. As he attempted to repeat the trick the other way, a soldier gave him a shove, sending him tumbling down to the ground. Immediately, one of his comrades delivered a heavy blow to a soldier using a wooden club – and, in the same instant, a hail of rocks flew towards the rest of the soldiers behind the gate.

I, like hundreds of others, turned tail and fled, the sound of tear gas and stun grenades was enough to convince me that there were better places to be at that moment. I regrouped with my friends up on the hill, where we watched the ugly events unfold. Plumes of smoke criss-crossed the sky, as the soldiers fired tear gas at the stone-throwers. Youths gathered on the path below, hurling projectiles from their slingshots, and drawing the fire of the soldiers in return. There was sporadic rubber bullet fire too, though in the main it was restricted to tear gas versus rocks. As frightening as it might have been to an outsider, those who had seen it all before knew that nothing too serious was going to happen, other than a game of cat-and-mouse between the soldiers and their assailants.

At that point, my own rage was starting to erupt. As I watched the pantomime play itself out, I realised that this was all pre-meditated, orchestrated violence on the part of both sides, akin to football firms who arranged fights before and after a big match. Everyone knew this was coming; from the organisers, to the participants, to the army. It was never a matter of if, but when. The original rocks had not been scooped up in response to the soldier's actions; they'd been clutched surreptitiously well beforehand, in hands belonging to angry young men waiting for any excuse to launch them.

And for what? To give the border police yet more justification in treating the Palestinian populace with such heavy-handedness? To give the politicians yet more excuse to say "Look at these unruly natives – they can't even protest peacefully, so of course we need tougher security measures in place"? To give people like me – the uncertain, the unconvinced – reason to doubt the motives of those on the hard-left and yet more reason to think they just came to these events looking for a punch-up?

One thing was for sure – I wasn't alone in my reaction. Many of the protestors continued with their peaceful singing, even as the tear gas and missiles fell all around them, and the soldiers went easy on them in return. There were expressions of disgust at the antics of the stone-throwers by the same people who minutes before had been marching hand-in-hand with them to the fence. There was a general feeling of "not again... and not in my name" from those whose plans of a peaceful afternoon had been overruled once more by those set on letting their rocks do the talking.

No one won. No one lost. Sixteen people were injured. Plenty more commanders were able to tell their charges "see what kind of savages we're dealing with here?" Plenty more protestors were able to say exactly the same in reverse. And everyone went home, with their war-stories, their adrenaline surges, and their desire for more of the same the next week. Was that really what it was all meant to be about? It should not have been an afternoon's sport – this was real life. The ramifications would be felt long after the cameramen had wrapped up their filming, and the protestors had made it back to their respective towns. The wall wasn't going to come crashing down on the strength of what took place there that Friday; in fact, if anything, there would have been calls for it to have been built that little bit higher.

Whether Palestinians had the right to physically attack soldiers occupying their land was a moot point. It might have been legitimate, it might not – but it was definitely not pragmatic. For every rock thrown, there was a stun grenade coming the other way. But not only that;

there was another right-wing lawmaker who could cite the unruliness as reason to clamp down harder. There was another military tactician who could devise bigger and better methods of crowd control for similar future occurrences. And there was another wannabe-leftist writer who found himself wanting to distance himself even further from the hardcore who used peaceful protests as cover for their primal urges of violent revenge.

However, according to several readers, I had no right to criticise the Palestinians for exercising their right to protest, violence or none. The war of words spilled over into all-out accusations of me being a stooge of the Israeli government; a tool of the IDF; and all kinds of other assertions that I was trying to undermine the Palestinians' cause by pretending to care, and then sticking the boot in when I got the chance.

I had to deal with the abuse in two ways: firstly, by standing my ground on the CIF thread and explaining what thought processes had led me to my conclusions; secondly – and more privately – by coming to terms with the fact that the readers were often veteran I/P activists, aid workers, and so on, and that I'd do well to listen to their points of view as well, instead of just staunchly sticking to my own guns to save face.

That was easier said than done, and in the meantime I continued to be a middle-of-the-road moderate, refusing to plant my feet firmly in one camp or the other, much to the chagrin of both the right- and left-wing readers. My next port of call was a visit to East Jerusalem, to see the work undertaken by one of the co-existence groups in the region that sought to challenge the status quo and try to forge links between the youth on either side of the divide.

As I stumbled out of my block at an ungodly hour of the morning, I nearly fell over two early-rising dogs checking one another out after a chance meeting in the garden. They approached tentatively at first, before circling each other, and getting a feel for who they were up against. By the time I'd made it past them and onto the street, they were getting on famously – a portent of the day that lay ahead.

I was off to Bet Hanina, on the other side of the Green Line, as a guest of the Centre for Creativity in Education and Cultural Heritage (CCECH). Since 1991, the centre had been working with Israeli and Palestinian children in their schools, using folklore as a way of fostering contact and communication between the two groups. The fifth grade children visited their counterparts at their schools for organised activities, which included visiting each other's places of worship and learning the culture and traditions of their contemporaries.

On this occasion, children from the TALI School in west Jerusalem were to be the guests of the Bet Hanina School for Boys, who hosted the visit alongside pupils from the Shu'afat School for Girls. The group had met once before, at the TALI School in Bayit Vagan, and the plan was for them to meet four or five times a year, for the next two years at least.

Rivanna Miller, in charge of evaluation and programme development for CCECH, said that one of the basic aims of the project was "to get the two groups to feel comfortable with one another", but that if they ended up forming lasting friendships outside of the scheme, then that would certainly be a bonus.

The TALI kids disembarked from their coach, their nervous faces due to them being the "away" team this time, rather than down to fear of the Bet Hanina children. Within seconds, the welcoming party of Palestinian boys and girls were mingling happily with the Israelis, albeit stifled somewhat by the language barrier.

As Alex and I looked on, I mused on how many of the children would end up meeting each other at checkpoints in ten years' time, and whether their experiences here would soften their feelings towards each other when the time did come. From what I was witnessing, I surmised that this was the best way to end the hatred – the prevention, rather than the cure. Meeting at such an early age had to be better than trying to re-educate Israeli and Palestinian youths well into their teens or twenties, who would by then already be full of indoctrination.

Several parents from both groups were also present, since the day's activities centred round games that the parents had played as children. Their presence was vital, in my opinion, so that the children could watch their mothers and fathers – their heroes and role models – lead by example in mixing happily with the "other side".

Dr Simon Lichman, the centre's director, told me that one school principal had recently explained his participation by saying "I want my children to see the kind face of Israelis". This sentiment was also of utmost importance, to counter the kind of attitudes that led Ayaan Hirsi Ali[8] to express surprise upon first meeting a Jew that "they are made of flesh and blood too", rather than being the demons that she had been raised to believe they were.

And it cut both ways. Plenty of Israeli children would only ever see Palestinians on the TV news, viewing them as bombers and militants, rather than people with the same hopes, dreams and fears as themselves.

Erela, the form teacher of the TALI class, told me that some parents were reluctant to let their children attend due to security concerns – which was another reason these trips were so important. I could attest to this, having spent so much time in the West Bank on trips that not even Jenin's refugee camp intimidated me anymore, whereas most Israelis I know expressed horror that I even set foot there.

Of course, there was a downside to the project. As one Palestinian parent told me, the scheme itself was "wonderful – there's nothing negative to say at all". But that was just it. It was so good, and so necessary – yet there were only a handful of similar ventures in the entire country. That something so positive and empowering was not being repeated in every single classroom across the land was unacceptable. On the part of both the Israeli government and their Palestinian counterparts.

Granted, there was no tangible short-term benefit to the conflict that either side could use for political gain but, in the long-term, the potential for calming the tension was enormous. Politics would inevitably intervene at some point in the children's lives, but if they came well-armed with experiences such as these, then they'd be far less likely to give into polarisation in the future.

Funding was, unsurprisingly, limited for work of this nature. The government had better ways to splash its cash – arms procurement for example – but private donors knew better. From what I saw and heard in Bet Hanina, only good could come from events like these, and it also gave lie to the haters out there who were keen to level the old "apartheid" accusation at Israel. Whatever the policies of the current leaders of this land, this set up told a very different story.

The beaming faces of the group I spent the day with could have been translated into so much more in the future – if only we would let it bloom. But it was not going to be easy. "If I feed a poor man, they call me a saint", went the saying. "But if I ask why there are so many poor people, then they call me a communist". I had a feeling that the same would be said of CCECH. As Alex said afterwards, people might have seen it as all very quaint and cute whilst it was only a few schools taking part, but if it was introduced it on a national scale, the public would have been up in arms, accusing them of trying to destabilise the state. And how wrong they would have been.

The following morning, Alex called, exhorting me to accompany him on a walk round Silwan, a village in East Jerusalem we'd driven through on our recent ICAHD[9] tour. We met half an hour later at Jaffa Gate in glorious sunshine. We strolled through the Old City, then swung right past the Western Wall and down into the valley where Silwan is located.

There was no point to our trip; no political motive, no axes in need of grinding, nothing at all, in fact, save the chance to see the place for ourselves. We traipsed up and down the narrow backstreets, watching the natives at play. The natives being both Palestinian and Israeli; there were several settlements dotted around the village, no more than single houses flying the Israeli flag and surrounded by high walls and security guards. Settler children played behind the fence, too young to comprehend the resentment their presence caused in their neighbours.

Heading downhill, we passed a barber shop, whose owner was cleaning his equipment in anticipation of a busy day's work. Remembering the last time Alex had had his hair cut by a Palestinian (in Bethlehem, where he squealed like a stuck pig as his beard was trimmed with two pieces of expertly wielded taut string), I encouraged him to go in here. He did.

We went in, introduced ourselves, and the barber got to work. I interrupted him to ask him a few questions about life in Silwan, but his English wasn't up to the task, much like my Arabic. "Let me call my friend Ibrahim," said the barber, "He's a lawyer, and his English is perfect." Two minutes later, with the shop filling up by now, Ibrahim arrived – rotund, smiling, and ready to give his two shekels worth to the Englishman in the corner.

What began as a benign chat, soon morphed into a violent polemic by Ibrahim, punctuated sporadically by heated interruptions by Alex and myself. Whether Ibrahim realised that we were Jewish or Israeli, I didn't know, but due to our status we were able to engage far more passionately than the average, unconnected reporter might have done. What we heard provoked us to defend ourselves and our people in the face of such concerted rhetoric.

I led by asking Ibrahim about relations between the settlers and the Palestinian residents of Silwan, and was told that "Of course we don't get on. They lock our roads, refuse to buy from our shops, and treat us like we're insects. I call it a form of imperialism." He went on to say that the army did nothing to ease the plight of the villagers, since "the settlers are the army. They're the government. They're the judges, juries and courts."

I asked whether he thought there could be any change in the situation, given that he saw the tentacles of "settler power" reaching right to the upper echelons of Israeli society. Ibrahim scoffed at the suggestion, saying that "Israeli policy is based on racism and discrimination. They come to our shops in the Old City and destroy them. They think they're the masters of the world, with their noses in the air... For a solution, you need respect between people – but there is no respect from the Jews to the Muslims." He asserted that this phenomenon was not restricted to the Jews of Israel. "It would be the same in London. It is nothing to do with land. It is just racism."

I asked whether he thought that all Israelis felt like this, or whether he was prepared to accept that there was a section of intelligent Israeli society that wanted peace with their neighbours. Grabbing my knee, and staring me intently in the eyes, Ibrahim revealed that "I actually don't think that Israelis are intelligent. And anyone who tells you there will be a solution is a liar."

Were the Palestinians who seek a solution also liars, I asked? "Yes. Abbas and Fatah are puppets of the West – no one here supports them. Fatah belong to the US. The leaders of Hamas belong to King Abdullah, who in turn belongs to the US. I don't trust any of the leaders." He then went on to denounce, in turn, Marwan Barghouti, Mustafa Barghouti ("an atheist and a communist"), Muhammad Dahlan... in fact, anyone who Alex suggested to him might be a leader he could trust. Sheikh Nasrallah, on the other hand, "is much smarter. I like him far more than the others."

I was beginning to imagine Ibrahim's rage as akin to an abused child put into care. He seemed so mistrustful, so suspicious, that even those purportedly out to help him were dismissed with derision and scorn. Was this what we'd done, after forty years of occupation – turned even the well-educated Palestinians into such seething, angry individuals? Or was this what their own leaders had done, having promised them so much, for so long, and then never delivering?

We moved onto the subject of a shift in power in the Middle East. "Listen – a war is coming," said Ibrahim. "All of the Middle East thinks the same. Israel is very weak – look how she was defeated by Hezbollah in the summer. We need to take the power – only when we have power will there be justice," He maintained that a one state solution was the only answer and, even though he believed that all Jews' "mentality is racism and fanaticism", he was still willing to live alongside them in the new entity: "I do not believe in violence against them."

I picked up on this, and asked him if his declaration of being anti-violent meant that he had problems with what Islamic Jihad, and others, were carrying out in his name. But, it turned out, "I will not criticise them, because of what Israel does. The conditions make me stay silent and not protest. If F16s kill your kids, then what can you expect?" In the same breath, he told me that "Mohammed says 'Do not hurt Christians or Jews', and I say we can't kill civilians – especially women and children. Soldiers are another thing."

Confused as to his true thoughts about whether it was or wasn't acceptable to blow up a bus, I let Alex take over. He queried Ibrahim's assertion that "all Muslims are united already", citing the internecine violence between Sunni and Shia in Iraq as an example.

Ibrahim shot out of his chair, shouting "Don't talk to me about Sunni and Shia. I don't want to hear it. It is all untrue – lies by the US and UK." Alex mentioned the Samara mosque bombing, but: "All lies – the US was behind the mosque bombing. Forget about it. It has nothing to do with Islam. There is no way a Muslim would blow up a mosque."

His comments reminded me of Hirsi Ali's book, where she maintained that Muslims had no ability to self-criticise or be introspective, but instead sought to blame outsiders whenever things went wrong. That said, Israelis were often quick to do the same – deflecting criticism by denouncing it as anti-Semitic, when in reality they should have used the opportunity to wonder why the finger kept being pointed at them.

We ended the conversation on a low, with Ibrahim giving his take on the Holocaust – "Six million is a lie – I have many friends in Europe, and they tell me it was more like hundreds of thousands. But the Israelis and Jews are very active in the media – you might even end up getting killed if you deny the Holocaust." But, by that point, I'd had more than enough, and he had work to which to return.

Yes, he was only one man, and not talking on behalf of any group (save the barber, who told me he was "happy that Ibrahim speaks for me"). But, for all that Ibrahim the lawyer might have been an isolated case, he was an influential figure in Silwan, and the zeal with which he spoke left an impression on me as I headed back for West Jerusalem. When we talked of collateral damage, I thought, it ought not to have been just in terms of the number of dead and wounded, but should incorporate the number of Ibrahims we had created with our decades of oppressive policy.

Later in the week, I found a similar level of anger waiting to erupt from the mouth of an irate cab driver. Staggering along Jaffa Road, in the blazing midday heat, I managed to utilise the last of my strength and flag down a passing taxi. Collapsing into the seat, I was immediately told to "Shut up – the news is starting". Happy to oblige, I fell silent and watched the driver's face contort in ever-deepening rage.

Switching off the stereo, he turned to me and spat "They're all thieves, the lot of them". Assuming he was referring to the collective mass of Jerusalem cabbies, notorious for skinning tourists and immigrants, I concurred, and waited for him to go on.

93

But no. Instead, his ire was aimed at the cabinet, parliament and state machine in general. Following the recent scandals engulfing the hierarchy, from the rape charges against the president to the S+M ambassador,* and beyond, the public had been quick to condemn the ruling elite for their misdemeanours. On top of that, yet another public strike the day before – in protest at misuse of government funds and non-payment of salaries – brought home once more the extent of the corruption endemic in the system.

I was treated to an early-morning lecture from Ami, the driver who, over the course of our ten minute drive, proved once more that taxi drivers round here were finely tuned into the zeitgeist.

I told him that my mother shared his concern at the current state of affairs, even though she was all the way back in London. "She's a wise woman," said Ami. "I wish we could turn the clock back fifty years – there was a different spirit in this country back then. Today's society doesn't even compare."

"Look at us these days," he urged. "We've got no-one decent to vote for anymore; instead we have MKs[10] committing every crime under the sun. You name it, we've got it: rape, theft, harassment, bribery, and so the list goes on." I interjected to ask if he though the level of corruption was worse here than in any other country.

"Of course there's sleaze outside Israel," said Ami. "But we hold the number one spot on the charts." With a rueful smile, he told me that the best on offer now was "to vote for the one who's committed the fewest crimes. There's no black and white any more, only different shades of black. So we have to say 'he's only raped three girls, whereas the other one's raped five. So let's vote for the first guy.'"

I suggested that maybe it was because we were all too worried about the security situation, and thus let other

---

*http:/news.bbc.co.uk/2/hi/middle_east/6441461.stm

94

issues slide when really they ought to have been of equal importance to the public. "Yeah," said Ami, "maybe. But it's not as if we can even fight a war properly these days, is it?", reflecting the general opinion that we had got a seriously rude awakening in the war with Hezbollah the year before.

Pulling up outside City Hall, where I was headed, he stopped the meter and continued his speech. "What we need is a new generation. My one's finished; it's impotent. We need your generation to say 'we've had enough', and go back to socialist values." I nodded in agreement, though the chances of that happening were slim, in my opinion.

As I opened the door to get out, he grabbed my arm. "Look at the Ethiopians," he said. Here we go, I thought, expecting the cabbie racism – but instead he directed his hostility to the Israelis who had "corrupted the poor Ethiopians. When they came here, they were all such good kids," he maintained. "But we've given them the wrong values – now they run around in miniskirts, getting drunk and imitating the worst of Israeli youth." And with that, he flicked his dying cigarette into the street, and sped off to find the next punter upon whom to unload his woes.

Israel was entering into a period of national mourning followed by just as hearty a celebration, with three major annual events occurring within a fortnight of one another. First was Holocaust Remembrance Day, and then Yom Hazikaron (when fallen Israeli soldiers were commemorated), which segued into Independence Day.

On CIF, a British religious leader, Rabbi Tony Bayfield, wrote a piece essentially demanding everlasting "recognition" of the Holocaust by all of mankind, seeking to put it over and above other suffering around the world – a sentiment with which I immediately took issue. His one-dimensional article, Never Forget, attracted several critical responses from the readers as well, among them the following:

"Does anyone, honestly, believe that all of this looking backwards is benefiting anyone? It smacks of 'wallowing'.

All we can do is keep telling the kids about these atroci-
ties, keep showing them around museums which
document them, but what else?"

I wrote a reply to Rabbi Bayfield, in which I said I would
have to agree with the "what else?" part of the reader's
argument. Whilst Zionist youth groups regularly took
their charges to Poland for tours of the Nazi death camps,
they did more than just "wallow" in the misery of sixty
years ago: they learned from history's mistakes and came
back to their home towns determined not to let racism,
bigotry or prejudice blight their own particular worlds.

But that didn't mean that there was not still plenty of
Holocaust-wallowing out there. I had encountered just as
much during a recent exchange, which left me disgusted
with some quarters of the Jewish community regarding
the "untouchable" side of the Holocaust.

I had been to Jerusalem's Museum on the Seam, where
the exhibition on display, entitled Equal and Less Equal,
explored the relationship between the exploited and the
exploiters in the sphere of global labour. The art, by such
luminaries as Santiago Sierra and Sebastiao Salgado,
was extremely powerful and provocative, using video and
photographs to evoke a sense of shame, guilt and horror
every bit as powerful as a walk through the haunting cor-
ridors of Yad Vashem (Israel's Holocaust Museum).

In fact, that last sentence was exactly what I wrote in
the review I wrote of the museum, which I sent to the
forty or so people who read my unpublished pieces. The
review entreated us, as Jews, to open our eyes to suffering around the world, not just to that of our own people –
and to acknowledge that there were human rights abuses
out there just as atrocious as what had befallen the Jews
in Europe.

I might as well have denied the Holocaust had ever happened, judging by the abuse I got from a certain section of
my readers. Whilst most of them expressed agreement
with the message I was trying to send out, a few middle-

aged people (and I believed their age was important) went nuclear in their scathing attacks on the piece.

One told me that my article had compared Israelis to Nazis, just because I'd mentioned a video that showed browbeaten, dirt-poor Palestinian labourers as they traversed the Erez crossing on their way to work in Israel.

I had made no such comparison, of course – but, as a relative of mine succinctly put it, the Holocaust remains the "Blue Suede Shoes" of certain Jews. Namely, "You can knock me down, step in my face, slander my name all over the place" ... but don't you dare go near the sacrosanct Holocaust and compare it with any other event in world history.

Another reader told me exactly that "You can't compare *anything* to Yad Vashem," she wailed upon reading the apparently offensive piece. Well, I said, you can. To cut a long story a little bit shorter, we never looked close to agreeing on the main topic: namely, that the Holocaust was so untouchable, so unique – so "ours" – that nothing on this earth would ever come close to being worthy of compare. "Not even Bosnia, Cambodia or Rwanda?" I asked quietly. At which point I scored my only point of the match. "OK," she answered, "but not sex slavery or cheap labour."

"Why not?" I asked, causing her lips to go again. "Because," she asserted, "nothing's as bad as what went on in the camps: rape, torture, murder ..." "Hold on," I interjected. "What do you think happens to these girls in Tel Aviv brothels? Exactly the same thing. And there're thousands of them, too." She became apoplectic – even suggesting that some of them came of their own volition and that they were not forced to work at gunpoint. Her assertion is false.*

We could have gone on for hours, but she was missing my point. As I told her, my aim wasn't to cheapen the memory of the six million – quite the opposite, in fact: I

---

*http://www.catwinterinternational.org/factbook/Israel/php

was trying to honour them by showing that I had learned from the lessons of history and thus was not prepared to be doomed to repeat them.

There was a holocaust going on the world over, in all but name. Sex slaves, slave labour, forced segregation and caste systems: straight out of the camps, and as prevalent in today's screwed-up society as ever. Just because the Brazilian gold miner at least earned a few pennies for his toil, it didn't make him any less a victim than a Jew forced to sew buttons on to SS uniforms. Just because a sex worker at Tel Aviv bus station looked well fed and pretty, it didn't mean there wasn't a pimp with a gun behind the bedroom door. And the mental scars of the Auschwitz "good-time girls" didn't run any deeper than that of Natalya from Odessa, held against her will and constantly abused on the fourth floor of a Bauhaus block of flats.

In my CIF article, I argued that "the Holocaust is not 'our' exclusive preserve". Of course, the Jewish people were dealt an unimaginable injustice, but that didn't mean the evil in the rest of the world was not equally worthy of our attention.

And thus, while "never forget" was a worthy and worthwhile refrain, it rang a bit hollow if all we did was remember without taking the next step and actively confronting abuses, wherever in the world they flourished unchecked.

This had become a central tenet of my newfound approach to the situation in Israel and Palestine. For all that I understood the gut reaction of only caring about our own people – a twist on the maxim "charity begins at home" – I could no longer sit idly by when I knew the suffering was just as bad, if not worse, on the other side of the tracks. I felt it my duty to spend as much time seeing for myself what was happening to the Palestinians as I had done caring and worrying about Israel when growing up. If "Love thy neighbour as thyself" really was Judaism's central teaching, then there was no reason not to apply it here, just because one side was Jewish and the other not.

7 *The People on the Street: a writer's view of Israel* (Virago, 2006).

8 A Dutch feminist and writer, a prominent critic of Islam, author of *Infidel* (Free Press, 2007) and *The Caged Virgin* (Free Press, 2006).

9 Israeli Committee Against House Demolitions.

10 Members of the Knesset, the Israeli parliament.

Chapter Four

"Why are you writing a book about us?" From the Yemeni man in the pizza shop, to the 19-year-old soldierette on guard duty, to the mayor of the town grilling us in her living room, this was the first question on everyone's lips when they made our acquaintance.

We came to the *Shtachim* to spend two months meeting the people behind the stereotype; the ordinary folk who had, for whatever reason come to dwell on the other side of the Green Line. To the outside world, settlers were often seen in a homogenous light – religious zealots with a Bible in one hand and an Uzi in the other, hate in their hearts and God on their side.

The truth was far from uniform. There were to be found, of course, the type of settler described above, but there were also those who moved to Judea and Samaria for reasons entirely detached from religion and war. Ariel, for example, was a mini-city "packed full of Russians", according to one *sabra* (native born Israeli) settler we interviewed. The residents were largely there for economic reasons: the subsidies provided by the government, the cheap housing on offer, and the low cost of living all played their part in persuading immigrants from the former Soviet Union to set up home in Ariel. They were not concerned with the contentious politics of the region, but rather were just looking for anywhere cheap and comfortable to call home.

We spent our first week in Kedumim. The first settlement to be set up in the Shomron region, it had mushroomed into a crowded town of over 7,000 residents. Kedumim appeared to be a religious settlement, but scratch the surface and the cracks started to appear. The town had the same problems as any modern-day suburb.

Bored with the rigidity of orthodox living, some of the youth had rebelled, begun to break the Sabbath laws, and now escaped to the coastal cities of Netanya and Tel Aviv for nights on the town.

We met two Ethiopian girls who came to Israel on Operation Shlomo, the government-sponsored airlift from Addis Ababa, and who were at boarding school in the West Bank. "After all the hardship our families went through to get to Israel," said Yafa, "with people dying on the trek through Sudan, and so on – why would we want to give any part of this land back?" She complained about racism against the Ethiopian community by other Jews in Israel, but was quick to assert that "I'll never have Arab friends – all Arabs are just too frightening".

We met settlers who weren't religious, but their Zionist belief had led them to believe that their mere presence in the *Shtachim* was what fortified the borders and protected the country. "People in Tel Aviv see settlers as the ones creating the problems," said one young army captain we interviewed. "But I see settlers as the true patriots. Settlers keep the war away from the main cities of Israel."

And so it went on. We hoped to uncover, during the course of our trip, the entire spectrum of opinion of those who lived in the *Shtachim*, and by so doing to put colour into a region that was too often viewed in only black and white.

As two Jewish boys from north-west London, who had grown up on a diet of Zionism and solidarity with our co-religionists in the Holy Land, this trip was a living history lesson. It was our way of finding out the mentality of those whose entire raison d'etre was based on the victory of 1967, as well as those who came to live here more by chance than for any idealistic goal. It was a way to open our eyes, and the eyes of those who read our work, to what the consequences of the Six-day War were to those Israelis whose every waking moment was shaped by the battle's outcome.

101

First, however, we had to navigate the minefield thrown up by some ultra-defensive settlers who had got wind of our intentions. Underneath the screaming head-line "Beware of the Freedman Cousins", a resident of the Binyamin region had put out a warning to his fellow zealots, having decided that as *Guardian* journalists with previous for anti-settler tendencies, we were a threat to the quarter of a million settlers living inside the Occupied Territories. He ended by declaring that: "One or both of them may be getting in touch with Binyamin residents to ask for hospitality since they have been turned down by their original target. I've excerpted some of their own words so that you can decide for yourselves whether you really want to open your homes to this pair."

Despite his cautionary appeal, he was unsuccessful in his attempt to have us barred from the slew of settle-ments across the West Bank, as was one of the settler leaders in Hebron, who had warned me earlier in the year not to visit the city, telling me it was for my "own good" that I stayed away. His threats fell on deaf ears; after all, I was more than used to the menacing tactics of those on either side by now, and saw their hollow posturing as exactly that – long on noise and short on gravity, as far as I was concerned. I put my theory about Hebron to the test on a break from our settlement trip, and – as expected – had no trouble whatsoever gaining unfettered access to the hardcore of extremists who exerted so much negative influence over the beleaguered city.

For all that it resembled a ghost town – deserted streets, boarded up shops, abandoned homes – Hebron made a hell of a lot of noise. Whether it was the sporadic thud of tear gas canisters, the deafening calls-to-prayer from the minarets, or the dirge-like chanting from yeshiva classrooms, the ancient walls reverberated all day long to the sounds of a city divided. A city so frac-tured that it required being crudely bisected by concrete barricades. A city so holy that it could never be relin-quished by either side.

102

It was my fifth visit to Hebron in twelve months; for all that I hated the place in its current form, I was drawn to it. I'd been there in various guises since moving to Israel: as a religious worshipper, as a soldier, as a left-wing activist and as a tourist looking to buy a cheap carpet. But this time I was going in undercover, just as I had in East Jerusalem with JCDF.

Erika and I had signed ourselves up to a self-styled "politically incorrect tour" of the city, organised by The Hebron Fund. Donning modest garb in order to better blend in with our fellow passengers on the bullet-proof bus, we met at the Sheraton in West Jerusalem – where this time I found myself biting my tongue from the off.

"The Muslims have ethnically cleansed the Christians from Bethlehem and the rest of the West Bank," declared Yossi, our guide, with a mournful shake of his head. Clearly the irony of his statement was lost on the rest of the group, even though he had just advocated a programme of 'urban renewal' in Hebron, his phrase for kicking out the Arab residents and replacing them with thousands of religious Jews.

After a brief stop at Rachel's Tomb in Bethlehem, we headed for Hebron, a forty minute ride, which gave Yossi ample time to work his crowd into an Islamophobic frenzy. For the length of the journey, we were treated to a wide variety of Yossi's anecdotes – such as Arabs attacking Jews, Arab children attacking Jews, and Arabs attacking Jewish children.

Curiously absent from his monologue were the frequent and vicious attacks by Jewish settlers on Arab residents of the city, but then – as he'd so gleefully informed us at the beginning – "this isn't gonna be a politically correct trip, and I make no apologies for that". The others on the bus didn't seem too perturbed; the bulk of them were New Yorkers who'd flown in for a family wedding, and had decided to make use of Yossi's oratory skills as a way to teach their children the "real" history of Hebron.

The presence of such impressionable infants was the worst aspect of the trip, though I was hardly surprised that their parents saw fit to bring them along. After all, the Jesuit motto of "Give me a child until he is seven and I will give you the man" worked just as well when trying to indoctrinate Jewish kids to see the Arabs as no more or less than our eternal enemy.

We spent the best part of five hours wandering the streets of Hebron, including a visit to the Avraham Avinu settlement (actually just two portakabins), where we met Baruch Marzel, former right hand man to Meir Kahane, who now spends his days advocating the murder of left-wing activists, and stealing goats.

For my part, it meant I had now met both Zacharia Zubeida and Marzel, a feat that I couldn't imagine more than a handful of Israelis had achieved, and two extremists with far more in common than either would admit. Both had dedicated their lives to tormenting and attacking the other's people, and neither would rest until their goals had been achieved.

As I sat in the courtyard of another settlement compound in the city, I looked up and watched the yeshiva students traipsing up a series of staircases that could have come straight out of an MC Escher painting. The analogy seemed fitting, since both sides in Hebron spent the lion's share of their time climbing the endless stairs, never achieving their aims, and wasting their (and their children's) lives away in a futile quest for dominance.

Sitting at a Jewish café in the town square towards the end of the tour, Erika and I cornered Yossi and asked him to expand on how the "Hebron problem" could be solved once and for all. "Look, maybe we need to do to them what they did to us in '29", suggested Yossi, referring to the massacre of Hebron's Jews long before the State was established.

"I don't like to see people get hurt," he assured us, "but I don't see another way at the moment. The only way to stop Arabs running after you is to run after them, and then to keep them on the run." He went on to detail the ultimate goal of Islam, as he understood it: world domination, with everyone bowing down to the altar of Muhammad. As he saw it, it was a case of "us or them – and we can't allow the choice to be made for us".

"We have to smash them conclusively," he said, growing animated by now and clenching his fists in rage. "I know it sounds extreme, but Hiroshima and Nagasaki were actually good for both sides in the long term. They saved American lives, of course, but also countless Japanese lives as well, by bringing the war to an end and showing them who was in charge."

I kept my counsel; after all, I was only hearing his diatribe on the assumption that I was as rightwing and religious as the rest of the group. "We have to collapse the PA and retake control of the Palestinians," he told me. "Aren't you worried that that would affect the Jewish majority in Israel?" Erika asked innocently. "Not in the slightest – we just won't give them the vote," said Yossi decisively.

"Listen," he went on, "the average Arab mum with fifty-five children is no demographic threat, since she herself has no interest in democracy. If we don't give them the vote, they won't care – they're used to being ruled by others, so why should it be any different here?"

This was the meat of the trip; all the rest had been mere hors d'oeuvres. However incendiary his speeches had been up to that point, they paled in comparison to the rhetoric he was spouting now. And, for all that the JCDF tour had horrified me, that group seemed like Meretz[11] compared with Yossi and his comrades.

His plans for retaking the "Greater Israel" of Bible times made complete sense to the others, who lapped up Yossi's next offering. "It's all part of G-d's plan," he declared. "Why do you think that those countries that should be ours are also the same countries with such unstable governments?" He let that sink in briefly, before expanding on the theme.

"Egypt and Jordan – they're not meant to be ours, so they have strong leaders and domestic calm," he said, ignoring reality in favour of knocking square pegs into round holes. "Whereas Lebanon and the PA territories – all of which should be part of Israel, and will be – are collapsing around their populations' ears." The rest of the group adored that way of thinking; after all, whenever "G-d's plan" was mentioned, they found it unnecessary to apply logic, and just let their starry-eyed wonderment take over.

To me, the religious lunacy of Yossi was as beyond the pale as that of the Islamic groups who believed that Israel must be obliterated in order to fulfil the will of Muhammad. But, just because these groups lived on the edges of reality, it didn't mean they didn't play an enormous part in the destabilisation of this region, with their vast financial and human resources, and their willingness to stop at nothing to achieve their aims. And, for all that I loved my religion, some of my co-religionists made me ashamed to sport the same *kipa* as them, wear the same *tallit* (prayer shawl), and pray to the same God.

I recoiled just as fiercely from my fellow kinsmen a week later during a right wing demonstration in the settlement of Homesh, which my unit had helped evacuate during the Disengagment two years earlier to the day.

Standing precariously close to the edge of the mountain, the two boys gazed down at the town below them as they waved their outsized flags with pride. But they weren't a couple of valiant explorers who had successfully scaled a previously unconquered peak, and they weren't inviting the villagers below to share their sense of jubilation. What they were, instead, were two religious settler youths who'd come back to the abandoned settlement of Homesh and were taunting the townspeople below with the Star of David. Why? To, in their words, "show them that we're back – and that we're not going anywhere".

"Nothing can stop us," said Aron, the cockier of the two, when I asked him what message he wanted the

Palestinians below to get from their display. "I want them to see that after 2,000 years, the Jewish people have returned – and yeah, I hope waving the flags did wind them up, so that they know how it feels."

Another day, another display of settler racism – not surprising, given the trip Josh and I had embarked on, but this time the scale of the hostility was far larger. We had come up on one of fifty buses chartered to bus settlement supporters to Homesh, in the heart of the West Bank, which had been emptied during the Disengagement and which the settlers were desperate to reoccupy.

Marching under a six foot high banner proclaiming "We will not forgive, we will not forget", the thousands of protesters swarmed around the ruins of the former settlement, planting trees and preparing the ground for their "inevitable" return. The event was organised with the approval of the IDF, which prompted the more extreme branch of the settlement movement to boycott the march, in protest at the collaboration of the settlers with the same army who evicted them two years earlier.

In spite of the split in the movement, the settlers were out in force on the site where Homesh once stood. Bands played soft rock numbers to the mainly young crowd, people sang and danced in the overgrown fields, politicians gave speeches – and all under the watchful gaze of the army. One soldier we spoke to told us "I understand how the protestors feel – this was their home after all," as he nonchalantly described what his unit would do if the crowd refused to leave the hilltop at the allotted time. "We'll try to eject anyone who attempts to camp out here," he said, "but if they won't leave, we'll have to stay up here and guard them until they do."

Having witnessed, and participated in, the hard-line repression of Palestinian protests during my time in the IDF, the duplicity of the army when dealing with right wing protestors spoke volumes. It wasn't as though the military treated all Israelis gently; the left wing got it in the neck, often literally, at protests such as those held every week at Bil'in. For a supposedly impartial army, the tacit approval of such incendiary marches was shameful, especially with the world's media looking on.

It wasn't as though the Homesh crowd were just looking for a benign location to vent their frustration and despair. If they were, they could have arranged a gathering at Rabin Square in the heart of Tel Aviv, and avoided yet more heartache for the Palestinians living in the northern Shomron region.

Of course, that wasn't the aim at all, as the two flag-waving provocateurs on the hilltop proved perfectly. "We have three options for dealing with them," said Yitz, pointing at the village below with his flagpole. "Make them live in peace with us, let them carry on with their terrorism, or kick them all out. All the people down there want us dead – giving places like Homesh back to them isn't enough, in their eyes."

Sarah, who lived on a nearby settlement and had come to Homesh to make a similar point, gestured expansively to the hills on the horizon and declared "in the long term we'll be on that hilltop, and that one, and that one... and Gaza too. It'll be a slow process, but it will happen." She lamented the fact that "round the world people have an image of us as the bad guys – but they [the Palestinians] can build their houses anywhere and not get killed, whereas whenever we settle somewhere we need the army to come and defend us. It's ironic."

Regardless of her skewed interpretation of which side was more dangerous to the other, the fact that the army were once again opting to walk hand in hand with the settler back into the West Bank was an indictment of the political situation in Israel. For the Palestinian villagers looking up at the spectacle from down in the valley, "We will never forgive, we will never forget" could well have become their rejoinder next time they were asked to take Israel's overtures of peace seriously.

In his report that week, Alvaro de Soto suggested that "If Israel... was seen to be moving earnestly to end the occupation, I believe it would aid rather than handicap its legitimate fight against terrorism."* Aiding and abetting racist hilltop youth in their quest to do just the opposite gave a good indicator of the Israeli leadership's real level of commitment to forging peace with their neighbours.

***

"Yeah, we've got lots of famous NF leaders on the estate," said the mother of the household, bursting with pride. "He holds an annual dinner here, where he raises a lot of money from the neighbours to fund the NF Youth school over in Burnley." As we continued discussing the "Paki problem", as she so eloquently put it, she remarked "me? I hate all them Pakis. Well, I say all, but not that friendly one at the corner shop – he's the nicest Paki I ever laid eyes on. But as for the rest of them…"

Scratch the surface and the hate coursing through the veins came to the surface, as Josh and I were finding out time and again on our trip. The above exchange took place over a June weekend, albeit with "Arabs" replacing the word "Pakis" and "Kach" replacing "NF", and was made all the more chilling because of the lack of guilt with which our hostess spoke her piece.

She, along with the others who we'd met thus far on our travels, had successfully managed to override any feelings of shame or embarrassment about their unabashed xenophobia towards their Arab neighbours. They had done this by contextualising their hate and convincing themselves that it was permissible, even admirable, because of the nature of the conflict. Jew versus Arab. Jacob versus Esau. God versus the Devil.

They believed, with an unshakable conviction, that they were part of a Biblical narrative that had played itself out for several thousand years, and which was now being played out on the plains of Judea and Shomron

***

*http://guardian.co.uk/world/2007/jun/13/israel5

where they made their home. They gazed out of their hill-top caravans over the desert plains, surveying the city of Jericho far, far beneath them, and believing that it was their destiny to fight for the cause until their dying day.

"God told Abraham to settle the land of Israel, and that's what we're doing," explained our hostess when we asked why she'd made the move from New Jersey to the mountain range east of Jerusalem. "I came here when I was in my early twenties, and thought 'I just have to live here'. I never felt comfortable back home – when I came here and got off the plane, I fell on the floor and kissed the ground. I read in the Torah that this is where the Jews are supposed to be – I'm never going back."

Non-religious by birth, she and her husband got pro-gressively more orthodox, having six children – "six for the six million" – and then moving them all to Israel twelve years ago. The family changed their English first names to Israeli ones (she had been Ellen and was now Esther), and took it upon themselves to live out the com-mandment to reside in the Holy Land, "where I feel that I belong", she said.

The overriding "Holy War" element to her way of think-ing appeared to be the reason she was so happy to conflate the ethnicity of all Muslims into one homogenous "Arab nation". This was apparent when, on being asked what she would do to bring peace to the region, she espoused the views of Meir Kahane and said "I would pay the Arabs to leave and send them off to the Arab coun-tries all around us. Israel is so small," she said, "and their lands are so big – I just don't understand why they want a piece of our country too."

I pointed out that the "Arab countries" have appeared reluctant to take in the refugees thus far, to which she cried "exactly – *that's* the problem! They don't want them!", her face betraying her confusion at this state of affairs. There was no hint of recognition in her eyes that the Palestinians were not, by definition, Jordanian, Syrian, Lebanese or even Egyptian. Instead, she had them all down as "Arabs", who ought thus to have been dealt with and aided by other Arabs – and who certainly should not have been the responsibility of the Jews.

She hadn't always felt like this, she told us. "I was a liberal for the first forty-two years of my life," she said. "When I lived in the States, I didn't have an opinion on the Arabs at all. But when I moved here, and I heard all my neighbours saying 'I want to kill the Arabs – they're evil', I started thinking that there must be something in what they were saying. When the Intifada broke out and the terror attacks hit Israel, I began to think that perhaps they were right."

However, a couple of years earlier, she met Musa, an Israel-Arab physiotherapist who helped treat one of her elderly relatives who had suffered a broken hip, and her feelings towards "the Arabs" took another twist. "He was such a nice guy – well-educated, polite, a real gentleman. What the experience taught me was that everyone has to be judged individually – but the problem is that most Arabs aren't educated and can't get along with us."

That she could utter both halves of that sentence in the same breath was bad enough, but worse was the fact that she was clearly confused as to her feelings towards the "other side", yet appeared to be happy to err on the side of racism whilst she remained undecided. This was a woman who loved her children with all her heart and soul, who displayed an equal devotion to the land of her forefathers, who had taken in her husband's elderly aunt to look after for her autumn years – yet who could dismiss "most Arabs" as casually as if she were discussing the weather.

A woman who came here with "no opinion on the Arabs", and now believed there "must be something in it" when all of her settler neighbours derided them as evil and called for them to be killed. And her story was by no means unique, and by no means exclusive to settlements. It was the same story on council estates in Oldham to tower blocks in Bow and all the way up to the mountains overlooking Jericho and the Dead Sea. The rulers of the roost sucked in the weakest, chewed them up for a year or two, then spat them out in their own mould; and in closed communities such as these, there was no one around to counter the hate.

The deeper we delved into the settlers' world, the more apparent it became that the casual racism with which we were confronted was dwarfed by the overarching discriminatory practices of the authorities. By seeking to 'normalise' the settlements and convincing the residents that living beyond the Green Line was acceptable behaviour, the government was guilty of institutional deception and malevolence, to the detriment of the Palestinian victims of their crimes.

Thanks to the government's programme of subsidies and support for anyone who relocated to the West Bank, the settler population was a far cry from the original, ideologically homogenous group that first set up home in the Occupied Territories.

It might not have been what people wanted to hear, it might have gone against all of their inbuilt prejudices about those who lived in the West Bank, but the truth about life on the other side of the Green Line had to be swallowed whole. Whether willingly internalised or merely by process of peristalsis, the various guises that the residents took was vital to anyone trying to understand the complexities of the situation, if they were to have any idea of how deep-rooted the settler phenomenon was.

Maaleh Adumim was a perfect example. A stroll through its lush parks and immaculate streets conjured up the immortal words of The Fabulous Micky C: "Jump in my car, who cares where we are – man, we can pretend this is Texas". Replace Texas with Jerusalem, and you had Maaleh Adumim down to a T. Ask anyone you passed about how they felt living in a settlement, and the response ranged from blank incredulity to downright amusement, since the majority of residents saw their city as merely another Jerusalem suburb, and a million miles away from the settlement enterprise.

112

On closer interrogation, they would concede that yes, Maaleh Adumim was over the Green Line, hence could be classed as a *yeshuv* (settlement), but they still wouldn't call themselves settlers. And why should they have done so? The government had duped the inhabitants into believing that they live in as politically acceptable an address as the Germany Colony or Katamon.

Other than the casually-manned checkpoint on the outskirts of the town, Maaleh Adumim looked and felt like any other location inside Israel proper. An enormous shopping mall stood proudly on one side of the ring road, facing the country club and outdoor pool on the other side of the hill. Thousands of brand new homes were crammed together in uniform arrangements, and schools, libraries and other amenities were conveniently placed within walking distance of the main neighbourhoods.

Nothing would sway the average Maaleh Adumim resident from believing they had every legal right to live in the city; at least, not whilst their own government continued to indulge them by turning the area into an idyllic retreat a mere stone's throw from Israel's capital. This was the turning of dream into reality, as far as the expansionist plans of Israel's leaders were concerned, or – from the Palestinian point of view – turning nightmare from fiction into fact.

And then, at the other end of the scale, came the assertion I heard at the Shabbat lunch table that "the government will always turn a blind eye to new settlements being built". Josh and I were guests at a family who, in the host's words, "never thought about the politics of the *Shtachim* until we came to live here". Now it was a different story for the family. "We are products of this place," smiled the man of the house. "Ever since we moved here, we've realised how important this land is to Israel, and how we must keep constructing *yeshuvim* here to strengthen our claim to it."

We asked him how he felt about the new hilltop settlement a couple of miles from his home, which even the

Israeli government had branded illegal (although as yet hadn't done anything about dismantling). "The one percent of settlers who live in illegal *yeshuvim* could be seen as problematic to our cause," he replied, "since they give us a bad name and they're the ones that the media focus on."

"However," he went on, "every single settlement began as an illegal one – even ours – and therefore I have to recognise how vital it is that the one percent carry on with their work. If we consider all this land to be ours, which we do, then it is vital to keep on building on every hilltop in the region."

He was not a particularly religious man, nor particularly extreme in his politics on the scale of characters we'd come across so far on our trip. However, he – along with his wife and children – was a perfect example of how easily the average Israeli could be convinced of the "need to settle", once they'd set up home in the region and let the politics of their neighbours do the rest.

The bulk of the blame lay at the feet of the government. It was the government which turned a blind eye to illegal hilltops being constructed, and it was the government which then rubberstamped the hilltops' expansion. And it was the government which showered the residents of the settlements with discounted tax rates and rent subsidies to coerce them into continuing to live in such contested areas, thus creating the 'facts on the ground' that were so vital to the quest to keep hold of the land.

Then, once hilltop became settlement, and settlement outgrew its borders and gave birth to satellite hilltops of its own, the process was well underway for the next Maaleh Adumim metropolis to be fashioned on the desert plains. And, as every clued-up Israeli would firmly declare, Maaleh Adumim "can never be given back – it's far too big for that". Four or five more strategically located Maaleh Adumims would be all it would take, and suddenly the settlement juggernaut would have rolled too deep, too fast, and the whole land-for-peace concept would be mere roadkill on the route to Greater Israel.

Out at lunch at a friend's house a few days later, his six-year-old son commandeered me to read to him from his favourite book whilst the others got stuck into dessert. He shoved into my hands a slim volume with a picture of a saintly-looking Jewish boy on the front cover, surrounded by baying dogs and vicious looking Cossacks with pitchforks and bayonets aimed in his direction. Intrigued as to what kind of story had so captured the attention of my friend's child, I sat down on the sofa and read the book out loud from cover to cover.

The story centred around the child on the front who, on finding himself stranded in a Russian synagogue as a pogrom raged around him, decided to entrust his salvation to G-d – and was predictably delivered from harm in the final chapter. As my one-man audience listened enthralled to the tale for the umpteenth time, he turned to me and pointed at a picture of the Russian soldiers who were leading the assault on the Jewish villagers. "They're Christian," he told me in a conspiratorial whisper, his wide eyes drinking in the violent scene on the page. "Is it true there are lots of Christians where you come from in England?"

I wasn't sure how to respond, given the terror that the word "Christian" evidently struck into him. "Yes, there are," I replied, "but we all get on pretty well with one another, and certainly nothing like this ever happens." Looking confused, he stuck his thumb into his mouth, then settled back to hear the rest of the tale of salvation and redemption unfold.

A couple of days later, I was getting lunch ready with another friend, who assured me that "the world can't fuck with us anymore now that we've got Israel". By "we", he meant the Jews, and by "fuck with us", he meant the various attempts at annihilation of the Jews that "the world" had attempted throughout our 2,000 year history (presumably including the efforts of the Cossacks, as portrayed so graphically in the illustrations of the religious story book earlier in the week). My friend told me that we – "the Jewish nation" – couldn't rely on any other country or people to come to our aid, since their apathy to our plight had been proved over the centuries.

He cited England's failure to do anything at all when confronted with aerial photos of the death camps midway through the Second World War. "They could have saved us, but chose to act like they were blind and ignore what was going on," he spat, his eyes blazing with indignation as he ruminated on the injustice. "So why should we care now when England decides to boycott us, chastise us, and tell us how to behave in relation to the Palestinians?"

Right or wrong, in essence these examples of paranoia and siege mentality needed to be addressed by those outside the Jewish camp if they were to be able to understand how to get their message through to Jews, and by extension Israel. For my part, I didn't think that anti-Israeli sentiment necessarily equated to anti-Semitism, however I didn't feel that my views were in any way representative of the majority of Israelis and Jews. There was a growing feeling amongst the Israelis I knew, as well as the Diaspora Jews with whom I grew up, that the vast amount of world attention paid to Israel was totally disproportionate, and was born out of anti-Semitism.

An old man I spoke to in the next settlement we visited told me that the world's obsession with castigating Israel was anti-Semitism pure and simple. "It might not be as bad as that of the Nazis, but it is anti-Semitism nonetheless," he sighed. "If 100,000 people die in Sudan," he said, "it's news for two days. But if an Israeli soldier slaps a Palestinian, it's headlines for a month". Warming to his theme, he asserted that the world's hostility is "probably subconscious, and we're doomed to remain on the receiving end of it forever – there's nothing we can do."

He recounted a well-polished anecdote of his that he believed more than proved his point. It centred around the signing of the Oslo Accords in 1994, which included the handing over of Jericho to Palestinian control. "France sent a football team to play a friendly match against Arabs from

116

Jericho," he remembered, "which was all well and good, and not done with any bad intentions – at least, not consciously." However, according to my narrator, "over a hundred countries have received independence since the United Nations was formed, and when did France ever send a team to play against any of them in celebration?" He sat back in his armchair, satisfied that he'd amply got the message across to his young audience – and, in a way, he had.

I'd certainly got the message – thrice in as many days – that the winds of fear and paranoia were swirling around my compatriots at an alarming speed, and that every little story concerning Israel could and would be twisted to suit their frightened outlook. And when the sky looked like it was falling in, be it on Israel or the Jews at large, then the already-entrenched would dig even deeper, the alarm bells would peal out even louder, and the wagons would be rearranged into a protective circle until the danger was seen to have passed.

Jews had spent years kowtowing to the will of ruling nations and host countries, and the scars of recent atrocities were still fresh and raw in many Jewish memories. That didn't excuse any of Israel's many misdemeanours but, when the world chose to haul Israel over the coals day after day, month after month, they should have been under no illusions as to how their reproaches were viewed by millions of Jews around the world.

Israel was created as a Jewish state, for better or worse, so it shouldn't have been difficult to understand that – in the eyes of many – to criticise the Jewish state was to criticise the Jewish people. What was far harder was to find a way to separate the two entities sufficiently to pacify the fears of a deeply suspicious and untrusting people. But that needed to be done, and soon, if any real progress was to be made in convincing Israel – and the Jews – that the world was truly balanced in its dealings with the State of Israel.

A *Guardian* reader asked me later in our trip whether the settlers we'd met have an issue with putting their

117

children in the line of fire by raising them on the other side of the Green Line. His question gave voice to the largely-held belief that life in the *Shtachim* was akin to residing in a war-zone, and that settler parents were doing their offspring an injustice by exposing them to a daily diet of violence and fear.

However, as I replied to him, the residents themselves saw their security set-up as anything but precarious. "During an Intifada, it's far more dangerous to live in the cities than in a settlement," declared one man we met in Kedumim, before going on to provide statistics to back up his claim. "Suicide bombs killed six or seven residents of my home town Petach Tikva – whereas no one was killed on our *yeshuv*," he said, knocking on the wood of his chair to ward off the evil eye.

The assuredness that he displayed was a common trait of those we encountered – and it reached far beyond their confidence in raising their own flesh and blood in the *Shtachim*. Many settlements had set up schools and study retreats for residents of Israel proper, and the students attended in their hundreds. The intentions of the settlers were noble enough – wanting to provide a quiet environment in the countryside conducive to study – but, at the same time, there was a marketing ploy going on.

Yakov, a long-haired, post-army Israeli with dreams of India and Laos, was a student at the *midrasha* in Kfar Adumim, where he had spent the last four months studying philosophy, religious texts and other material with a group of fifteen others. He had no connection to the *Shtachim* before taking up his place at the school, yet he now was seeking to extend his stay on the settlement well past July, when the study programme was due to end.

He spent most of his free time swimming with his dog down at the *wadi* (gorge) near the school, and his love of nature combined with the tranquillity of the surroundings meant that he could see himself spending another six months living and working in Kfar Adumim. Politics played no part in his desire to stay – and that was just what was so alarming about his decision to remain.

Through a combination of accessibility to the West Bank and stimulating activities once they arrived, the students were left with the impression of life in the *Shtachim* as no less appealing than English students might have found a similar retreat in the rolling hills of Devon. There was no talk amongst the attendees of fear of attack, nor any politicised polemics about whether the land should be retained by Israel. Instead, they had been entirely normalised to the area during their four month sojourn there.

A similar situation existed in Kedumim, the settlement near Shechem (Nablus) where we'd stayed at the beginning of our trip. Twelve years ago, one of the residents set up a school exclusively for Ethiopian girls who live in 'bad' neighbourhoods throughout Israel. His intention was that they should be able to escape the negative influences present in many development towns – drugs, crime and the like – as well as be provided with extra-curricular tuition, something that many Ethiopian parents were unable to provide at home. Again, the intention was nothing short of laudable – but, at the same time, throwing the girls into the heart of the conflict had effects other than just providing them with better schooling.

Mazal, a seventeen year old religious student on the programme, repeated the assertion that she felt safer in the West Bank than back home near Tel Aviv. "Here, it is only Arabs that cause problems, whereas in the city, even Jews might attack you – the city is far more scary," she told us.

Staying on the theme of fear and loathing, her friend Yafa then chose to interject and tell us that "I'm scared of all the Arabs". I asked her what she would say if someone told her they were "scared of all the Ethiopians". "I'd laugh at them," she said, but wasn't prepared to accept that her take on "all Arabs" was equally hard to hold up to scrutiny.

"The image we have of Arabs is the problem," said Mazal. "For example, the other day there was an Arab worker fixing the roof at school, and he had two *shomrim* [security guards] standing next to him the whole time. That made us think he must be dangerous". She conceded that "there must be some good Arabs", but said that the impression they had of "bad Arabs outweighs any impression we might have of good ones". With no contact between them and Arab students of the same age, it appeared that the only Arabs they would come across whilst in Kedumim would always be surrounded by armed guards, thus reinforcing their perceptions of Arabs as dangerous.

Both girls had become both politically active since joining the school, and took part in protests against the disengagement of Gush Katif in 2005. Mazal told me that "of course land-for-peace doesn't work – just look at what's happening in Sderot". She said that she would happily live in the *Shtachim*, as and when she got married, "assuming that my husband doesn't mind".

This was what happened when the settlement doors were thrown open to the rest of Israel. Youths who would otherwise have little or no connection to the political situation found themselves drawn into the arena, exposed to the minutiae of life behind the Green Line, and – in many cases – were chewed up and spat out in the mould of settlers-to-be.

The settlement enterprise thrived on the illusion of normality and, to all intents and purposes, much of what these students experienced in the *Shtachim* was normal – on the surface at least. However, the peaceful atmosphere in which to study, or the still waters of the *wadis* in which to swim, could be easily branded *trompes l'oeil* when it came to the wider implications of living on such contested land. But, as long as all looked rosy to the influx of wide-eyed students who flocked to the region, they were easily conditioned to see the area as exactly how the settlers wanted them to see it. Just another part of the State of Israel, and a part that was as integral to the country's make-up as Jerusalem and Tel Aviv.

***

We'd been warned that Nadia was something of a firebrand and, as we walked towards her front door, it appeared that our advisers had been spot on in their assessment. Her battered Chevrolet van was swathed in scores of political bumper stickers, professing hate for both the Palestinian leadership and Israeli government alike, and there was a huge orange flag flying on the well-kept front lawn. Sitting at a table to the side of the house sat Nadia herself, barking into the mobile phone clamped to her ear, and scowling with frustration at the person on the other end of the line.

When she saw us, she mellowed somewhat, breaking out into a well-polished smile and motioning for us to sit down opposite her. A couple of her kids peered at us curiously from the front door, then Nadia hung up the phone and we got to work. The next hour was spent with her firing off soundbites as we struggled desperately to keep up with the transcription. She packed as much rhetoric and opinion into the interview as she possibly could, adamant that she'd make the most of this opportunity to spread her message, given that she didn't enjoy the best of relations with the Israeli press.

"They're very left wing," she told us, "especially the state media. Anything that Peace Now say gets straight into the papers here, whereas whenever I put out a release, it just gets ignored." She was the head of Women in Green (WIG), an activist group that she founded along with her mother-in-law in order to "protect the Jewish people's right to this earth, so that our great-great-grand-children can still live in the Land of Israel."

The group was made up of both religious and secular Jews; Nadia called herself orthodox, yet was wearing trousers when we met her – and this dichotomy was reflected in WIG's policies. "Our ideas are based on both the religious and historical connection between Jews and the Land of Israel," she stated, "however, we're not just doing it for the Jewish people's benefit..."

121

Here we go again, I thought, knowing full well what was coming next, thanks to my recent tour of duty with both the Hebron Fund and JCDF. "It's in the world's interests that we stand up and be strong against the Arabs," she assured us, getting more and more animated as she warmed to her theme. "The Arabs won't stop if they get the *Shtachim*, they won't even stop if they get all of Israel. No, that would just be the first course in their quest to take over the world."

According to Nadia, as well as far too many others I'd met recently, this was the opening salvo in "the war of Islam versus Judaism and Christianity. The Arabs have a saying – 'first the Saturday people, then the Sunday people'. If we cave in, then the next step will be turning Europe into Eurabia." Explaining her family's presence in the salubrious West Bank settlement of Efrat, she told us proudly that "we're the bullet-proof vest for the rest of Israel, and – by extension – the world."

This idea of selfless sacrifice permeated the rest of the interview, with Belgian-born Nadia declaring that she knew far better than anyone else what was best for this troubled country and how things could be righted, if only she had some kind of power. However, since she was staunchly "extra-parliamentary" (due to her disgust at the "corruption of the Knesset, which is in the hands of the left-ist elite"), it was hard to see how she ever hoped to wrest control of the political reins and bring her plans to fruition.

She appeared, to all intents and purposes, to be yet another frustrated extremist, sidelined even further by a self-imposed ostracism from the mainstream. However – and this was where she and her followers differed from the kind of people who just sat around bemoaning their fate – the most alarming part of WIG's hysteria was how pro-active they were in seeking to take on the powers-that-be.

Nadia herself had been slung into jail for her protest-ing "many, many times" and, at the end of July of that year, the group planned to flood onto a contested hilltop called Givat Ha-Eitam to "build a settlement there, in

122

order to counter the government's policy of retreat and capitulation to the enemy". She spoke defiantly of the inevitable confrontation with the army: "It's up to them if it descends into violence, but we'll turn out in force regardless".

And this was only the start, according to Nadia's grand designs for the future of the conflict. Citing the world's opinion of Israel as being based on anti-Semitism, she maintained that "we can only counter their views by being proud Jews". She declared that "no one respects a person who crawls – the only time the world looked up to us was after the Six Day War, when we crushed the Arabs decisively. It's a psychological thing. People respect those who respect themselves."

If she had her way, "during the next war, we must get rid of all the Palestinian leaders, just as Europe destroyed the Nazi Reich. We must kill all of Hamas, all of the PA, all of the PLO, and smash their infrastructure, just as the Allies did in Dresden. It's either that, or being wiped out ourselves." She apparently used to believe in coexistence, but "now I've become radicalised thanks to the new generation of Arabs who can't fathom the idea of a Jewish state where Jewish sovereignty rules the people."

She explained away the entire left wing camp in Israel as being "mentally unwell". "They have a sickness," she said with a sad shake of her head, "and it's called 'beaten wife syndrome'. Whenever the Arabs attack us, the left think it's their own fault, and try to do everything they can to appease them – such as handing over land and power to them." And nowhere was safe when this mentality took hold, according to Nadia. "Peres and the other architects of Oslo* are responsible for 9/11," she stated flatly. "They gave legitimacy to Arab terror, and made the

*The 1993 Oslo Accords were intended to be a framework for the future relations between Israel and the anticipated Palestinian state, when all the outstanding final status issues would be resolved in one agreement.

Arabs believe that they could forever get what they want through slaughter."

She delivered these words without the slightest trace of irony in her voice. The same woman who moments earlier had been advocating the mass extermination of the Palestinian command was now declaring that the Arabs shouldn't be allowed to get their own way through the language of war. And so it went on. The cycle would continue forever, as long as the likes of Nadia and her mob stayed convinced that it was "us or them", and as long as the likes of Hamas and Co. on the other side were saying the same thing to whip up their own followers into a hate-filled frenzy. Those in the middle might as well throw in the towel, it seemed, for all the difference their mild sentiments made when pitted against the fanatics whose actions often match their violent words.

Out pounding the streets of Efrat a day after meeting Nadia, Josh and I walked past a building site where a few labourers toiled away in the afternoon sun. As we turned the corner, we saw another group of workers sitting down in the shade of an olive tree eating his lunch, so we stopped and struck up a conversation with him. What we learned from the brief chat served to reaffirm to us the atrocious state of affairs that existed for Palestinians who were 'lucky' enough to find employment with Israeli contractors, who shamelessly exploited them with no regard for anything other than their own profit margins.

Clad in a ragged t-shirt emblazoned with the logo of an Israeli building company, Boel [not his real name] glanced furtively around him, then agreed to talk to us for a few minutes while the coast was clear. The coast needed to be clear for him to be able to converse with strangers, since in Efrat Palestinian labourers were banned from every activity other than silently doing the job that they were employed to do. Contravention of the rules would result in his permit to work being instantly withdrawn, said Boel, "and I'll end up sitting outside my house all day, with no way to feed my family."

"If I want to go to collect supplies from the gate, the guard must come with me," he told us. "If I want to go to the toilet, the guard must come with me too. If I want to speak to anyone other than my fellow workers, the guard must be present. In fact, I can't even walk more than twenty metres away from the guard, otherwise he'll call the police and have me kicked out of the area." Boel was afforded as much freedom as a dog chained to a gatepost; his invisible shackles were closely monitored by the gun-toting guard, upon whose whims rested Boel's entire livelihood, and who had to be treated with suitably fawning respect by Boel as a result.

Boel received one hundred shekels a day for an eight-hour shift – equivalent to the pittance that the underpaid menial workers (known as the 'Basket Children') earn in the Mahane Yehuda *souk* (market) in downtown Jerusalem. However, even though the Basket Children's wages were pitiful, it was somewhat more understandable given that they were underage, unskilled workers. Boel, on the other hand, was in his mid-thirties and had a wife and kids to feed, plus he'd been working in the building trade for years.

Naturally, given the indifference of his employers, as well as that of the government – who refused to enforce the labour laws – there was no insurance policy in place to assist Boel and his friends in the result of accident or injury. Boel laughed bitterly at the idea that anyone would care enough to provide such cover; "If I get hurt, then I don't work and I don't earn," he said. "Plus I have to deduct any medical expenses from the hundred shekels I earned that day."

Despite all of this, Boel actually felt fortunate to be working on the Efrat project. There was no work whatsoever for him in his home village, and the alternative to this job would have been to seek employment illegally in Tel Aviv or Haifa. There, he said, the exploitation was even more severe, where those hiring knew that they had the workers over a barrel, since Palestinian ID-holders weren't allowed in those areas at all.

"Over there, the work isn't even fit for dogs or donkey," Boel said. "And any Arab who tries to sleep on the site overnight will get attacked by the soldiers on patrol. I have a friend from my village who was heavily beaten with a stick by a soldier – he ended up in hospital, and he can't even see anymore, let alone work".

The abuse wasn't always physical, Boel told us. "Here in Efrat, the guards empty out my food containers every day searching for weapons, even though they've known me for twenty years. Everything that the Israelis do to the Arabs is no good," he stated flatly, instantly conflating his parochial experiences with a far wider assessment of how the two sides interacted. "In the Koran, it says that the Israelis will do this to us for years," he said, finding solace for his predicament through his religious learning. "But it also says that our time will come. This won't go on forever."

The situation in the region meant that both sides could excuse their own abhorrent behaviour towards one another. Efrat residents we met told us "it's a shame we have to treat the Arab workers like that, but they've attacked us from within before," referring to several murders that were perpetrated by Palestinian workers over the previous few years. And, on the other side, when the likes of Boel saw and experienced the racism and oppression that he was on the receiving end of every day, it was little wonder that the more militant amongst his community rose up against their subjugators.

There was no way out of the impasse whilst these perceptions persisted. If we kept Palestinian workers chained up while they worked, we were never going to win their hearts and minds. If they, in turn, resorted to indiscriminate violence against Israelis to exact revenge for their mistreatment, they'd find their pleas for a better life falling on deaf ears amongst those who once might have heeded their calls.

In the meantime, however, a wage increase and insurance cover for workers such as Boel would have gone some way to alleviating his concerns that his Israeli employers couldn't really have cared less about his welfare. However, he – along with anyone else familiar with the status quo here – wouldn't be holding his breath for change anytime soon.

***

The two horse race for leadership of the Likud party that August pitted Binyamin Netanyahu against one of the Israeli establishment's biggest pariah figures. Under the banner "Moshe Feiglin – because he has a G-d", the much-maligned challenger hoped to overcome the heavily-stacked odds against him, wrest control of Likud, and turn it into a party of "Jewish Law". The man convicted of sedition less than ten years earlier was back on centre stage that summer, and was already causing tremors amongst the Netanyahu faithful.

Statistics and hard facts came a distant second to otherworldly belief for Moshe Feiglin and his supporters. When Josh and I met him at his house, he was sanguine about his position in the polls, telling us "it might look bleak now, but miracles do happen – especially in Israel". Assuring us that he was only in Likud in order to "steer it in a new direction", he spoke confidently of becoming prime minister of Israel in the future, and heralding in a new dawn of proud Jewish identity amongst its citizens.

Years on the outside looking in had taken their toll on Feiglin's ability to trust others and court favour amongst his political colleagues. Speaking over his shoulder as he hung up his family's washing in their modest back garden, he told us casually that "I don't care whether the other Likud politicians are nice to me or not – I see myself as part of their party, but with my own agenda entirely." When he first joined Likud, "the others realised that I was a big force, and tried to draw me near to them – but, once they saw I was totally independent, they fought me and tried to keep me down."

His star's ascent had proved difficult to halt, however. Coming third in the primaries eighteen months ago, he was now the only real challenger to Netanyahu, and he had gone from 14% in the polls a month ago to over 25% last week, sending alarm bells ringing in the Bibi camp. And, from what I gleaned during our hour-long interview, the sirens should have been sounding far beyond the offices of the Likud Central Committee.

His plans for Israel's future seemed fairly harmless – at first. "Every child will have to study Jewish history," he said. "They won't have a choice, just like you didn't have a choice learning maths and English when you were growing up." He spoke of reaffirming family values, sounding like the quintessential conservative politician, but quickly returned to his *cause celebre*, the purification of the Jewish state. He took aim at the "half a million immigrants from the former Soviet Union who aren't even Jewish", getting more and more indignant as he spat out his words.

"Why was it so important to bring them all here in the first place?" he asked. "It's because they [the government] don't want Israel to be Jewish. There's a war in this country between two dreams – those who want a Jewish state and those who want a secular Israel." He cited Shimon Peres's declaration that Israel should be "the Singapore of the Middle East", apparently meaning that the country "should have no flavour of Judaism whatsoever". Feiglin's plan was to "return the country to the people, seventy percent of whom see themselves as Jewish first and Israeli second."

The right of return law should be severely tightened, he went on. Currently, anyone with one Jewish grandparent qualified for citizenship but, according to Feiglin's plan, "only those who the Torah says are Jewish will be allowed to come [i.e. only those whose mother is Jewish]". He was reaching his crescendo at this point, and I decided it was as good a point as any to try and burst his bubble. What about an Israeli man who married a non-Jew and had a child, I asked – would Feiglin deny that child citizenship too?

Flustered at the interruption, as well as at his inability to reply coherently, Feiglin stammered that "I don't have all the answers yet, I don't have all the details. Maybe the child would have citizenship, maybe not... I'm just laying down principles for now, trying to point in the direction we should head". Going back to the "Russian problem," he told us that he hoped "many will convert, and that the others will understand that there is no place for them here and find their future somewhere else."

Next in Feiglin's line of fire was, predictably, the Arab population of Israel. "There's a state within a state growing here," he said, shaking his head sadly. "We've got to stop fooling ourselves, look in the mirror, and deal with the problem head on." He said that sixty percent of the territory within the Green Line is controlled by Arabs, "who build where they want, take over more and more land – and we need to start explaining to them who this country belongs to."

In Feiglin's utopia, the Arab population would only have been allowed to vote in municipal elections, and would only have been consulted in civic affairs, "such as sewage". National security, and all the other concerns of parliament, would remain the exclusive preserve of Jews – but not just Israeli Jews. Proposing a two-house system modelled on the United States, he said that the upper house "would be elected by both Israeli Jews and Jews from all round the world, since Israel belongs to every Jew on this earth – all of whom should have a say in how it operates."

The family dog, Scud, was getting impatient for his afternoon walk, so we wrapped up the interview, with Feiglin saving his best for last. "When Jews are proud of who they are, then the Arab problem will disappear," he assured us, rising from his chair and ushering us through the house to the front door. Another day, another diehard Jewish supremacist; and, for all that my CIF detractors castigated me for allegedly only showing the extreme side of Israel, the fact that Feiglin was Likud's number two leadership candidate was worryingly revealing of the state of the middle ground. The likes of him, Nadia Matar and the other firebrands we'd met so far, had done little to convince us that there wasn't a real cyclone brewing on the periphery of Israeli politics that was headed ever closer to engulfing the middle ground.

Once Nadia Matar got wind of the article I wrote about our meeting with her, her hysterical response had been to brand Josh and me as "Palestinian agents". She fired off a mass email to her acolytes, to this effect, calling for them to be vigilant against our espionage. Ignoring the thinly-veiled threats she'd made against us, we headed back into her lair again and witnessed what happened when Nadia was allowed to pull the strings of a few thousand puppets in the heart of Jerusalem.

Her Women in Green organisation was behind the July 2007 march round the Old City of Jerusalem. The march, now an annual event, coincides with Tisha Ba'av, the saddest day in the Jewish calendar. By fasting, and reading the Book of Lamentations, Jews around the world commemorate the series of tragedies connected with this date that had engulfed the Jewish people over the centuries (including the destruction of the First and Second Temples, the expulsion from Spain, and the Holocaust).

However, subdued mourning and introspection did not appeal to Nadia Matar and her merry men. Instead, they hijacked the event in order to disrespect the Arab residents of East Jerusalem by way of their inflammatory march.

It was the Mediterranean equivalent of the Orange Order parade in Drumcree in Northern Ireland. Even the colours were the same, thanks to the presence of the anti-disengagement crowd whose orange t-shirts and flags bore their latest, shamelessly sectarian slogan, "The Land of Israel for the People of Israel". Two thousand people gathered in Kikar Safra, West Jerusalem, where Nadia worked herself and the crowd into a frenzy, stalking round the square in her trademark green baseball cap while preaching her message of hate and war through a microphone.

I asked a passing demonstrator if he was worried that the Arabs might react badly to such an incendiary march, but was reassured that "they know better than to mess with a crowd this big". He strode off into the distance, whilst Josh, Alex and I debated the wisdom of our three-man CIF cell spending the next two hours in such delectable company. Trying to spot Nadia in the crowd before she clocked us was like playing a real-life game of *Where's Wally?*, and in this furtive manner we made our way down to Damascus Gate to begin the parade.

The roads were cordoned off and manned by a huge police presence, meaning that the protestors were free to strut their stuff as provocatively as they liked – and they did. One burly man, dressed in sackcloth in honour of the occasion, spotted a group of Arab youths on the other side of the road, and purposefully stormed over to wave his flag in their faces as he smirked triumphantly. Resisting the urge to connect my right fist to his temple (first or second – either would do), I decided instead to approach my new friend and casually enquire as to what he hoped to achieve with his actions.

In a booming American accent, Eliyahu told me "I don't hate them, I just want them to understand that they can only live here under Jewish rule." As I struggled to keep up with his frantic pacing, I asked him whether he thought this method of getting his message across was likely to do more harm than good in terms of Judaeo-Arab relations. He exploded like a cluster bomb. "Look," he screamed, "I don't care whether they like it or not. They need to understand that they lost the war – we won, they lost. Why it's taken them forty years to get the picture I don't know, but we're not going to stop until they understand who's in control."

Warming to his theme, he went on to deride "the chutz-pah that the Arabs have – they demand that we can't even live in their midst and want us to withdraw. You're from England, so answer me this – what if all the Pakistanis in England said we don't want any whites living in our area, they've all got to go? What would you say to that?"

For all his incendiary posing, Eliyahu was by no means a major player at an event like this. That accolade belonged to the rightwing Member of Knesset, Arieh Eldad, whose speech in front of his adoring audience was as frightening as it was surreal. With the walls of the Old City lit up behind him in a fluorescent glow, he bellowed out his message: "We must take back the Temple Mount, if we are to avoid another *Churban* [Destruction] befalling the Jewish People. We are doomed unless we bring in a strong Jewish leader to rule a land which is meant for Jews, a land which is not meant for Arabs." He left the stage to thunderous applause, the crowd hanging on his every word.

What disturbed me most about the entire evening of marching and sabre-rattling were not the protesters themselves, since our recent trip had left me rather immune to their ranting and raving by now. Instead, it was the absence of counter-protest by fellow Israelis who *knew* this event was going ahead, yet were either too apathetic or too intimidated to do anything to stand up to the fascist face of the Israeli far right.

When I was young, my parents would regularly take me on anti-National Front rallies in Trafalgar Square. They instilled a firm belief in me that standing by and doing nothing made you (almost) complicit in the crime itself. The extremists marching round the Old City were by no means representative of the Israeli mainstream, but they were far better organised, far more passionate, and far more prepared for action than any other section of society here.

With the likes of Nadia Matar and Arieh Eldad at the helm, an event like that on Tisha Ba'av should have sent an urgent warning to their opponents that it was time to stand up and show the world that this type of hate would not be tolerated.

By this point, we had been travelling for weeks round the settlements of the West Bank. Whilst the pieces that

I'd written for CIF had focused on the extremists and radicals who we'd encountered along the way, the vast majority of people we'd come across had been anything but fanatic.

Granted, the majority of the settlers fell firmly to the right of the political spectrum, but that didn't mean that they spent their days spitting venom and preaching war, nor that they wished any ill towards their Palestinian neighbours on the other side of the tracks. Almost every settler we interviewed spoke of their previous good relations with the Palestinians with a sense of *recherché de temps perdu*. They reminisced fondly about the pre-Intifada days when they shopped in the *casbah* of Shechem (Nablus), the markets of Hebron, and the villages adjacent to their own homes.

With a sad shake of the head, our interlocutors would tell us that "it'll never go back to the way it used to be", but that they wished it would, so that both sides could pick up the pieces and return to living peacefully side by side. Most of them had enjoyed close relationships with local Palestinians, in contrast to the racism that was supposedly endemic in the settler culture. I was the first to lay into the settlement movement as an occupying force and a provocative entity, but the sentiments I encountered did not match the misconception of bloodthirsty settlers under which many observers laboured.

On the contrary, in fact. We were welcomed with open arms by every family that we stayed with, whose adherence to the Biblical concept of *Hachnasat Orchim* (welcoming guests) spoke of their charitable and generous nature. For all its faults, the settler community was like one big family, and it was important for the layman to be aware of this before making judgments about the type of Jews who made their home in the West Bank.

Doors were thrown open wherever we went, drivers slowed to offer us lifts whenever we trudged along the motorway in the midday sun, and the warmth belied the cold-hearted image that the settlers' detractors loved to project onto them. What saddened me most about these people was precisely the fact that they *were* so kindhearted in their day to day lives, that they *were* so concerned about their fellow man's welfare – but that they still persisted in antagonising the Palestinians by virtue of living where they did.

However, there were important distinctions to make about why they chose to reside on the 'wrong' side of the Green Line. Whilst their detractors may have written off their actions as merely selfish and callous, most settlers would have justified their decision in quite differing terms. Many saw their presence as the height of self-sacrifice, believing that they were fulfilling the Biblical commandment to settle the land of their forefathers, and were prepared to selflessly risk their lives in order to please G-d.

This was not an issue that could be resolved overnight, as some people would have liked to believe. Whether one believed in their cause or not, there could be no doubt that the settlers too had suffered from the years of mortal conflict between Israel and the Palestinians. Everyone in the settlements knew at least one person who had been killed by suicide bombers or sniper fire, and the scars were still fresh.

We met people who expressed genuine confusion that the Palestinians they had worked alongside for years in the fields of the West Bank were the same figures who downed tools and took up arms as soon as the Intifada erupted. The reasons might have seemed clear to the outsider, but to the people on the ground, the events of the previous few years made little sense at all.

I was not suffering from Stockholm Syndrome, and starting to identify with my "kidnappers", nor was I about to begin championing the settlers' cause, but I was aware that I needed to provide some kind of context to my previous writing on the topic. I abhorred the vicious sentiments as expressed by firebrands like Nadia Matar, but at the same time I was aware that she was by no

134

means representative of the settler community at large. Nor was she even representative of her own community, in fact, where several people we met spoke dismissively of her extremist views and quietly wished that she'd take her rabble-rousing elsewhere.

When I published an article on the subject of the less extreme settlement residents, I was not making a plea for readers to embrace the settlers and clamber aboard the expansionist bandwagon. Instead, I was merely attempting to represent the quiet majority inside the settlements, whose desire to live in peace was far stronger than any imagined urge to fight to the death. From what I'd seen up to then on our tour, there was far more reason to be hopeful about rapprochement than I'd imagined before we first set foot inside their world. Their hearts were in the right place, for the most part – it was just their houses that weren't.

---

[11] Left Zionist political party

Chapter Five

Tolstoy's declaration that there were only two stories in the world – "a stranger comes to town" and "a man goes on a journey" – was perfectly encapsulated by the arrival of a new *oleh* (immigrant) to Israel. For the *oleh* himself, it was a voyage of self-discovery and rebirth, which would see him forcibly immersed into life in one of the world's most volatile regions, and which would open his eyes to the reality of the situation in a way that no amount of second- or third-hand testimonies could ever come close to doing.

For those Israelis who were tasked with aiding the *oleh's* successful integration, they were exposed to a refreshingly different take on their country, its politics, and its reputation, which – whilst they may have taken issue with the verdict – couldn't help but put into perspective the way that they viewed their homeland compared with how those abroad saw it.

That summer, I had marked the third anniversary of my moving to Israel, and the overarching theme of my entire time here had been "walk a mile in their shoes". Of course, I had come here with preconceptions about the people and places I was about to encounter, but at the same time, the knowledge that all my information had been gleaned from other people rather than personal experience forced me to approach it all with an open mind.

My original decision to enlist in the IDF stemmed as much from wanting to get inside the mind of the average Israeli, and understand why they thought what they thought and did what they did, as it did from wanting to take up arms to defend the country. For anyone who truly wanted to comprehend the Israeli psyche, it was of paramount importance to experience what all Israelis went through during their national service.

From donning the uniform for the first time, to throwing a grenade during training in the desert, to tearing round a Palestinian village in an armoured personnel carrier, the lessons learned and information obtained were essential to being Israeli; to seeing the situation through the prism of a native. Those on the outside who railed against the aggressiveness of the Israeli soldiers they encountered at checkpoints, were incapable of comprehending the fear of the new recruit as he spent his first day on active duty, not knowing if the next Palestinian car to speed up to his sentry post would be the one that detonated in front of him and his comrades, blowing them all to kingdom come.

Equally, on demobbing, one of the first things I did was head off to the Palestinian side of Hebron, to see for myself the destitution and penury in which the non-Jewish residents of the city lived. Granted, I was still seeing their situation through an observer's eyes, but – compared with the majority of Israelis, who wouldn't have dreamed of crossing the tracks to see life on the other side – it was massively instructive.

I spent much of the next year traipsing round the villages and refugee camps of the West Bank, making use of my dual citizenship to avoid the restrictions placed on Israeli Jews from entering places such as Jenin, Ramallah and Bethlehem. Areas that I'd previously seen only through the sights of my M16 as we patrolled the streets now seemed far more benign, and far more tragic, than they'd been portrayed by my commanders during our tour of duty.

Stopping and talking to the Palestinian locals about life under Israeli rule brought home the true meaning of oppression. The hollow expression in the world-weary eyes of parents who saw no hope for their children's future was every bit as haunting as any Oxfam appeal for starving African villagers, and every bit as shameful as it ought to have been to an Israeli who witnessed it first hand. At the same time, however, the vengeful rhetoric spouted by some of those I met, who thought they were talking to a non-Jewish, non-Israeli foreigner, appalled me in a way that all but made me believe that these people really were our mortal enemies, and that resolution was a pipedream whilst the likes of Hamas were in charge.

Finally, several weeks touring the settlements of the West Bank and listening open-mindedly to the hopes and dreams of the residents gave me more food for thought than any dismissive, damning report of "the settler movement" ever could have done. The variety of settler, the differing politics of each one that I met, and their diverse takes on the conflict all combined to tear apart the prejudices I had had about them and their ilk, and gave me far more hope for the future than before.

Not every *oleh* had the luxury of spending as much time touring the country as I did, nor did every *oleh* have the inclination to try and experience as many of the facets of Israeli and Palestinian life as me. However, to those on the outside who made it their mission to get involved and take up the cause for one side or the other, they would have been well advised to think about both sides of the coin before banging a drum for their chosen team.

The International Solidarity Movement (ISM) activist who had never met an Israeli Jew, let alone listened to their concerns and fears for their own safety and their country's security, had no right telling the world what Israelis should and shouldn't think. Likewise, the straight-off-the-boat religious American youth who brazenly waved his flag at Palestinian villagers from atop the ruins of a dismantled settlement had no place preaching hate and war against a people whose hardships he couldn't even begin to comprehend.

No one would ever see the whole picture, and nor could they have claimed to be able to, however long they'd been here or however hard they tried. But, the act of walking a mile in someone else's shoes was as good a way as any to open one's eyes to a reality that was all too often distorted by one-sided, closed-minded prejudice – of which both sides were equally guilty.

For an area as sensitive and volatile as this to be over-run by hordes of self-righteous yet intentionally ignorant activists and *olim* was a travesty, and it served to wreak yet more havoc and polarisation between the two camps. If those who wanted to make a difference couldn't take it upon themselves to see the situation from every available angle, then it was better that they kept quiet, or – even better still – kept as far away from the conflict as possible. The Israelis and Palestinians would have fared far better without them.

Ever since I'd begun writing for CIF, I'd found myself under the cosh when it came to my chosen platform for disseminating my work. I never expected anything less, especially given the almost fanatical disdain with which some people treated the *Guardian* and trumpeted its alleged hatred of the State of Israel. Of course I'd encoun-tered the abuse in spades on the discussion threads, but lately it had also surfaced in face-to-face confrontations in Israel, and my friend's wedding towards the end of the summer proved no sanctuary from my detractors' ire.

It began before I'd even arrived at the venue. A burly South African boy sitting near me on the hired coach scoffed when he heard who I wrote for, and quizzically asked how I, a Zionist Jew, could justify giving my mater-ial "to an anti-Semitic paper like the *Guardian*". I asked him if he was a regular reader of the paper, given that he was so secure in asserting its antipathy to Jews. He replied, predictably enough, with: "I don't need to read it to know that, do I? Everyone knows its position – it's hardly a secret."

Confronted with such impeccable reasoning, I left him to his own devices and sought shelter further back on the bus. His line of argument was nothing new, of course, but just because I'd heard it all before didn't make it any less depressing. The *Guardian's* standing amongst the major-ity of my peers in Jerusalem, as well as a large section of

139

my friends back home, was on a par with the much-maligned and detested BBC. What was worse was that the hatred was now so embedded that some people didn't even feel a duty to discover the facts for themselves before aiming their poisoned darts, nor would they entertain any refutation of their wild allegations.

At the wedding itself, I found myself outside with a Swiss girl, whose nicotine craving overrode her desire to carry on dancing the *hora* with the rest of her religious comrades. She told me she worked for a think-tank and, when I asked whether it was right- or left-wing in nature, arched her neatly-arranged eyebrows at me and looked at me askance. "I'm Jewish, right? So my politics are hardly going to be left-wing when it comes to international politics, are they?" "Well," I replied, "I'm Jewish too, but my politics are left-wing; to the point that I even write for the *Guardian*".

That was always going to be red rag to this particular specimen of conservative young lady. "But they hate Israel," she cried, giving me the look of horror usually reserved for child-killers and crack-pushers. I didn't have the energy to bang my head against a brick wall for the second time in as many hours, and – since the bride and groom had now taken centre stage in the middle of a particularly frenzied dance circle – I bowed out of the opportunity for another pointless row and headed back inside.

I expected my work to be judged on its own merits, not on the merits of the medium in which it was published. However, that was not the way it worked; although I understood why I couldn't escape my work being conflated with the *Guardian* party line, I still took issue with having to discuss allegations that fell way outside the ambit of my role as an opinion writer on CIF.

Later that evening, drenched in sweat after another round of frantic dancing, I felt a tap on my shoulder and turned around to find an orthodox-looking boy facing me, asking "Are you Seth? I always read your pieces on CIF..." Here we go again, I thought, and prepared myself for another round of unfounded criticism, either of me or the paper. But, despite the form so far at the wedding, my interlocutor wanted to encourage me to keep on writing, and used the *Guardian's* reputation as the main reason to continue. "You've got a great platform to get an Israeli moderate's views across," he said, "like the line you used about the settlers – 'their hearts are in the right place, it's just their houses that aren't.'"

In my wine-induced haze, I smiled shakily at him as he all but mirrored the thoughts I had when justifying to myself the reasons to ignore those critics who use the *Guardian* itself as a stick with which to beat me. We embarked on a lengthy debate about certain lines I'd taken in my pieces, and why not? That was why I wrote, in order to provoke a reaction about why I said what I said – rather than where I chose to say it.

What the more conservative couldn't stomach, no matter how many times they encountered it, was that it was perfectly acceptable to love Israel yet cleave to left-wing politics and principles when it came to resolving the bitter, never-ending conflict. And if, as in my case, I wanted my opinions on the issues at hand to be in the public eye, and if the *Guardian* were happy to publish them under their banner, then that made us pretty comfortable bedfellows.

Just as a couple didn't have to have entirely synonymous views and attitudes to make their marriage work effectively, likewise with my views and those of the *Guardian* editors. In any relationship, there would be areas where the partners' views widely diverged, as well as issues on which they held entirely similar opinions. In this case, there was enough common ground to merit giving the marriage a decent shot and, given my political leanings, it was where I was happiest airing my views.

A successful relationship didn't require the two parties to agree on every subject. They may well have ended up influencing one another's opinions during the course of their relationship; equally they could have spent their future agreeing to disagree without the call for separation and divorce. Only the couple themselves would ever fully understand the intricacies of their relationship and attraction to one another. Which was why all the raised eyebrows and muttering from the sidelines about "why on earth did they marry in the first place?" wouldn't have had the slightest effect on this particular newly-wed.

I was by now back to my usual, pre-settlement trip routine, seeking out individual stories on which to report to my readers on CIF and with which to further my own understanding of the situation. However, one article I penned after a harrowing morning with a group of left-wing activists prompted David Horovitz, the editor-in-chief of the *Jerusalem Post*, to request permission from the *Guardian* to reprint it in his own decidedly more conservative paper. The *Guardian* duly allowed the article to appear in print in the *Jerusalem Post*, where it received an unsurprising barrage of criticism from outraged, right-wing readers – but their abuse was water off a duck's back. Far more important that they should be exposed to the realities of what was going on in their names, I felt, than for me to worry about the "self-hating" seal of disapproval that they hoped to brand on me as though I was defective livestock. I'd written the piece the moment I got home after my morning with the activists, and it was the most heartfelt article I'd written to date.

Slumped against the concrete slabs of the graffiti-covered security wall, I drifted off to sleep as I waited for the line of Palestinians to shuffle forward towards the checkpoint. The sun shone weakly through the dark early morning clouds, a cold wind did its damnedest to extinguish the cigarettes that hung from almost every pair of lips, and the only sound was the rustle of paper bags as the workers ate their breakfasts al fresco – as if they had a choice... Welcome to rush hour at the Bethlehem checkpoint, where the difference between a day's paid work or a wasted morning's queuing followed by a mournful trudge home all rested on the whims of the bored teenagers manning the turnstiles inside their bullet-proof sentry boxes.

My own presence in the midst of the interminable line of labourers was down to my guides for the day, three Israeli women from Machsom Watch who had encouraged me to use my British passport to pass through the checkpoint into Bethlehem so I could time how long it took me to return to the Israeli side. A trio of middle-aged Charlie's Angels, the women came every Thursday morning to the checkpoint at the crack of dawn to keep an eye on the army's treatment of those crossing the border, and to intervene when required on behalf of the helpless Palestinians whose own complaints went unanswered.

As the queue edged forward agonisingly slowly, I looked around me at the world-weary faces of the men in their tattered work clothes as they stared helplessly at the red and green lights that hung above the turnstile. Those at the front of the semi-dark hall were bathed in the luminous glare of the red light, as it beamed out its warning to stand still and not come any closer to the booth ten metres ahead. A couple of muttered cries of "open another window, please" punctured the silence, but had little effect on the stony-faced soldiers manning their posts.

All of a sudden, the green light flashed into life, and the crowd surged forward as though scrambling for a place on the last helicopter out of Saigon. Five seconds later, and the light was cruelly switched back to red, with less than a dozen people having managed to make it through to the promised land. Eventually, the floodgates opened once again, and this time I was propelled forward by the swell as we pushed our way through the iron doorway.

As we rounded the corner, the men began removing their belts and holding up their trousers pitifully with one hand, as they clutched their valuables with the other. When we reached the x-ray machines, paint-spattered work boots were kicked off and placed on the conveyor belt, along with bags of food and bundles of clothes. Forgetting my current status as merely another body to be searched, I walked through the metal detector without removing either my belt from my waist or my keys from my pocket. The siren screamed out its annoyance at my slip, and I retraced my steps and tried again.

Again I failed, thanks to the lighter in my back pocket, and the men behind me angrily motioned for me to take the situation more seriously. This was no good-humoured queue of holiday-makers making light of inconvenient airport security; this was real life, and time was money to

143

the impoverished men desperate to get through to find work on the other side.

Once I'd reattached my belt and rejoined the queue, I stood morosely in line for another fifteen minutes. Those ahead of me had their hand-prints read by the computer monitors and handed their papers to the soldiers through the gap in the glass. Brandishing my British passport like a shield, I strode up to the cubicle, where the bored girl gave my maroon-encased papers a cursory glance before nonchalantly waving me through, evoking jealous stares from the green-ID-carrying masses behind me.

On my return, I rejoined the three Machsom Watch women and we spent another half hour observing the machinations of the checkpoint. When it became clear that there were not enough windows open to deal with the number of people crossing, Ruti phoned the local army commander, who agreed to send a soldier to man another stall. I was standing next to the door of the troop's barracks, and a sharp blow from behind announced the arrival of the extra soldier dispatched to deal with the crowd, as she kicked the door open and strode into the hall.

Expecting her to apologise for knocking me sideways, I looked plaintively at her, and received a glower and "nu, what?" in return. I responded in kind, but she'd spotted our Machsom Watch badges by now and knew full well who was responsible for the sudden end to her break time. She sneered at me and flounced away, gun swinging from her shoulder in time with her footsteps.

Every now and then, an incoming Palestinian would stop and greet Ruti and her comrades, exchanging pleasantries and thanking them for their work. Outside the reception hall stood half-full minibuses, and those exiting the checkpoint hurled themselves at the bus doors, fighting one another for a coveted place aboard that would guarantee them a day's income on a building site in Jerusalem.

As the queue finally thinned, our observation job was nearly done for the day, and we got into the car and headed off into the hills for the next stage of the proceedings. We drove to Neve Yunis, where two Palestinian men were stranded after receiving fines from the police. Thanks to yet another malicious trick on the Israeli authorities' behalf, a Palestinian who got a speeding ticket, for example, would have his papers confiscated

144

*until he paid the fixed penalty at the appropriate office.
Except, of course, he couldn't get to the offices without his
papers, since the army wouldn't let any Palestinian
through a checkpoint without his ID documents. No payment, no papers; no papers, no payment – which was
where the women of Machsom Watch came in.*

*Ruti and her colleagues played the middleman in this
game, ferrying the money and the papers between the two
sides until the situation was sorted, and so it was that
morning. The two grateful men poured out their hearts in
thanks, before clutching their documents to their chests
and heading off down the dirt track towards their village.
Next up was a visit to the DSO offices, where a large
crowd of young men stood resignedly outside, waiting for
a chance to plead their case for a permit to work inside
Israel's borders.*

*As we approached the group, a white-haired man called
out to Ruti, hurrying over to her and begging her to help
him. "I've been put on the Shabak[12] list," he cried, "and I
don't know why. They say I'm banned from entering
Israel, and they won't give me a hearing to put my case to
them. I've got six children to feed, and all my work's in
Israel – I don't know where to turn". Trying to calm him,
Ruti thrust the phone number of her colleague Sylvia into
his hand, who was well-versed in intervening with the
security services in cases such as this. "I've spoken to her,"
he replied, running an anxious hand through his thin-
ning hair, "but she hasn't been able to do anything so far."*

*"It's getting desperate now at home," he went on. "What
am I meant to do?" Save for encouraging him to try Sylvia
again, Ruti was unable to give him any other practical
advice. Afterwards, she told me that often Shabak waited
until people like him are on the verge of penury, and then
approached them quietly and told them their troubles
could all be over – if they'd just provide them a name of a
terrorist in their village. Even though their quarry might
not have a clue who was or wasn't on the extremists'
books, he'd often give any name just to get his papers back
and regain the chance to work, and thus the cycle continued.*

*As we drove back to Jerusalem, Ruti waxed lyrical
about such criminal deeds. "Occupation has to involve
dehumanisation", she told me. "If you have feelings, you
can't kick someone down – so we've conditioned our soldiers to have no feelings for the Palestinians. We've*

145

brought up this third generation [of Israelis] to act like conquerors, and to have contempt for the conquered."

I suggested that the plight of the Palestinian workers was similar to that of battery chickens. No one liked to think of the conditions battery chickens were forced to live in, instead they preferred not to dwell on the issue at all, so long as they got their cheap meat (or cheap labour, in this case). Ruti agreed, saying "Israelis just don't want to know what goes on, they don't want to see themselves as the bad guys. People need to feel good, so they simply close their eyes to reality."

Which was what made the work Machsom Watch did so crucial to breaking the silence. These women and their colleagues were all Israeli Jews, and their publicising via the Israeli media the atrocious conditions for Palestinians meant that their message reached parts that international activist groups couldn't reach. At the same time, "we show the Palestinians that not all Israeli [Jews] are enemies, and that's a vital part of our work," said Ruti. "Once, at Qalandiya checkpoint, a man brought his six year old daughter to meet us to make her understand that there are good Israelis as well as bad. She was reluctant to meet us, and shied away at first, but he soon got her smiling and talking to us."

The army and the authorities would always be able to justify the tight security measures they used to keep the Palestinians at arms' length, and so too would the Israeli public themselves. However, what they wouldn't, or couldn't, see was that it was the daily humiliation and hardship that bred the next generation of bombers, and that guaranteed the hatred was passed down from father to son and beyond.

The man who returned home without a day's pay to a hungry and desperate family wouldn't blame anyone but the lackadaisical soldier who didn't switch the light from red to green in time for him to clamber aboard the minibus, and neither would his children. The man with no means of getting his ID card back other than coming cap in hand to a group of volunteers from Machsom Watch wouldn't ever forgive the authorities for the misery through which they put him and his family. And the man forced to turn collaborator just to put food on the table for his six kids wouldn't ever forget the cruelty of the occupiers who put him in such a predicament.

If we didn't want terror on our doorstep, we would have done well to treat those over the garden fence with at least

146

a modicum of respect and consideration. If we didn't; if we refused to retreat from our entrenched position of mistrust, mistreatment and misanthropy, then there was no hope for any kind of resolution that didn't involve more bloodshed for years to come. Unless the call was heeded soon by those with the power to help the Palestinians, a bitter harvest would once more be reaped by the very people the army was meant to protect with their actions.

That the average Israeli neither knew, nor – consequently – cared, about the trauma of daily life on the other side of the security barrier was rammed home to me less than a week later, and only bolstered my determination to continue trying to bring as many stories of the occupation to light as I could.

Friday lunchtime in the upmarket strip of Dizengoff Street, Tel Aviv was like walking onto the set of a Vogue shoot. Every girl strutting by looked like Nicole Scherzinger, and seeing and being seen was the only thing on their minds. People sprawled on sofas outside cafes, eyes hidden behind aviator lenses and mobiles permaclamped to their ears as they whiled away the opening act of another weekend's languorous performance.

That afternoon, right in the heart of the whole show, a small group of earnest activists gathered around a cluster of olive trees on the corner of Ben Gurion and Dizengoff, hoping to draw the masses' attention to their protest. Organised by the Coalition of Women for Peace, they were marking the opening of the olive harvest season by performing a symbolic reaping in the centre of Tel Aviv from trees they claimed were stolen from Palestinians.

Their cause was just, their aims were true… but they never stood a chance when it came to waking the beautiful people from their apathetic slumber. Part of the problem was that they were hidden from view by exactly the trees that formed the centrepiece of their demonstration, meaning that most of the passers-by didn't have a clue that any kind of action was taking place yards from where they walked.

However, even those who sat eating their lunch at the outdoor tables on the same strip of the boulevard were utterly uninterested in what was going on next to them. Turning their noses up at the flyers being proffered by the hopeful protesters, they went straight back to admiring one another's clothes and fawning over their latest partners. They were, as Alex put it, "far too busy being

147

agonisingly beautiful to worry about Palestinians' trees being stolen".

I'd been olive picking with a similar group in the West Bank a year earlier, and I was full of admiration for those dedicated to aiding the Palestinian farmers. At the same time, however, they must have known that their latest exercise was doomed to fail in terms of rallying public support for their cause. This generation of bourgeois Tel Aviv residents just didn't care, and the disinterest was endemic the length and breadth of Israel.

For a country that used to brim over with political activists and protestors, the speed with which the youth had turned indifferent and lethargic was as alarming as it was dangerous. Alarming, because it showed how swiftly a state founded on zealousness and enthusiasm could morph into just another lackadaisical Westernised country. Dangerous, because the majority's ennui left a vacuum in the political sphere, which the extremists were only too eager to fill with their own zealous beliefs. In Israel's case, it was the right wing who had seized on the opportunity quickest and most effectively, as was evident in the way they mobilised their youth to demonstrate in defence of the settlement enterprise.

Watching the complete disdain with which the Tel Aviv public treated a serious political protest shocked me, given the gravity of the conflict which had engulfed these Israelis their whole lives.

If they were forced to think about the issue of the IDF wantonly destroying Palestinian olive groves in order to annex their land, most of the Dizengoff diners would likely have expressed some sympathy for the farmers' plight on a humane level. However, it was precisely because they were too busy with their cappuccinos and tuna salads that they weren't ever made to address what was going on on their own doorstep.

The right wing knew this, and capitalised on it in spades. When they put on a protest – such as the incendiary march I'd witnessed in Homesh – they did so knowing full well there wouldn't be a counter protest by their opponents. They were also gradually wresting control of the army too, with forty-five percent of officers now coming from the 'knitted kipa' religious Zionist camp.

And, like it or not, their ability to play the game was paying off big time. As reported in the Guardian that week, the expansionist policies of the government were

148

continuing unchecked; the stranglehold of the security wall was still firmly in effect; and the punitive measures taken against the Gazans were barely opposed by the people on the Israeli street.

That didn't mean to say that the left-wing weren't alive and kicking. They were; all of today's protestors would doubtless spend much time over the next few months getting their hands dirty as they helped the Palestinians gather their crops. Likewise, the grassroots projects of the likes of Machsom Watch, Yesh Gvul[13] and their counterparts would continue at their usual pace, helping the people who really mattered at the heart of the conflict.

But the dispiriting spectacle I witnessed in the heart of uptown Tel Aviv left a bitter taste in my mouth. The silence of the majority left the field wide open for the fervent and dedicated minority to impose their will on the political course that the country charted. I genuinely didn't believe that most of Israel's citizens wanted to pursue a path of war, intolerance, expansionism and injustice, regardless of how many times my readers told me just that on the CIF threads.

What I did believe, instead, was that too many Israelis – especially amongst the younger generation – had just stopped caring. The post-army opium-trail through the Far East quickly detached them from what they'd witnessed during their national service, and by the time they came back to reality they were too busy with careers and bettering their own statuses to care about the conflict. And when the only olives they cared about were the ones adorning their fettuccine alfredo, all the flyers in the world weren't going to paper over the cracks in their consciences.

***

My first trip to Ramallah took place during my pre-CIF days, one month after I'd demobbed, and was one of the most sobering experiences of my three year sojourn in Israel. Having spent the previous fifteen months swaggering round the West Bank clutching a shortened M16 to keep my nerves at ease, being confronted with tooled-up Palestinian militiamen as I slunk unarmed around the city was quite a shock to the system, and one I had been in no hurry to repeat.

149

However, after an aborted attempt to visit a museum in Abu Dis which was closed for Ramadan, a recently-emigrated friend and I and headed back into the heart of the Palestinian Authority. With no agenda other than wanting to soak up the sights and sounds, we brandished our British passports and headed tentatively to Ramallah.

Mindful of Ramallah's previous when it came to hosting Israeli visitors (namely the two reservist soldiers lynched there in 2000), we did our damnedest to assume the identities of wide-eyed Christian Brits-on-tour, and thus did we make our way round the bustling streets of central Ramallah for the rest of the day.

My care not to insult the Ramadan-observing Muslim populace by eating or drinking in public did not extend to curtailing my smoking in the street, and my ignorance of the rules was quickly seized upon by a vegetable vendor we passed in the heart of the *souk*. Grabbing me by the arm, he entreated me to put out the offending cigarette, then spent the next twenty minutes treating us to a local's-eye-view of the town he called home.

A burly man of about forty with sunken eyes and a gruff expression, Sam told us that he had recently come back to the West Bank from Chicago, where he'd been living for years. Within seconds, his hackles were rising, as he cursed the "fucking racism" of the Israeli authorities, who "won't let me or my children into Israel, even though we're American citizens". Eyes blazing with righteous anger, he asked us "how would you feel if you knew your passport could get you into any country in the world except the one that was stolen from you?"

As we played dumb and pretended not to know the first thing about the regional politics, he got into his stride and told us why he and his fellow residents felt such antipathy and hate for the Israeli powers-that-be. "We can't take being in a prison this long," he declared angrily. "All our movement's under the eyes of the army, and we can't take it much more".

150

Continuing in the vein of ignorant first-timer, I asked him innocently if Israeli tourists or shoppers ever came to Ramallah on business or pleasure. "Israeli Jews can't come here by law," he replied, "and anyway, if they did they'd probably be killed." I tried to elicit who would do the killing, and why they'd be so minded to murder in the first place. He clarified his position somewhat, stating that "only some of the youths here would cause trouble to Jews if they came into town, whereas plenty of others would stand up for the Jews and not let any harm come to them."

He declared that "we don't hate the Israeli Jews as people – the problems are all between the two sets of leaders," Gesturing at the heaving market streets all around us, he said "we're not all terrorists, you know. The media like to paint us as such, but the [world] media is owned by the Israelis. Look at these people – do you see any terrorists here? Even the police don't carry guns," he stated, pointing at a tired-looking traffic policeman standing across the street.

This assertion didn't quite ring true, given the enormous arsenal of weapons I'd seen on my last trip to the town, and, as we made our way up the road, it was clear that the police still packed a fair bit of heat in these parts. Out of nowhere came a blood-curdling shriek from behind us, and we turned to see three men beating the living daylights out of a fourth man who was being held over the bonnet of a car.

Within seconds, dozens of onlookers burst into the car park where the fight was taking place, and pandemonium ensued for a few seconds, until a squad of AK47-wielding policemen smashed their way into the fray and dealt blows to the main protagonists of the fight. As the vengeful mob swirled around us, we decided to make a swift exit from the tension-filled street and the nervous policemen trying to keep order.

We headed off by taxi to Arafat's grave, in the all-but-deserted Muqata compound which was guarded by a bored-looking crew of soldiers with little to do, given the complete lack of tourist activity in the area. We walked reverentially across the bleached white concrete to the impressive marble structure and stood in contemplative silence for a few moments at his tomb. Pilgrimage made, we headed back to Jerusalem by taxi, spending over an hour waiting in the stifling heat for the soldiers on the checkpoint to vet those ahead of us in the queue.

Earlier, Sam had stated that "every year gets worse and worse for us", an almost word-for-word repetition of the assertion made by the theatre director I'd interviewed in the Al Aida refugee camp a few months earlier. The difference between the slums of the Al Aida camp and Ramallah's comparatively upmarket boulevards may have been massive in terms of affluence, but the sentiment expressed by the locals was tainted by exactly the same resignation.

Brand new 3-Series BMWs may have driven past opticians selling the latest Gucci sunglasses in Ramallah, but when they got stuck in the interminable queues at the checkpoints, their drivers' rage and hostility towards their Israeli masters was every bit as tangible as that felt by the penned-in poor in Bethlehem. And that, coupled with the total lack of interaction between ordinary Israelis and Palestinians thanks to the wall and the climate of fear in which it had been erected, meant that the polarisation would only grow more acute as the years passed.

The militants of Ramallah didn't do themselves any favours with their actions; the lynching, for example, will be seared on the consciousness of Israelis for decades to come. Just as the punitive measures of the Israeli army were hardly likely to win over the hearts and minds of the moderates such as Sam and his ilk. In the meantime, the fact that visiting Arafat's grave was something only a handful of Israeli Jews could – or would – do, spoke of the gulf that separated the two sides as much in 2007 as it ever did.

***

"WARNING!", screamed the flyer being thrust into my hand by a concerned-looking young religious man as I entered the

152

hall. "American Jews are in danger!", it continued. "Countless Neo-Nazi groups are spreading their venomous [sic] message... at public demonstrations calling for violence against Jews... and praising Hitler as a 'true hero'!"

Fair enough, I thought; that was a pretty sobering prospect, and something worth taking heed of as a Jew who cared about his brethren, and who hated to think of them in danger. That the same boy was then in the midst of a 500-strong crowd yelling "Arabs out! Arabs out!" less than an hour later, and screaming deliriously at footage of the late Meir Kahane, was as ironic as it was despicable.

"Who is wise... those who see the future," was written half way down the same flyer, quoting Pirkei Avot in an attempt to exhort the endangered American Jews to make *aliyah* to Israel and escape the Nazis' evil clutches. The wise man also saw the present though – and knew when to call a spade a spade. Which is why I had no qualms whatsoever about describing the baying mob at tonight's Kahane memorial as the closest thing we Jews had to home-grown fascists.

Rabbi Kahane had been the leader of the Kach party in Israel, and his politics included advocating the forcible expulsion of all Arab citizens of Israel. A former member of Knesset – until his party was banned in 1988 – he was gunned down after giving a speech in the United States in 1990. His followers had been responsible for numerous terror attacks against Israeli Arabs and Palestinians, most notably Baruch Goldstein's bloody massacre at a Hebron mosque in 1994.

At the memorial service, the mere mention of Goldstein's name received thunderous applause from the audience, all of whom were ultra-orthodox, and all of whom had not the slightest remorse at singing the praises of Israel's most notorious mass-murderer. Dozens of men wore t-shirts emblazoned with the slogan "Now everyone knows... Kahane was right", a message every bit as repulsive as a group of German neo-Nazis wearing similar attire with Hitler's name replacing that of Kahane's.

153

The politics of Kach and those of the National Socialists were similar in their vicious racism and call to arms. Footage of Kahane's more incendiary speeches were shown throughout the ceremony, as he ranted and raved to his enraptured acolytes, fists clenched and raised in triumph whilst he spat his venomous message of hate.

"There is no such thing as an Arab village in Israel," he thundered from beyond the grave, "only a Jewish village that is temporarily inhabited by Arabs." The crowd went wild, stamping their feet and giving piercing whistles, regardless of the fact that most of them had seen the footage countless times before. An impromptu chant of "Kahane still lives" was started by a boy in the row behind me, and soon the entire hall was singing as one, from the youngest school-children to the most gnarled and wizened old men in the room.

The women, on the other side of the curtain *mechiza* (divider), were no casual bystanders to the furore. The delirium was just as fervent amongst them in response to the various speakers at the dais whipping the audience into a frenzy. One rabbi, well-known in Kach circles, took to the stage with a huge orange Star of David pinned over his heart, to the delight of those looking on. (In a sick send-up of the Yellow Star that the Nazis forced Jews to wear during the Holocaust, the far-right, anti-disengagement settlers had adopted the emblem for themselves, in protest at the detested IDF and Israeli government's evacuation of Gush Katif).

The service went on for nearly two hours, and showed no sign of abating when I'd had my fill and headed for the exit. Interspersed with the speeches were video montages put together by Kach propagandists designed to reinforce the feeling that their underground movement was the victim of obscene oppression on the part of the authorities. Like something out of *A Clockwork Orange*, film of riot police beating settlers and religious youths was juxtaposed onto a soundtrack of plaintive Jewish song, as children looked on in horror and their fathers shook their heads mournfully.

154

"But we're not beaten," cried the next speaker up. "We've got to mobilise better – every one of you here must spread the word of Kahane, and only in this way will we bring about the true Jewish State that he dreamed of." That same state, according to Kahane when he was in Parliament, would have included a ban on all sexual activity between Jews and non-Jews, and seen only Jews eligible as citizens of Israel.

His assassination in New York in 1990, and the subsequent murder of his son and daughter-in-law at the hands of Palestinian terrorists, only strengthened the resolve of his die-hard followers, who formed the Kahane Chai offshoot which was currently listed as a terrorist organisation by the FBI. It was similarly viewed in Israel too, although the blurred boundaries between Kahane Chai and the original party meant that the police were powerless to ban events such as that evening's memorial.

For my part, I was glad they didn't, since the opportunity to witness the fascist hordes for myself was massively instructive as to how low certain elements of Israeli society had sunk. By hailing Baruch Goldstein as a latter-day saint, they were every bit as repulsive as the Hamas supporters who revered Sheikh Yassin, or the far-right Europeans who mourned Hitler's passing every year on his birthday.

As much as I regularly sang the praises of Israeli peace activists in my articles, so did I just as passionately hate each and every one of those sitting alongside me at the memorial event. These were *our* extremists, these were *our* terrorists – and this was *our* dirty secret that was a stain on the state that was founded as a refuge from similarly-minded fascists. If the likes of the Kachniks got their way, then the wheel would truly have come full circle, when the hunted became the hunter and history repeated itself once more.

---

[12] Israeli Security Agency, also known as Shin Bet.
[13] "There is a limit" – the peace bloc led by Uri Avnery.

Chapter Six

As the year drew to a close, I returned to London on a family visit, relishing the opportunity not only to see my relatives and friends, but also to spend a fortnight far away from the ever-more depressing situation with which I was confronted whenever I headed into the West Bank. However, I couldn't escape the conflict entirely, even on the day I packed my bags to head westwards for London.

As I sat in my house waiting for my cab to the airport, I came across a small article in the Israeli press announcing the cancellation of two upcoming "peace concerts" in Jericho and Tel Aviv. Citing security concerns as the reason that the Jericho show was called off, the paper reported that "Palestinian participants were threatened", requiring the organisers to pull the plug on the event.

The concerts, organised by the OneVoice organisation, hadn't appeared on my radar up until I read the article, but reading of the cancellation put me in a defeated mood as I headed off to catch my plane back to London. This seemed to be yet another case of extremists taking umbrage with a centrist movement's pleas for rapprochement, and putting the frighteners on the organisers until they caved in and cancelled their efforts.

Nothing new, I thought to myself. It had been this way for years in the region; the minute anyone put their head above the parapet, the snipers came and silenced their opponents through violence or threats. It was as though the moment a light of hope flickered to life in the gloom of the interminable conflict, hordes descended on the flame, blowing furiously to extinguish it and leave the situation mired in darkness once more, just as the fundamentalists liked it.

In the case of the Jericho concert, it was Palestinian extremists who had headed off the event's organisers at the pass, but at the same time, the report stated that Chief Rabbi Metzger had also been leant on by his flock to withdraw his support from the Tel Aviv show. He had initially agreed to participate because he "thought [OneVoice's] goal was to voice moderate views on the conflict", but after being harassed by right wing rabbis and MKs, decided to step back due to the group's "political agenda which includes territorial compromises".

So, here was a movement with apparently massive support from both the Israeli and Palestinian camps, trying to unite the two sides and getting a kicking from every angle in return for their efforts. A year's work organising the summits, which were to have had Bryan Adams perform as well as local artists and were due to be screened around the world, was up beyond repair. As I found out when I contacted the organisers upon my return to London, the whole debacle was the result of a thoroughly orchestrated, and thoroughly misleading, smear campaign by the hard left, One-State camp.

According to Jake Hayman of OneVoice, members of the boycott-Israel group PACBI decided that OneVoice were pushing a "secret agenda" advocating the Palestinians give up the right of return, among other things. They issued a release effectively denouncing OneVoice's efforts in the region, which was immediately picked up by hard line groups, including the intransigent ISM.

"Some of the boycotters got hold of a set of surveys we did five years ago," said Hayman, "and have changed questions into statements and manipulated them to suggest that we do have a secret agenda of our own final status negotiation". By distorting the facts in this way, he said, the boycotters had set into motion a chain of intimidation and intense pressure that resulted in the safety of the OneVoice people involved being put in intolerable jeopardy.

Hayman also commented that "they missed the point entirely that we are about empowering the process instead, because – as it stands – even with the perfect 'answer', the leaders are too weak and hardliners too strong to see it implemented". That was the *raison d'etre* of OneVoice, and made the theoretical argument that derailed the summits look even more absurd than it appeared at first glance.

"It's heartbreaking," Hayman said. "Not only has the Palestinian street been conned, but also the Israeli public and international community, who will now think that the Palestinian grassroots won't even attend a conflict-resolution event such as this". OneVoice's efforts had, thus far, been making significant inroads into the region's consciousness, with over 600,000 Israelis and Palestinians having signed up to the group's Mandate.

Hayman's distress would doubtless have been shared by everyone connected with the organisation, but it was the people the group were trying to reach who would also suffer the consequences of the concerts' stifling. The events would have bolstered the confidence of the moderates on either side of the divide, making them believe that the middle-ground peace camp was gathering momentum and taking centre stage in both the Israeli and Palestinian populations.

Instead, those – like me – reading of the event's cancellation in the national press would shake their heads in disappointment before turning the page and reading of the 'success' of other, more violent groups as they pushed their own solutions on the troubled area. And, when it turned out that those purportedly helping the Palestinian cause (ISM, PACBI[14], and the like) were the ones who had done the most damage to OneVoice's pleas for peace, hopefully people would realise that it was time to ignore the extremists once and for all.

From the right-wing rabbis to the ISM, there had to be a mass awakening that neither side would ever have their every last demand met when it came to a conflict as complex as this. As Tony Klug[15] pointed out in a brilliant analysis of the situation, there would need to be very heavy, and very painful, concessions from both sides before peace really had a chance to envelop the region.

Until they did, however, the lights of peace would continue to be snuffed out wherever they were lit, and the likes of OneVoice would continue to be beaten down whenever they tried to bring the warring factions together. If they were kicked down every time they tried, one day they would just stop bothering anymore; and when that day came, the ISM and Israeli hardliners would only have themselves to blame for what followed.

Once I returned to Israel, intrigued as to how OneVoice would regroup and recover, I made contact with their Jerusalem branch and spent an evening interviewing their leadership.

In a small flat in downtown Jerusalem, a group of bright-eyed, eager young men and women leaned forward in their chairs, listening to their leader instruct them in their quest. "We split them into independent cells," said Adi, the woman in charge of proceedings, "and they know their mission, though they have free rein in how they achieve their goals."

If successful, these operatives, along with their colleagues in the Ramallah branch, would make a significant impact on the future of the Israel-Palestine conflict. Through their actions, they aimed to overthrow those currently leading the people, in order to wrest control of the course of the conflict and bring power to the streets. Eyes blazing with righteous zeal, they fired one another up for the long battle ahead as they relished the challenge that lay before them.

"OK," said Shani, from the other side of the room, "we had a major disappointment with what happened last time, but we're looking to the future now and we're going to come back stronger and harder this time." Sitting on a couch nearby, Maya agreed with those sentiments. "For the first time since I joined the group, I had to deal with the reality of the situation hitting me in the face, but it just made me proud to carry on, and more determined to succeed next time."

As I listened to the group talk about their quest, I realised that the militant analogy was an apt one to choose to describe them and their goals. Even though they could not have been further from urban terrorists, their methods and training were no different from the clandestine meetings Ed Husain described in his whistle-blowing account of Islamist fanaticism in London*.

But these activists were the antithesis of extremists, and using violence and terror to achieve their aims was the last thing on their minds. These were the young volunteers from OneVoice Israel, and these were the people who were about as likely to break the deadlock in the interminable conflict as anyone else in the region. Leaving personal politics to one side, they came together as right-wingers, left-wingers, Jews and Arabs, all determined to combat the extremists and preach a message of moderation to the masses.

The Jerusalem cell were tasked with spreading the OneVoice ideology throughout the 27,000 students at the Hebrew University campus. Having undergone intensive leadership training, they were equipped with the skills and the dedication to promote dialogue and debate between their peers on the Palestinian and Israeli sides of the divide. Despite the massive setback caused by their Peace Summit's recent abrupt derailing, they had lost none of their enthusiasm.

"The reason OneVoice is so amazing is that its main concern is ending the conflict, regardless of your political views," said Yaniv, who had just returned from a promotional college tour in the US with a fellow OneVoice leader, a Palestinian girl named Shada. "I can come back from a month in my *miluim* [reserve duty] combat unit and return straight to my work at OneVoice without it being any kind of contradiction," he explained. "I lost too many friends in battle for me to ever love the other side, but that doesn't mean I don't want the conflict to end."

---

*The Islamist (Penguin, 2007)

Adi, the head of OneVoice's leadership programme, agreed with Yaniv's assessment. "It's not about peace and love," she said, "and it's not about pretending that we can all get along. But we have to work together to solve this. I can live with it if the Palestinians don't love us, so long as we can put an end to the conflict and have a safer future for our children." The intention of OneVoice was purely "to empower the moderates to take back the agenda which has been hijacked by extremists", and to show people in Israel and Palestine that those on the other side wanted peace to break out too.

The only political stance of OneVoice was that any settlement had to be based on a two-state solution, which was hardly out of step with what most rational observers called for at that time. "We're not taking a view on the rest of the details", said Adi, "since the two sides are not even at the stage where negotiations are taking place," explaining that it was therefore not timely for OneVoice to get involved in the minutiae either.

On the strength of the volunteers I met in Jerusalem, being cowed by the fanatics was not something that would put off the dedicated members of the group. As much as they were gutted at what had happened to the project they'd worked so tirelessly to organise, they were just as proud of what they had achieved so far.

Whilst full of indignant anger at the way in which OneVoice had been muscled off the scene in Ramallah and elsewhere, I – by virtue of voicing my opinion on CIF – had unwittingly set into motion a sequence of instructive events which reshaped my entire view of so-called 'coexistence groups' and their underlying philosophies. An angry response to my original OneVoice article was posted by Ben White, another contributor to CIF, who made it clear exactly why OneVoice was viewed with such disdain by many Palestinians.

By seeking to "assume equality between occupier and occupied", he wrote, groups like OneVoice denied the reality on the ground, instead sugar-coating the status quo and pretending that things were nowhere near as bad as they were for the Palestinians. Whilst I took issue with his critique at first, I also realised that I was in no position to comment from the perspective of the Palestinians, and so decided to seek the opinion of West Bank residents myself the next time I set foot in the area. What I heard forced me to rethink whether such ventures as that of OneVoice were the best way forward; for all that I promoted putting myself in the shoes of those on the other side (be they settlers, Palestinians, or soldiers), it appeared I had not done so in this case up until now.

I went back to Ramallah at the invitation of an apolitical youth organisation, although politics was, as usual, never far from the minds of all who I met whilst there. A day earlier, I'd been in Neve Yakov, a suburb of Jerusalem the wrong side of the Green Line[16], to interview the director of the local Computer Clubhouse, an Intel initiative for children in underprivileged neighbourhoods around the world. To date, the programme had been an enormous success, with over one hundred clubhouses up and running across the globe. The children were given access to the latest computer programmes and technology, and encouraged to express themselves in whatever way suited them best using the software at their disposal.

Gail Breslow, the woman in charge of the whole operation had flown in from Boston, in order to check on her charges in the various centres round the Middle East. With three clubhouses in Israel, one in Palestine and two in Jordan, it occurred to me during the interview that there could be a valuable opportunity to promote dialogue between Israeli and Arab children in a forum devoid of political pressure and rhetoric.

When I asked the director of the Neve Yakov branch how his members would take to sharing ideas and projects with their Arab peers, he told me that thus far no official connections have been made. "The population of this town are fairly suspicious," he said, "as well as being

162

pretty rightwing. Their sentiments translate to the youth as well, so [dialogue with Arab youth] is not something they'd necessarily be into."

Whilst I wasn't particularly surprised to hear his response, it still seemed pretty depressing that a non-partisan, extra-political movement with a foot in both worlds wasn't being used as a means of getting children on the two sides together. However, the sentiments on the Neve Yakov side of the divide were nothing compared with the stonewalling I received when I suggested the same thing to those running the Ramallah branch.

When we got to the gleaming premises of the Ramallah Clubhouse, we spent a harrowing half hour watching videos that some members had made using the sophisticated equipment at the Clubhouse. Every film centred around the security wall and its effect on the children's lives, and there wasn't a dry eye in the house at the end of the screening. The kids had spoken frankly, and heartbreakingly, about their daily struggle to deal with the humiliation and hardship they suffered at the hands of the IDF on their doorsteps.

To me, this material was worth its weight in gold if it could be put on the Clubhouse intranet and shown to the Israeli members, so that they could see for themselves what life was like for their counterparts only a few miles up the road. Part of the problem, I believed, was that Israelis were ignorant of what Palestinians went through under occupation, because they couldn't or wouldn't go and see the situation in Palestine for themselves. To paraphrase Ice Cube in Boyz 'n the Hood, "either they don't know, don't show, or don't care about what's going on in the Territories"; and, whilst the blind-eye-turning continued, they were never going to have to face up to just how awful life was for the Palestinians.

But, even though the Ramallah directors agreed that dialogue could be beneficial, there were far too many barriers and prejudices on their own side to justify pushing the issue to their members. "We'd lose all credibility

163

amongst the refugee camp's residents if we were seen to make contact with the Israeli Clubhouse members," I was told as we sat having lunch in a local restaurant. "The conflict isn't just political to those living in Ramallah – it's their day to day lives," said Talal, who worked for the Youth Development Programme. "They live with the occupation every minute, and the last thing they'd want to do is engage with the occupiers."

Talal was a veteran of several joint Israeli-Palestinian workshops and discussion forums, and was pretty sceptical about the value of any such initiatives. "They [the Israelis] need to first admit what their country's doing if they want any kind of dialogue with us", he said bluntly. "If they don't admit that they are the ones occupying us, that they are the ones making our lives a misery, then there's no point whatsoever in pretending we can get along."

"Peace doesn't work on a foundation of lies," he continued. "And whilst Israelis continue to kid themselves that this is some kind of balanced conflict, then no progress can be made at all." His co-worker, Hala, went even further, telling me that there was no branch of Zionism with which she could engage, "since violence against Arabs is integral to the concept of Zionism. If you go back to the original Zionists – the Stern Gang and Hagana – they called for, and carried out, extermination of Palestinians, so how can we say there is the opportunity to make peace with Zionists?"

Meanwhile, back at the Clubhouse, the kids were revelling in their activities and delighted to be let loose on the computers and hardware that Intel had provided. Just as in Neve Yakov, the centre had become a haven for children looking to while away their after-school hours in a productive, educational fashion.

However, behind the façade of seemingly identical programmes that could have had great potential for cross-over dialogue and cooperation, the spectre of the conflict loomed, and its presence remained an insurmountable obstacle for both sides. Whilst Gail and her staff had reaped enormous dividends in terms of improving the individual lives of those who frequented the centres, the Clubhouse was as powerless a model as any other when it came to being of use in solving the conflict.

Having interviewed the kids and heard for myself the pain and anguish that they felt living under Israeli rule, I didn't blame Talal and Hala for not wanting to engage with the children on the other side. There was no reason that the Palestinians should be brought to the table as equals of Israel when it came to talking it all over. We were the oppressor and they the oppressed; until we recognised that and treated them accordingly, it was no wonder they were neither willing nor able to sit down and hear the other side of the story.

I asked Talal about the OneVoice scandal, and he confirmed Ben White's basic premise in strident terms. "We considered taking part in their initiative to be collaboration," he told me, "which is why we opposed the event." He said that OneVoice had suggested, via their survey and in other ways, "that the Palestinians are ready to compromise on the right of return [since OneVoice supported a two-state solution], which is simply not true."

He also said that OneVoice believed "in equalising the occupier and the occupied, by [their simplistic] condemnation of 'the violence on both sides'". This suggested that the underlying issue was not the oppression of the Palestinians that had been going on for years, he said, but rather an issue of violence between the two camps – which was a thesis unacceptable to most Palestinians. The more I thought about his, and others', words on the subject, the clearer it became to me that no principled Palestinian was likely to be brought to the table under the guise of being equally to blame for the hostilities.

Over the coming weeks, I wrote two articles admitting to my earlier lack of insight, both of which prompted an enormous response amongst my readers, with just as much praise heaped upon me as there was criticism levelled in my direction. Whilst I wasn't, at that point, ready to revise my views on whether two-states was the only viable solution, I was at least prepared to see why it *had* to be Israel who made the first move to ending the stalemate. Expecting the Palestinians to do so, given the subjugation under which they lived, was not only unrealistic but unfair as well. The first article I published was inspired by yet another organised tour of the West Bank that only confirmed how deeply entrenched the occupation had become with every passing year.

Standing on a dusty ridge on the edge of East Jerusalem, the sun blazed down mercilessly as our guide struggled to make her voice heard above the howling wind. Sweeping her arm expansively over the hills that lay beneath us, she gave a blow-by-blow account of how Israel was expanding ever eastwards, and ever deeper, into land that had ostensibly been earmarked to form part of a future Palestinian state.

For all the overtures that successive Israeli governments had made towards peace; for all the 'painful concessions' they had supposedly made to assuage the suffering of their neighbours, the truth was laid out in front of us as far as the eye could see. Far from retreating from the contentious territory that was the cause of such bad blood between the two sides, it was clear that the authorities were marching ever onwards with their plans to grab more and more land in their pursuit of a Greater Israel.

The worst part about the area, E1, that we were being taught about on the Peace Now tour, was the effect that its annexation would have on forming a viable Palestinian state. E1 was the zone between occupied East Jerusalem and the vast settlement metropolis of Maaleh Adumim, and covered twelve square kilometres of land. However, the impact of its appropriation by Israel went far beyond the size of the territory.

If, as was currently shaping up to be the case, E1 became the final link in the chain between Jerusalem and the settlement bloc around, and including, Maaleh

Adumim, then it would result in the near bisection of any Palestinian state that was declared in the West Bank. That prospect wasn't likely to encourage the Palestinian militants to lay down their arms and rush to the negotiating table with Israel.

After all, it was not as though they were asking for the moon in desiring a state based on what little of their land remained to the east of the Green Line. If a two-state solution was ever to come to fruition, both sides would have had to make sacrifices in scaling back their ideal demands of what they should be given in a final settlement. On the Israeli side, the people would have had to realise that the only way that they could expect the Palestinians to honour a peace agreement was by pulling back to the '67 borders, regardless of how many illegal settlements had to be uprooted in the process.

Similarly, painful as it may have been, the Palestinians would have to recognise that the right of return that they held so dear was not something that could, in its current form, be considered by their opponents if Israel was to retain its status as a Jewish state. Instead, they would have to make do with forming a state in the West Bank and Gaza. But they couldn't be expected to do that if Israel slices up the region into ever smaller units and subdivided cantons.

In the meantime, however, all the diplomatic talks and secret negotiations between the two sides were rendered meaningless whilst Israel made a mockery of its commitment to peace by continuing to plough on with its settlement programme. Even the most cursory glance from atop the hilltop at the level of expansion in E1 belied any government suggestion that it was freezing settlement activity whilst it negotiated with the Palestinian Authority.

We drove to the site of a controversial police station that was nearing completion deep in the heart of E1, and which represented the mendacity of the Israeli government. It had been built in direct contravention of orders

167

to halt construction in contested areas of the West Bank, and its erection was another example of Israel's rush to create 'facts on the ground' before the US or Europe could finally put a halt to their misdeeds.

As one settler told me during my tour of the region that summer, "every settlement began as an illegal one", and that once they became "too big to dismantle", then they had done their job in having annexed yet another slice of the West Bank to the body of Greater Israel. The Palestinians weren't stupid; they could see full well what was going on in E1 and elsewhere, and it was no wonder they were up in arms about the massive scam to which they were bearing daily witness.

In the grander scheme of things, it might have seemed insignificant that Israel had opted to build one more police station, given the vast number of IDF bases already dotted around the country that had been there for years. Supporters of the construction would have also argued that if the Palestinians refused to reign in their militants, then it was no wonder Israel needed to build more and more security installations to combat the threat.

Given the utter imbalance between Israel as occupier and the Palestinians as occupied, someone has to show good faith and that someone has to be Israel, as much to soothe the Israeli collective conscience as to alleviate Palestinian suffering. Adhering to international law doesn't need to be seen by the nationalist Israeli right as some kind of climb down or retreat, but rather as a step to protect the long-term security of the Zionist state.

Israel has no right to do what it was currently doing in E1 and throughout the rest of the West Bank; namely, signing up to peace talks with one hand whilst frantically digging foundations for further building all over the Territories with the other.

When I first moved to Israel, I had been prepared to play my part by enlisting in the IDF and serving in the West Bank. Whilst there, I saw for myself the effect my mere uniformed presence had on the Palestinians I encountered on a daily basis. Every interaction took place with me holding all the cards: it was me with the loaded gun in my hands; it was me barking instructions to "stop or I'll shoot", "lift up your shirt", "don't come another step closer"; it was me playing with my quarry as though they were puppets on the end of short, taut strings.

However, I still believed that we "did what we had to do", since it was a case of us or them, and we could never ease up in our actions for fear that the next Palestinian we encountered was the one with a bomb strapped to his chest. And so it continued, bursting into buildings to round up the residents and lock them in their own basement, so that we could take over the house and grab a few hours' sleep in the middle of a mission; all perfectly acceptable in the context of war.

Once I left the army, my forays into the West Bank were on more equal terms, as I sought to meet the very people whose towns I'd previously patrolled, to hear their stories about life under military rule. From Jenin to Bethlehem to Ramallah and beyond, the extent of the suffering and the depth of the torment was exposed to me time and again.

The unspoken truth that every Israeli knew, uncomfortable as it may have been to admit, was that occupation bred terror. Every incursion, every raid, every curfew and collective punishment, drove the moderates into the welcoming arms of the militants, who promised to return their honour and their wounded pride by fighting the oppressors' fire with fire of their own. That fact alone should have been enough to shake Israelis awake and realise that the occupation had to end, as much for our own security as for the sake of the Palestinians that we were subjugating.

Even those who only cared about the safety of the Israeli people, and to hell with the Palestinians, should have been backing the withdrawal of troops to the Green Line. They should have known that the labyrinthian network of checkpoints was not making them safer, but was there just to make the Palestinians' lives a misery, thus endangering Israeli lives further in the end. And they should have recognised that whilst Israel's presence continued to fester in the Palestinian territories, there was little chance that the Palestinians would seek rapprochement and dialogue with their neighbours.

That meant that any coexistence projects – such as those promoted by OneVoice, the Clubhouse network – were doomed to fail whilst the occupiers refused to acknowledge the plight of the occupied. Israel has the upper hand and to treat the situation as somehow balanced was to overlook the injustice of it all.

Of course, the Israelis have suffered decades of terrorism at the hands of extremist Palestinian groups, and as such have every right to demand their government protects them from similar atrocities in the future. But, for all that Israelis have had it bad, they haven't seen every facet of their lives systematically destroyed at the hands of an uncaring occupying force. They haven't seen their economy run into the ground by border closures and sanctions; or been denied freedom of movement between their homes and farmlands; and they haven't had to beg soldiers to let their wives through checkpoints in order to give birth in hospital.

At the same time, the settlements are as much of a problem to a viable Palestinian state as anything, thanks to the watertight security their presence demand from the army, restricting Palestinian movement and cutting the West Bank into tiny ribbon-like strips. As one Palestinian said, in Emma Williams' essential book on the region[17], "thanks to the settlers and their infrastructure, we're locked so tight into the State of Israel we're like a bug in concrete."

But still the expansion continues, and still the stranglehold on the Palestinians persists. Whilst the Israeli public stay silent; whilst their taxes swell the government's coffers, they are aiding and abetting slow torture on a national scale. On top of the sporadic killing that the

170

occupation inevitably causes, the killing of an entire people's hopes and dreams takes place 24 hours a day, 365 days a year.

And it has to stop. Even though it is no doubt too late to pull many of the current generation back from hate and enmity, there is still time to ensure that today's resentment don't have to be instilled into the children of tomorrow. Playing the 'fighting terror' card might win Knesset votes, but it doesn't push things forward, nor work out how to pave the way towards long-lasting future peace.

Israel has to leave the Territories, and they have to do it soon, whether accompanied by concessions on the Palestinian side or not. The occupation is illegal, it is abhorrent, and it is counterproductive if its aim is to bring security to Israelis. Anyone who ventures into the Palestinian towns and cities, who witnesses the devastation for themselves knows this.

Nowhere on the Israeli side is this more apparent than in the embattled town of Sderot, where Kassam rockets fall on a daily basis as the militants of the prison-like Gaza Strip make their protests felt in deadly fashion. That autumn, I visited the city for the first time, and what I saw and heard was as harrowing an experience as any trip I'd been on to the equally-beleaguered Palestinian towns in the West Bank.

"There's something in the air," shrugged the café owner when asked why the plaza was deserted at noon on Friday. What should have been his busiest spell of the week – Friday lunchtime, when pre-Shabbat shoppers usually swarmed round the city centre – turned out to be as dead as any other day of the week. The reason was, as he said, down to what was in the air, or looked at another way, what could have been arcing its way through the air en route from Gaza at any moment. This was Sderot, and this was the other side of collective punishment; an entire town held hostage by the actions of an enemy across the border.

At the behest of a friend who had taken issue with an article I'd written calling for the army to refrain from collectively punishing Gaza's population, I took him up on his offer to drive me down to Sderot to witness life under near-daily rocket attack. What I found there could have been straight out of Studs Terkel's chronicle of Depression-era America; a town utterly devoid of hope, a people feeling completely abandoned by their government, and an air of resignation that things weren't going to get better any time soon.

Kassams or no Kassams, Sderot has never been a prosperous place to live. Isolated from the more salubrious parts of Israel, its mainly-immigrant population is decidedly blue-collar. Consequently, the seven year long barrage of rockets had dragged Sderot's already precarious economic situation into the realms of disaster. Factories have closed, businesses have relocated out of range of the onslaught, and no company in its right mind would think of investing in such an imperilled area.

Whilst the casualty figures have, fortunately, remained relatively low (thanks to the crude nature of the missiles being fired), the town is under constant siege, with no one knowing when, where or why the next barrage will be launched. Pockmarked pavements and shattered buildings bear the scars of war, and the dozens of ugly concrete bomb shelters on every street are a constant reminder.

One heavily-pierced teenaged boy I spoke to painted a bleak picture of the future for him and his friends. "There's nothing for us here," he said, as he languidly smoked a cheap cigarette. "We all want to leave after we've finished the army. Where would I go? Anywhere – it doesn't matter. Just as long as I don't have to live here." Two of his friends appeared, and – after they'd all kissed one another's cheeks in typically flamboyant Sephardi fashion – they concurred with their mate's opinion.

"Anyone with money gets out of here," said one boy. "There's no work here, especially now the Kassams are raining down." The day before nine rockets had been fired at the town, but the boys were reluctant to think about the political climate that was breeding such hate on the Palestinian side. "I don't understand why they do it," said the most vocal of the trio. "And I don't care either – I've got enough problems of my own here [to worry about what they're thinking in Gaza]." He said his nephews had begun to stutter, and that other children had started wetting their beds, all as a result of the constant state of fear that gripped the town.

The boys' gallows humour came out as they told of a major gaffe on the part of phone company Cellcom. Earlier in the week, Cellcom – who had donated a lot of money for youth activities in Sderot – decided to put on an impromptu firework display for the residents, without telling a soul of their intentions. "Everyone went mad, thinking the Kassams were coming," laughed one boy. "People called the police, ran to the shelters – you can imagine the scene."

Whilst many companies and individuals had been quick to donate money to the embattled town, the residents complained bitterly of apathy on the part of the government. Racism, elitism and plain indifference to an "unimportant" town were among the various accusations levelled at the authorities, with people scornfully asking if anyone would have let bombs fall on Tel Aviv for seven years running. "Our blood is different," stated bitter graffiti sprayed on one shelter in the heart of town. "We are not second class," it continued, reflecting the deep resentment many felt for those meant to protect them from the terrorists.

At the emergency room, Sderot's chief paramedic preferred to praise the town's Blitz spirit rather than dwell on the government's half-hearted response to the situation. "We all know that we have to be strong in the face of the terror," he declared, "and we must not hold up our hands to those trying to kill us." He reminded us that "Israel is the strongest country in the region now, when once we thought the Arabs might make it all the way to Tel Aviv [in the 1973 war]."

"We don't have any other land," he went on, "so we have to fight for every inch." Although he hoped his children would grow up to join combat units of the IDF, he still said that "we have to believe that peace will happen, and that we'll one day live side by side." His front line work, treating the rocket victims, meant that he could "go to bed every night knowing I've done a little bit more for my country."

Fortunately the terrorists were having a day off whilst we were there, so Avi had plenty of time to talk to us about his take on the conflict. But, a day later, the bombs were back and the town was clearing up the debris once more. Collectively punishing the Palestinians was still not the answer, however frustrated the Israeli government was at being unable to halt the rockets. However, those who point the finger at the IDF for proposing, or carrying out, war crimes against the Palestinians ought to be just as vocal in their condemnation of the Kassam launchers.

Too many people play the numbers game, suggesting that things were not anywhere near as bad in Sderot as they are in Gaza because fewer people are dying violent deaths. But that view was myopic, as well as unhelpful in solving the crisis. Whatever the casualty figures, there is an entire town suffering, and an entire generation of children whose only experience of the Palestinians is terror and hate. They deserve as much sympathy as those trapped in the quagmire of Gaza.

After returning from Sderot, the issue of coexistence soon returned to the forefront of my work, underlining how hard it is to forge any links between potentially suitable groups of individuals on both sides whilst the overarching occupation continued to be maintained.

As a phalanx of heavily armed soldiers prowled along King David Street, the buildings were bathed in blue neon light from the police vans and jeeps parked on every available inch of pavement. The natives weren't particularly restless; after all, the King David Hotel and its

174

neighbour, the Citadel, had long been the bases of choice for the never-ending stream of visiting dignitaries to Israel's capital.

When the clock struck seven, the already tight security was upped another notch, as two groups of delegates ducked out of side exits and made their way into waiting motorcades. In the first party was Condoleezza Rice, the outgoing US Secretary of State, en route to making yet another plaintive appeal to the region's leaders to give peace a chance. In the other, slightly smaller group was a similarly high-powered entourage, made up of myself, my friend Nic, along with two Israeli Arab friends and an eminent sheikh's son from East Jerusalem.

Whilst Ms Rice sped off under heavy guard to the Saban Forum*, we made our way somewhat less ostentatiously to the Mount of Olives, where we were to spend the evening locked in discussion with a group of Palestinian community leaders. Our meeting was no less tense, nor any less sensitive, than the one Condoleezza was attending, and the experience gave me a real taste of just how hard it was to make any headway between the two mutually suspicious sides in the conflict.

The group of gap year students that Nic worked with were embarking on a project to clean the dilapidated Muslim cemetery in central Jerusalem's Independence Park. To that end, they were seeking a similarly-aged group of Palestinian children to work with, in order to foster dialogue between the two sides and try to break down the prejudices that both groups had of the other.

However, just because the proposal seemed simple enough on paper didn't mean a thing when it came to trying to get the idea off the ground. Months were spent in negotiation with the Jerusalem Municipality, who were far from helpful even at the prospect of free labour

---

*Organised by the Saban Center for Middle East policy/ Brookings — a gathering of US and Israeli leaders

in a park that fell under their jurisdiction. They viewed the project with suspicion, as well as with an unhealthy dose of apathy, and it was only the month before that they finally gave approval for the work to begin.

Trying to find suitable partners on the Palestinian side proved even harder, as I witnessed for myself that evening. Via the assistance of a prominent sheikh to whom he had been introduced, Nic thought he'd made a breakthrough with the heads of a Palestinian youth club in East Jerusalem, who seemed interested in sending some of their charges to join the project. However, they weren't happy to rubber stamp their participation until they'd ascertained Nic's motives, so they called him in for a face-to-face meeting.

Ten of us crowded into the meeting room on the ground floor of the sprawling building deep in East Jerusalem. Six men from the village were there, headed up by Abdalla, a stern-looking man who held court from behind his thick wooden desk. Dozens of impressive trophies adorned the shelves, testament to the club's members' sporting prowess. In a huge framed photo behind me, a young Yasser Arafat decked out in military attire beamed down from atop a sleek stallion.

Nic gave a long introduction to the project, via the translating skills of Rashad, one of the Israeli Arabs who had come with us. He explained the importance of fostering communication between Jewish children who would most likely one day make *aliyah* and Palestinian children who would never otherwise encounter Jews in such a positive forum. Whilst his interlocutors appeared interested, there was also a sense of apprehensiveness evident as they weighed up the proposal.

"Explain to us about your group's background," Abdalla instructed Nic, as the room filled up with smoke from the cigarettes hanging from everyone's lips. "We're a British, Zionist youth movement...", Nic began, although it was clear that he'd said more than enough in just that half sentence. Lips began pursing, as they digested the fact that the children weren't just Jews, but Zionists to boot.

More glasses of thick Arabic coffee were brought and the debating continued long into the evening. What had seemed to me to be a straightforward session of getting to know one another had taken on a far more political edge, as Abdalla and his men considered the implications of sending their charges to work alongside supporters of the Zionist regime.

Although, in Nic's words, the Zionism his group promoted wasn't one that viewed Palestinians as second-class or sought to colonise their lands, to Abdalla merely defining themselves as Zionist implied an outlook that did not rest easy with him. Things continued in this vein until the sheikh himself arrived, and the others listened deferentially to his views of the project.

By the time we wrapped things up, the only progress made was that Abdalla and his aides had agreed to think about the plans over the next week. Whilst they were right to deliberate over their involvement, it would have been a sad day for all involved if such a groundbreaking scheme was to be derailed because of suspicion one side harboured towards the other.

Most Zionist gap year programmes take little interest in rapprochement with their Palestinian counterparts, thus the cemetery project was a rare chance for both sides to break the wall that exists between them. But the silence had already bred mistrust, and – unless the deadlock was broken soon – the next generation would find themselves as mired in polarisation as the one before them was at present. And the next generation's Condoleezza would be no better positioned to act as peacemaker than today's secretary of state has proved.

---

[14] Palestinian Campaign for the Academic and Cultural Boycott of Israel.

[15] A British member of Independent Jewish Voices writing in the Fabian publication *How peace broke out in the Middle East: a short story of the future.*

[16] The 1967 border between Israel and the Territories.

[17] *It's Easier To Reach Heaven Than the End of the Street: A Jerusalem memoir* (Bloomsbury, 2007).

Chapter Seven

Later that month, Britain's former prime minister Tony Blair announced four projects designed to kick-start the ailing Palestinian economy. One of the plans was to revive the tourism industry in Bethlehem, by easing the restrictions on entering the city and making the town centre more appealing to sightseers. However, noble as his intentions no doubt were, from what I gathered on a visit to Bethlehem, the residents weren't holding out a great deal of hope for his vision.

After making my way through the bottleneck of the checkpoint – where two long queues on either side of the border converged on one harassed-looking teenaged soldier – I headed for the dilapidated Aida refugee camp on the edge of the city. Once there, I went to meet Abdel-Fattah Abudsrour, the head of the Al-Rowwad Theatre Centre who had left such an indelible impression on me when I first interviewed him in May.

On my way to the centre, I had begun to convince myself that Bethlehem was undergoing something of a mini-revival since my tour of duty there two years earlier. Dotted around the edge of town, new shops and hotels were tentatively springing up like the first flowers of spring pushing their way through a blanket of snow. But, once I was settled in a chair in Abdel-Fattah's office listening to his bleak outlook on the situation, my optimism evaporated along with the steam from his coffee.

He had been pretty despondent six months earlier when we had talked, "but now it's even worse," he told me. "Despite having nearly completely cut us off with the wall, the army still comes into the camp every day – and if they're not on a raid, they throw sound bombs instead, which leave a severe psychological impact on the residents." He said that the children he worked with had been showing more and more signs of the trauma of the incursions. "They've become much more violent with one another over the last couple of months," he noted dejectedly, "hitting each other in class and starting fights, to the point that some of the battles have escalated so much that their families come to blows as well."

Unemployment was still at a staggering seventy percent in the camp, he said, with factories closing all the time due to their employees being unable to get to work through the crippling network of checkpoints. When I asked if he thought Tony Blair's plans could have had any positive effect on the city, he shrugged half-heartedly at the suggestion. "Firstly, we have no confidence in Blair whatsoever," he replied, "thanks to his complete alliance with the US over Iraq, and the lies he told to justify the invasion."

"As for his ideas for regeneration in Bethlehem, what can I say?" he asked, rolling his eyes heavenwards. "All we hear are promises – we listen, we hear, but we never know whether any of them will come true. After all, they've been promising us our own state ever since Oslo, and all that's happened in the meantime is that Israel keeps raising the bar for our compliance – and the world just looks on."

He said that he was doubtful that any increase in tourism would have much effect on the Bethlehem economy, unless the fundamental way in which tourists visited the town changed significantly. "At present, the buses bring the groups in, they visit the Church [of the Nativity], jump back on their bus and are gone," he said. "That means that they don't sleep here, so the hotels are empty, as are the restaurants, and none of their tourist money filters down to the street. They just use Bethlehem as a passageway".

A Palestinian policeman I spoke to outside the Church of the Nativity was equally unenthusiastic about Blair's proposals. Shivering in his bomber jacket and felt beret,

179

he said that "I don't know what it is he wants to do here, but I do know that you shouldn't trust what you read in the media. We've heard nothing about spending on the tourist industry – they talk about putting money in, but the tourist policemen sleep with the mice."

He wasn't exaggerating, he said. "We sleep in an underground building, with rats everywhere, and we don't even have enough money for guns," he complained, patting his waistband where his pistol was conspicuous by its absence. "We didn't get our salaries for fifteen months," he continued, "and even when we did finally get paid, they didn't cover the debts we'd accumulated during that time." Where did that leave him? "I've got five kids – and no cash," he replied flatly.

Despite the storm clouds overhead and the fierce November wind, Manger Square was heaving with tourists from as far afield as Russia and India. However, also present were their coach-shaped chariots, reinforcing Abdel-Fattah's assertion that the tourists might have been there in person, but that it was little use to the stallholders and shopkeepers whilst their cash never left their pockets.

Whether or not Tony Blair's tourism drive manages to inject life back into Bethlehem's collapsed economy, the main obstacle to financial health was the far more significant problem of the wall and the checkpoints. "Most people can't even leave their own cities anymore," Abdel-Fattah told me, "and that has a devastating effect on their ability to find work". The prime minister of the PA, Salam Fayyad, said the same thing when unveiling Blair's plans, stating that the private sector wouldn't recover until roadblocks were lifted to permit the passage of goods and people.

Until that happened, Tony Blair's idealistic proposals seem like nothing more than window-dressing, given that the West Bank's problems are far worse than a mere dearth of tourists in Bethlehem. "Peace be with you," read the cynically-placed Israeli Tourism Ministry billboard where tour buses pass through the security wall to enter Bethlehem. But, until that same wall is opened up just as

180

freely to the Palestinian people, then the last thing that would be bestowed on the people was peace, and the situation will continue to deteriorate as steadily as before.

***

After every round of doing battle with readers on my CIF threads, it was easy to forget that the underlying debate centred on a real and urgent issue, rather than a trivial matter that we discussed to pass the time. The arguments sometimes felt as though they were no deeper than a group of people discussing the best formation for the Arsenal first eleven or the best wines to complement their dinner party menus. The Israel-Palestine conflict was, to some, no more than a way to let off steam and an arena in which to sharpen, and wield, their intellectual swords.

I was as guilty as the next person in that sense; at least, I was when I first began writing for CIF. Now, as I reached my hundredth piece after being let loose on the site almost a year earlier, I looked back and couldn't believe the change that had come over me since my very first comment (which, embarrassingly, had ended with "whatever, mate – I write, you read…").

Twelve months getting down and dirty in the CIF bear pit had taught me far more than I was willing to let on at first. In fact, it had proved the perfect foil to living in Jerusalem, traditionally the stamping ground of the more right-wing, religious section of Israeli society. What had begun as an opportunity to spread my message to an audience somewhat wider than Alex's site False Dichotomies allowed, soon turned on its head, and I found myself the one being educated and challenged for my previously-held beliefs.

Although I fought against it at first, in the end I had to concede that most of my sacred cows were well overdue a good slaughter. Of course, I came at the conflict from (what I thought was) a fairly left wing position to start with, but it was soon evident that I was deluding myself when it came to the intricacies of the situation. That was not to say that I had performed a complete volte-face when it came to my politics, and there was no reason that I should have done, whatever some of my more vociferous detractors might have said.

For instance, I still had no time at all for the sickening aggression I witnessed in Bil'in, even though I now accepted that it was the Palestinians' legal right to violently resist the occupation. I still thought that their behaviour was reprehensible, and – more importantly – counterproductive to their cause. However, I was forced to confront the reality of the events that led to their rage by virtue of the incandescent readers I encountered on the ensuing thread.

Similarly, I was heartened to read that, time and again, readers came onto the threads to tell me that their own minds were being changed when it came to the conflict, thanks to the pieces I was submitting. Whilst there were still those who would never be prepared to see the conflict through the prism of an Israeli, those who weren't too entrenched in their views were exactly those I was proud to be able to reach through my writing.

That was, for me at least, the beauty of a forum such as CIF. Thanks to the heavy stress put on participation in the threads, it forced both writer and reader to engage with one another and challenge each other relentlessly for three days straight. Gone were the days of readers writing prim and proper 'letters to the editor', waiting to see whether their missive was chosen for publication, and then hoping against hope that the writer saw their complaint in print.

Now, instead, the gloves were off; there was no standing on ceremony, and the debate became a duel in real-time, with instant results and a fluidity to the exchange that no print medium could hope to match. And, most importantly, this format bred results. I would never have expected myself to dismount my high horse as many times as I had done, especially of late, and that was entirely down to the efforts of those reading my pieces in hauling me over the coals whenever they saw fit.

When I wrote "Spare the rod...", I realised that I had to follow through on the sentiments I was expressing, precisely because it was in Israel's best interests for its citizens to approach the conflict honestly and not be held back in their self-criticism by partisan loyalties. In the microcosm of CIF at least, this approach had paid off.

Commentators like Trueleft (the screen name of one of the most popular readers) were constantly held up as exactly the type of Israeli citizen that outsiders could trust, as well as inspire them to believe that all was not lost in terms of Israeli intransigence and hyper-defensiveness.

The world was not going to change overnight just on the strength of the intellectual arm-wrestling taking place on CIF, but, if a year's experience on the site had taught me anything, it was that if previously sworn enemies could come together over the threads, finding even the smallest area of common ground and building upon it, then so too could it work in the non-electronic world.

Those who grew exasperated with the hardliners they encountered on the threads should have looked at the bigger picture; that CIF's loyal army were far less interested in war than peace when it came to slugging it out on the screens. For me, at least, the whole experience had been instructive, and done more to open my eyes to the true feelings on both sides than any other forum could ever have hoped to have done. Whilst my education was far from over, the first hundred threads had proved an incredible learning curve for this particular Zionist.

However, my own experience of engaging with my political opponents and accepting that I was far from an expert in the field did not tally with the likes of the *mavens* (experts) of the Israeli right. You could approach outsiders' hostility towards Israel in two ways. Some, usually those who weren't prepared to lay culpability at the feet of the Israeli government, liked to batten down the hatches and convince themselves that "the whole world's against us". They often extrapolated this logic to the point that they claimed that all critics of Israel were motivated by anti-Semitism, and thus did they sleep easier at night; safe in the knowledge that no matter what Israel did or didn't do, they would never be able to win round the pack of racists baying for Israeli blood.

Then there were those, like me, who preferred to incorporate the "ten bar theory" into their thinking. Namely, that if you walked into a bar and someone started a fight with you, the chances were that they were the one with the problem. But if you walked into ten bars and each time someone wanted a piece of you, then it was more than likely that you were the one doing something wrong.

Proponents of each way of approaching anti-Israel criticism were quick to accuse their opposite numbers of deluding themselves in one way or another. The latest event I attended was no different, as I found whilst sitting in a convention hall just outside the walls of the Old City, listening to the keynote speakers at the NGO Monitor Conference entitled "Preparing for Durban II".

Six years on, the Israeli right was still licking its wounds in the aftermath of "Durban I", the stormy conference which was dominated by the passing of several high-profile motions which condemned Israel for its policies. One of the knock-on effects of the event was the springing up of groups such as NGO Monitor, an organisation that dedicated itself to holding to account NGOs that operated in the Israel/Palestine sphere.

According to its executive director, Gerald Steinberg, "nobody gets a free ride", a concept which was ostensibly the modus operandi of his group, an organisation that has appointed itself unofficial watchdog in the NGO sphere – in itself an important and necessary role. They called for NGOs to be transparent in any political agenda that they may have been pushing, and to take an honest and balanced approach to the conflict. Which was all well and good, except that – on the strength of what I heard at their conference – they, and their supporters, were in

184

danger of tarring all left-leaning NGOs with the same accusatory brush.

In his speech, Professor Steinberg employed some pretty hysterical analogies when making the case against various NGOs, from the home-grown Peace Now to Amnesty International and beyond. He accused the groups of producing "pornography, in the way that they use and abuse the language of the Holocaust when they criticise Israel". A strong allegation indeed, especially since the terms he was referring to were "war crimes", "indiscriminate bombing", "collective punishment" and "violation of international law"; phrases which no one would have expected him to associate with the Nazis if applied to any other country in the world.

However, to an audience hanging on Steinberg's every word, it all made perfect sense; yet more fuel to fan the flames in which all criticism of Israel was motivated by rabid anti-Semites hell-bent on eliminating the Jewish State. He said as much himself, when claiming that Oxfam's (now-withdrawn) Blood Orange boycott poster was designed to "appeal to the base anti-Semitism still present in the European community", rather than seeing it for what it was; a provocative campaign that had been used in one form or another against far more countries than just Israel.

Once he'd said his piece, he handed over to Shimon Samuels of the Simon Wiesenthal Center*, whose rabble-rousing employed exactly the type of Holocaust rhetoric that Steinberg was so quick to condemn on the part of the NGOs. Warning them of the inherent dangers if they treat Durban II with apathy, he claimed that "Hitler's [political] campaign was a prelude... we can't allow Durban II to be a prelude as well."

In the eyes of Samuels and Steinberg, it was unthinkable that Israel itself may have been to blame for some of

---

*The Los Angeles based Simon Wiesenthal Center has little connection with the Nazi-hunter Simon Wiesenthal.

the accusations levelled against it, and for the unenviable reputation it had forged for itself in the human rights sector. Instead, it was far more convenient to play the man and not the ball, when faced with the volley of criticism levelled against Israel by countless humanitarian organisations which studied and worked in the field.

Whilst they were quick to demand an end to opaque practices on the part of the NGOs they monitor, they were not keen to apply the same standards to their own work. On a banner to the right of the stage, they described themselves as "promoting critical debate and accountability of human rights NGOs in the Arab-Israeli conflict", suggesting that they were as concerned with pro-Israeli NGOs as they were with those who criticise the State.

However, as panellist Arik Ascherman from Rabbis for Human Rights pointed out, NGO Monitor "is only concerned with those organisations that oppose Israeli policies, and thus their own propaganda is in fact disingenuous". In reply, Professor Steinberg declared that "in the post-Durban world, the most important thing is to defend Israel from attack", effectively agreeing that his own organisation had a long way to go before it too did exactly what it said on the tin.

His sentiments spoke volumes about the level of defensiveness that still reigned on the Israeli right, often overriding logic and rational thought when applied to those considered inimical to Israel. Perversely, the more that the world took Israel to task, be it at Durban I or Durban II, the more entrenched these groups would become and the less likely they would be to take seriously the accusations levelled against the country. Because they would rather believe that every time they walked into a bar and were set upon, it was purely down to their ethnicity, and no one would ever convince them otherwise. It was on street level rather than in an auditorium that I next witnessed this intransigence, and the results and implications for the future were just as disturbing.

***

It was the archetypal Israeli demonstration; sun blazing away in a cloudless sky, a busy intersection in the heart of Jerusalem choked with traffic, two opposing camps of protesters separated by police lines and a few metres of tarmac. In the blue corner, the peace activists of Women in Black were gathering to celebrate the twentieth anniversary of their non-violent protests against the occupation. In the red corner, a counter-demonstration of rabid religious men and women poured scorn on their opponents across the road.

And, diving into the fray with well-rehearsed investigative curiosity, stepped Alex and I, not ones to miss an opportunity to join in the fun. My first port of call was a woman brandishing an outsized poster of Palestinian gunmen in the direction of the oncoming cars, whose scowling visage marked her out as just the person to explain her group's rage.

I strolled over and asked her whether she had a problem with one of her fellow protesters clutching a sign with "Israel for the Jews" scrawled across it. "Don't you think that sends a bit of a racist message?" I enquired, suggesting that if I'd seen people holding "England for the English" banners in my youth, I'd have been understandably upset. "Of course it's not racist," she replied through gritted teeth. "Look, you have to understand that they want to kill Jews…" she declared, pointing angrily at the fairly placid-looking Women in Black over the road.

"They support a caliphate," she continued, straying further and further from the question I'd asked her to answer. I could see what was coming, and took out my right-wing bingo card which I carried for occasions such as these. "They want to dissolve Israel," she said, as I checked the right box on my form. And so it went on: "they've got twenty-two countries of their own" (*check*), "there's no such thing as Palestinians anyway" (*check*), "they teach their children hate" (*check*), and then the

187

coup de grace: "you should know what I mean – you're from Londonistan, aren't you?"

Stifling the urge to shout "*house!*" and claim my prize, I patiently explained that the world according to Melanie Phillips wasn't necessarily in tune with reality, however much my new friend would have liked to believe it was. "Don't think I don't read the papers," she said defiantly. "I read eight newspapers every day – in fact, I was just reading in the *Daily Mail*" – check – "this week about the Muslims wanting to have a public call to prayer in Oxford." Pausing dramatically to see my reaction, I disappointed her by saying: "So? How's that any different from church bells calling the faithful to prayer?"

"It *is* different," she exclaimed sulkily. "For one thing, church bells are softer...". Defeated by that impeccable logic, I made my excuses and went to see how Alex was getting on. He was surrounded by baying middle-aged men throwing lame soundbite after lame soundbite in his direction, in a relentless attempt to wear him down with a barrage of catchphrases. "Every time there's a ceasefire, we cease and they fire," one man exclaimed triumphantly, as though he'd just given Confucius a run for his money.

Another wise man, waving a placard reading "Death to the traitors – black is the colour of death," chimed in with: "Anyone against Jews in the Land of Israel is morally bankrupt," which signalled him as another rapier-like wit with whom it would be enlightening to cross swords. "But don't you think claiming Israel is just for the Jews smacks of racism," I asked. He exploded like Vesuvius: "I *will not* hear anyone accuse Israel of being racist," he thundered. "Not when the Arabs have been racist for hundreds of years." But we're not talking about "the Arabs", I replied, "I was asking whether you thought perhaps Israel should not sink to racist levels in its dealing with its non-Jewish citizens."

"I don't care if it *is* racist," he responded, swiftly changing his position as his blood pressure rose. "Israel's not

188

meant to be some kind of multi-cultural democracy – this isn't England," he sneered. "Non-Jews shouldn't have the vote, otherwise we can't safeguard Israel's future," he carried on, well into his stride by now. "I bet you think the Arabs want peace", he asked rhetorically. "Well, let me educate you, as someone with experience – they don't. When they say they do, they're lying."

I conceded that I was obviously devoid of the same kind of "experience" as him, observing that he clearly had a far greater depth of understanding of "the Arabs'" collective psyche. "Listen," chimed in a woman in our little debating circle. "Mohammed broke his *hudna* (ceasefire) in Medina after two years – that's the kind of attitude we're up against."

By now, Alex was embroiled in an even-more heated exchange next to me, up against a man flailing his arms like some kind of amphetamine-fuelled windmill. I joined in on Alex's side, at which point a burly policeman decided to get involved, wading in and demanding we tell him "which side" we were on. "We're not on any side," I replied, "we're just interviewing these people about their politics." "Well, do it without shouting," the policeman instructed, as though keeping order in a classroom.

We decamped to the other side of the road at this point, seeking refuge amongst the "Jew-killing" Women in Black, who calmly dismissed the allegations of their friends across the street. "Most of us believe in a two-state solution," said Gila, one of the organisers of the protest, when I asked her to respond to the claims that they promoted the "dissolving" of Israel. "This protest is about ending the siege of Gaza, and the occupation in general," said another woman. "No more, no less". "We don't even bother trying to explain ourselves to them," said another, nodding to the crowd over the road. "There's no point; nothing we say will convince them of our true intentions."

I could well believe her, having witnessed for myself the complete irrationality and disregard for logic only moments earlier. It was nothing new; I had encountered plenty of extremists on both sides dozens of times since moving here, but it never ceased to amaze, and depress me, how intractable many people's positions were when it came to the conflict. That Friday's protest was just another example of how, even though they were only feet apart from one another, the gulf between the two camps couldn't have been wider, and the distance grew ever further as the years went by.

Defying the stares of the disapproving masses, I bravely read the *Guardian* from cover to cover en route from London to Tel Aviv two weeks later, including Ahmad Samih Khalidi's weighty critique of the post-Annapolis situation. In his article, he took aim at Ehud Olmert's apparent attempts to force the Palestinians to "give up their history," by encouraging them to settle for a two-state solution rather than allowing them the right of return to Israel.

Whilst there was no denying his logic, by focusing merely on the Palestinians' aspirations to return to their land there was an implicit suggestion that the right to live in Israel was something to which only the Palestinians were entitled. If ever there was a time and place to counter this opinion, it was on a flight into Ben Gurion airport, witnessing the unchecked anticipation and excitement of the Jewish passengers as the plane touched down on the tarmac.

There was a palpable sense of joy as the pilot taxied along the runway, as spontaneous applause broke out, and the more exuberant on board began impromptu singing of *Hava Negila*. So it was that Thursday, and – as the "leftwing by Israeli standards" man next to me remarked – it was because "this is our land, after all". According to him, "the only proof we have is that it says so in the Torah," but that was enough to convince him that relinquishing control over the territory was anathema to the survival of the Jewish people.

Once I had collected my luggage and boarded a *sherut* (a shared taxi) to Jerusalem, I was treated to a similar view by a particularly over-excited American man in his forties. It was clear from the off where he stood politically, after we passed an army jeep and he forcibly swivelled his young son's head towards it, shouting: "Look, look, look – there're our boys, God bless 'em." He repeated the trick as we caught sight of the security wall for the first time. "That's what Ariel Sharon built to keep us from being blown up by the Palestinians," he informed his son proudly.

Turning to me, he asked if it was my first time in the country, clearly looking to impart some of his wisdom to as wide an audience as possible. I casually remarked that I'd served in the army, assuming that such an admission would be the best lubricant to grease the wheels of our acquaintance. "Did you hear that?" he cried to his son. "This boy's a hero too! He did God's will by fighting against the dark Nazis for us."

"Who are the dark Nazis?" I inquired, though it was clear what he meant. "That's what I call the Palestinians," he replied smugly, evidently delighted with the epithet he'd conjured up for our neighbours. "I mean, I know they're not all dark, but it sums them up pretty well otherwise." I observed that they weren't all Nazis either, but was too late to stem the inevitable tide that poured forth from his lips now that he was in full flow.

After a fortnight in the relative calm of London, his diatribe was a sobering reminder of the aggression and passion that coursed through the veins of those with even the most tenuous of links to this troubled region. My new friend hailed from Atlanta ("though I'm desperately trying to convince my wife that we should move here"), and relied on a heavy ratio of clichés to reason in order to overrule any objections I made to his shaky logic.

"They're all animals," he assured me, after I'd opined that perhaps the violence wasn't a one-way street as he would have liked me to have believed. "In fact, they're worse than animals, since animals only kill in order to eat." I asked if that meant he could never get on with

Palestinians himself. "If you were an Arab," he replied, with pleading eyes, "I'd beg you to stop hating me just because I'm a Jew. The problem is that they're all taught to hate us from the minute they're born, and nothing we can say will convince them otherwise."

I asked whether he could see a similarity in their supposed blanket hatred of us and his definite generalisations about them, but he couldn't. "Look, I don't hate them – I just don't want to be a victim. I don't want them to chop my head off." Getting beheaded was evidently a major concern to him, as he worked the "head-chopping" scenario into a further three doomsday scenarios that he painted for my benefit.

In the twenty minutes that followed, he managed to dismiss the UN as "the children of the people who tossed us into the gas chambers", accused Muhammad of "twisting the Torah in order to steal the land from us", as well as assured me that Jewish extremists "are not following God's word, so they're not really our problem". As the driver pulled up to his stop, he gave me a personalised blessing "that God should protect you when you encounter those savages", before bidding me goodbye and stepping out into the Jerusalem night.

As I digested his words, which were neither particularly unique nor particularly unexpected, I realised that, love it or hate it, the man's devotion to the concept of a Jewish state in Israel was every bit as tangible as that of his Palestinian counterparts. Whilst I abhorred many of the sentiments he expressed – just as I despised the rhetoric of the extremist Palestinians – there was no doubting that his claim to the land was no simpler to dismiss just because it was based on an earlier period of history than that of the Palestinians.

And, from the commentators on CIF to the likes of Ahmad Samih Khalidi and beyond, there had to be a collective realisation that if Israelis were expected to take the Palestinians' yearning to return seriously, then so too must they respect the desires of the Jews both in Israel and in the Diaspora. To do otherwise was, to paraphrase Khalidi, "to demand that the Jews give up their history", and to go down that route was as unconscionable as forcing the Palestinians to do the same.

At Friday night dinner the next day, the conversation inevitably turned to politics, and the table split neatly into two camps across generational lines. As the adults took a conservative stance on the Israel-Palestine conflict, the younger guests stuck to a far more left wing agenda, which was quickly picked up on by one of the older men. "You'll see," he declared confidently, "as you get older, you'll find yourselves coming over to the right. That's just the way the brain works."

With that in mind, there was something even more unusual about Combatants for Peace (CFP) than first met the eye. The group was, as its name suggested, made up of ex-soldiers and ex-militants who had come together in search of peace, and they took their message to the streets, as I found out for myself. CFP had convened a meeting in Tel Aviv's Secular *Yeshiva*, bringing their campaign to the attention of a group of pre-army teens who studied there voluntarily, having completed high school.

Sitting in a large circle in a classroom, with the sounds of downtown Tel Aviv threatening to drown out the proceedings, the students spent two hours enthralled by the stories of war and peace being told. Two ex-combat soldiers sat alongside an ex-Fatah militiaman, and waxed lyrical about their own personal journeys from being teenaged fighters to grown-up peacemakers. The session seemed to be as much for the benefit of the speakers as for the audience, as they exorcised their demons by speaking out about the violence and aggression that had blighted their formative years.

Itamar Shapira, a twenty-seven year old Israeli who was demobbed six years earlier, spoke of the mental torment he had suffered ever since rejoining civilian life. After a fraught tour of duty, including participation in the notorious Operation Defensive Shield[18], he spent a year in "blackout", using drugs and alcohol as an escape from the memories of what he'd experienced during his service. "It can send you crazy," he stated flatly, hollow eyes trained on the middle distance. "You ask yourself 'who am I to have killed someone?', and you even start to question what Zionism is about at all."

As though participating in a truth and reconciliation commission, he spared the hushed room no detail about the grisly action that he saw during his spell on the front line. His lurid descriptions of opening fire on a jeepful of suspected terrorists was chilling, but was only half the story that he was trying to convey. He wanted the students to understand that, whilst in the short term their counter-terrorist actions may have seemed successful, in the bigger picture all of their efforts were in vain when it came to ending the cycle of violence.

"You go to catch a bomber," he said, "and during the mission someone unconnected starts shooting at your squad. So we respond and kill him, and then a week later there's another bombing, and it turns out to be the brother of the man we shot. And so it goes on [dragging more and more people into the fray]." He had been instrumental in founding CFP, hoping to redress some of the damage that the conflict had wreaked both on his own psyche as well as on the others who had shared similar experiences.

Usama, a stocky middle-aged Palestinian from Ramallah, was one such person who fitted the description. After being arrested for "throwing rocks and Molotovs" in the first Intifada, he spent three years in jail, finally being released at the age of seventeen. "I grew up fast," he said. "It was such a harsh punishment for someone of that age – when I was released I felt like I was already a man of twenty-five". By the time the second Intifada erupted, he'd decided that non-violence was the only route to bringing peace to his people, and opted not to take part in the uprising.

However, he then began to feel that "it was not enough just to abstain from violence – I had to be part of the peaceful solution as well." He attended the first meetings of the embryonic CFP, and gradually came to be an integral member of the organisation. Whilst optimistic about the work that CFP did, he admitted that there was much work to be done convincing fellow Palestinians of the group's worth, "since many don't believe in peace groups at all, as a result of years of occupation", a sentiment I'd heard expressed several times lately.

Once the speeches were over, the students piled in with their questions, eager to glean as much from the speakers as possible in the hour they had left. "Where's the anger gone after your jailing?"; "How can we get to the point where we live side by side in peace?"; "How did you make the first move to the militants on the other side?" – the questions flooded in thick and fast, and were dealt with skilfully by Itamar, Usama and their fellow CFP founder, Ory.

Whether one regarded CFP as an effective tool against the warmongers or not, ultimately it filled a vacuum that may otherwise have been occupied by less peaceful groups on both sides. Especially when working with children who were going to be the soldiers of tomorrow, and as such required as much first-hand knowledge of the situation as possible in order to be well-armed mentally when it came to their own national service.

In order to take down the organs of war, the word had to continue to be spread to Israelis and Palestinians of all ages and all persuasions. Which was why CFP was so vital, in order to promote 'another way', rather than just allow people to subscribe to the dominant notion that the only way to resolve the conflict was through violent means. So, even though they were older and wiser than they were when they were front-line combatants, it was to the CFP team's credit that they didn't become more entrenched and right-wing with age – and to the benefit of the entire region as well.

[18] An IDF offensive in the wake of suicide attacks during early 2002

Chapter Eight

Almost all the ingredients were there for a first-class demonstration against the illegal settlement of Migron. Over a hundred vocal Peace Now[19] protesters; dozens of banners and placards unfurled in the January wind; and a sizeable press pack on hand to record the proceedings. The organisers whipped the crowd into life, shouting into loudhailers to get the chanting going, as others clapped and cheered the speeches of various left-wing luminaries.

However, the one missing element was also the most crucial in terms of taking on the settlers and showing them that not all Israelis were willing to turn a blind eye to their misdeeds. Namely, access to the settlement itself, which the police had decided was out of bounds for the busloads of demonstrators who had flocked in from Tel Aviv and Jerusalem.

There were almost as many policemen and soldiers as there were protesters; so seriously did the authorities take their duty of preventing a head-to-head meeting between the two camps. Instead, they restricted the marchers to a desolate, windswept patch of ground a full kilometre away from the edge of the settlement, all but negating the impact of the protest on the very people at which it was aimed. In the event, they needn't have worried about a clash, since that was never on the agenda of those running the show.

I'd seen it all before: the left-wing making a lot of noise, whistling and stamping their feet in condemnation of the settlers' expansionism – and meanwhile the settlement juggernaut rolled on deeper and deeper into the West Bank. What difference was a protest in the middle of nowhere going to make, if not a single settler was there to feel the force of their opponents' rage? It was like the proverbial tree falling in a forest – if no one was there to hear, then whether or not there was a noise was a pretty moot point.

However, according to the organisers of the Migron protest, this one was staged entirely for the benefit of the media, and neither party was let down on that front. Timed to coincide with President Bush's first visit to the country, the leaders of Peace Now were well aware that all eyes were focused on Israel that week, and realised the potential for exposure that such an event would offer.

The more incendiary the placards, the more the press lapped it up; filming and photographing the gathering for both local and international media. The police looked on benevolently, having realised that this was to be no more than just a photo opportunity for the left, and not in the slightest bit likely to turn tense or violent.

However, amidst all the stage-managed chanting and ever-so-civilised protesting, there were murmurs of discontent amongst the crowd, many of whom wondered whether their actions would have any real effect on curtailing the ongoing illegal construction. "I'm not very comfortable with this," one man told me as we looked up in the direction of the Migron outpost. "After all, does our presence even register with the settlers over the hill?"

"Where's the direct action?" asked another. "When they [the right wing] decide to take a stand, they throw up a new hilltop settlement overnight, and the army just look on. We need to fight fire with fire, rather than just moan about it a few weeks later." I agreed wholeheartedly – I'd said as much after my tour of the West Bank the summer before. However, according to one of Meretz's leaders, non-confrontational protest was still the watchword of the Israeli left, "since we don't want to come across like a bunch of hooligans."

"I'm not sure whether it's the right decision," he told me, "but it's the strategy that we've chosen." I suggested that they could disrupt illegal settlement construction without violent means, such as by staging sit-ins on the site of planned outposts. If the army chose to evict them rather than the settlers, it would prove in a most explicit fashion that the authorities did tacitly support the settlers' activities. And, if the press were on hand to record such a scenario, it would at least have had the effect of seriously embarrassing the government when confronted with the evidence.

"It's not a bad idea," he replied, as though considering it for the first time. "Why don't you go and suggest it to Noa [one of the Peace Now organisers]?" I was amazed they hadn't given this idea some thought before, but on reflection realised that this state of inertia amongst the left was hardly news to me or anyone else. Instead of using the same hands-on tactics that had made the settler activists so successful – they were instead happy to sit back and take the easy option in order to salve their consciences.

They had the press in their pockets – a few emails and text messages, and they could mobilise as many reporters and camera crews as they desired, guaranteeing that they would get good coverage in the next day's news. Which was all well and good, and clearly served them well in the publicity stakes, but it had a negligible effect in limiting further settlements.

Whilst the intelligentsia were shaking their heads in sympathy with the protesters as they read *Haaretz* or watched BBC World, the settlers were busily constructing more and more 'facts on the ground' which proved impossibly hard to evacuate once they'd taken root. Nothing changed for the better, and the cycle continued for another week, another month, another year.

Bush's inaugural visit to Israel was the perfect time to show up the settlements and the left's opposition to their continued expansion. However, shying away from real action and just repeating the same tired old slogans seemed an unworthy way to mark the occasion.

Impotent chanting from the sidelines wasn't what was needed now; it had got much too late for that. Fighting fire with fire may have made for some uncomfortable alternative demonstrations but, since it was the only thing that would make the authorities really sit up and take notice, perhaps it was the only potent weapon left in the peace camp's arsenal.

Several other groups followed Peace Now's lead in making their voices heard during Bush's trip to Israel, capitalising on the opportunity to get their messages out to an international audience. However, as I discovered later that week, the pantomime atmosphere overshadowed any attempts to hold serious debate on the streets of Jerusalem...

"Now, children," our headmistress used to address us in assembly. "I want you all to be on your best behaviour today, because we have a ve-ry imp-ort-ant visitor, and I want us all to make a good impression." Her announcement would cue a frenzied burst of activity, as we smartened our uniforms, tidied our classrooms, and planned performances and acts with which to dazzle our honoured guest (invariably the local MP or one of his minions).

Fast forward twenty years or so, and the residents of my adopted city found themselves reduced to the same status of primary school children, as preparations were made for the arrival of the great hawk of the West. For weeks, municipal workers raced to scrub the streets clean, drape enormous American flags from every available lamppost, and bend over backwards to make his stay as amenable as possible.

At the same time, every group with a political agenda got ready, eagerly awaiting the chance to take the stage and perform in front of the world's press. Finally, after all the dress rehearsals and last-minute scene changes, the curtain finally lifted for them today – and they didn't disappoint...

I spent three hours on a cool evening watching the pantomime unfold, hot on the heels of the human chain round the Old City walls a day earlier, which was meant to reiterate Israelis' reluctance to divide Jerusalem. The latest show was a two-act performance, with the Israeli Communist Party gathering outside the American Consulate, whilst the Terror Victims' Association strutted their stuff half a mile up the road next to the Great Synagogue.

Fancy dress was the common theme, with both sides utilising their costume-making skills to devastating effect. The stars of the Communists' gathering were five women swathed in silky black robes and carrying cardboard sickles, weaving silently in front of their chanting and cheering comrades as the press pack snapped away feverishly. The two hundred strong crowd called for everything from ending the siege on Gaza, to dealing peacefully with Iran, to dismantling the settlements, as well as encouraging "Yankees go home".

(Although their final message fell on at least one pair of deaf ears, according to one charmingly naïve American girl watching the proceedings. "They mean the British, right?" she asked, before widening her eyes in disbelief when informed that Yankees referred to Americans. Fortunately for her, many of the other placards used pictures instead of words, meaning even she got the point of the dove holding the AK47.)

The crowd was matched man for man by a squadron of border policemen, who watched benignly from the sidelines as the crowd shouted themselves hoarse and sang to the beat of the drums. They showed no signs of abating by the time I got bored (there were only so many times I could bear to hear the childish refrain of "George Bush, we know you; your father was a liar too"), and I wandered up the hill to see how the right wing crowd were getting on.

Their dressmakers had really gone to town, kitting dozens of them out in stylish terrorist outfits: *keffiyehs*, toy machine guns and Palestinian flags on sticks. Posing behind a huge poster mocking Bush as the "Founding father of Hamastine", their *schtick* was "to thank Bush and Olmert for releasing us and for backing a terror state next to Israel".

I fell into conversation with their leader, Meir Indor, who insisted on speaking to me via a microphone, despite me standing face to face with him. "I want everyone in the street to hear our conversation," he told me, before launching into a well-rehearsed speech about why Palestinians "don't deserve" their own state until they promised to behave themselves.

His view was nothing new – I'd heard it all before countless times, most recently at the Women In Black demonstration a week earlier. "We gave them the freedom to choose their own leadership," he boomed into the microphone, "but then they elected terrorists, so we had to take that freedom away again. What choice did we have?" he asked, with the disappointed look of a parent who had grounded his child for breaking their curfew for the umpteenth time.

Our conversation took a bizarre twist, when he threatened to sue me for libel on behalf of Baruch Marzel, after I inferred that Marzel was an Israeli version of the very militants Indor was castigating for their crimes. Given Marzel's previous (including convictions for assaulting Palestinians, policemen and even Israeli peacenik Uri Avnery), I was more than happy to stand my ground. At least, until one of Indor's human puppets – dressed in an outsized American flag and Hamas headscarf – lumbered over and thrust his toy M16 into my chest, cueing my departure for the safer climes of the bar over the road.

Jerusalemites didn't need much of an invitation to stage protests and turn the streets into cauldrons of political rivalry, so Bush's visit was always going to be red rag to these particular bulls. However, as with the protest at Migron, how much of the demonstrating was for the benefit of the president himself and how much was meant to stoke the egos of those taking part was anyone's guess. Either way, until the Yankees finally did go home, there was to be plenty more pantomime to come, and plenty more starry-eyed pupils eager to strut their stuff on the Jerusalem school stage.

***

It was easy to claim that the pen was mightier than the sword from the safety of a university lecture hall, or a middle class soiree in a suburban dining room. However, in the bandit country that was Hebron, the adage rang somewhat hollow, as I found after spending a day out on patrol with TIPH[20]. What I saw during my six-hour shadowing of the dedicated yet – ultimately – toothless members of the TIPH team made me question the wisdom of their entire mandate in the troubled city.

Established in the wake of Baruch Goldstein's shooting spree in a local mosque, TIPH's job was to "monitor the situation in Hebron and record breaches of international law". In essence, they were stationed in the city to bear witness to the almost daily violent incidents that erupted between the Jewish settlers of Hebron and their Palestinian neighbours.

So it was on Wednesday, as I set out with Sibyll and Mortens, respectively Swiss and Danish TIPH workers, who were old hands at dealing with the situation using the limited tools at their disposal. Our first incident was fairly mundane by comparison with what we'd see later; a youth protesting to the pair that every time PA workmen came to try and fix a sewage blockage in the *souk*, Israeli soldiers ordered them to leave the area without allowing them to carry out their repairs.

"This is the third time we've heard this story in four days," said Sibyll, as she noted down the boy's complaint in her notebook. "All we can do is to try and get our liaison officers to try to intervene with the army and the PA, and attempt to get permits for them to complete their work [unimpeded]." Mortens concurred with her plan of action: "It won't happen overnight, though; we have to write a report, contact the DCO, and hope that they can

202

achieve results." In the meantime, the stench of raw sewage hung over the market and added to the sense of discomfort that the shopkeepers were forced to endure.

There had been reports that it was the settlers who had blocked up the sewage system, causing the problem, although that was hard for the team to verify. However, the next incident they were called to appeared far more clear cut. In a busy street underneath a barred window of one of the settlement buildings, a couple of tin cans with unidentifiable viscous liquid oozing from them lay on the edge of the pavement. "They tried to light it before hurling it at us," declared a middle-aged Palestinian man breathlessly, pointing up in the direction of the offenders' homes.

"They were sixteen or seventeen," he continued, "not small kids at all". Hanging from the bars of the windows were sandbags filled with stones, which Siybll said "are prepared by the children, who then throw the rocks down at the Palestinians. The IDF come, but always deny that anything has happened." All that TIPH could do in such circumstances was pull out their notebooks, log a record of the incident, and then file the report with the DCO, which did little to placate the injured parties and reassure them that anything tangible was being done to protect them.

"There's a feeling of real frustration amongst us," said Ghassan, a Swedish member of TIPH. "We can't intervene in a situation – all we can do is turn up and take photos." This caused resentment on the part of the Palestinians, he said, whilst others on the Palestinian side "don't like us because they're convinced we work for the Israelis."

As we continued along the route of the patrol, we came across a gaggle of teenagers surrounding a dishevelled-looking man sitting askew in a wheelchair. His t-shirt badly ripped from shoulder to shoulder and covered in bloodstains, he shook as he turned plaintively to Mortens and Sibyll and pleaded for their help. "The army did this", he began. "They beat me, and there are fifteen of them still in my house now – you've got to go and do something."

After taking photos of his injuries to use as evidence, we hurried off in the direction of his house in the company of one of the boys who was acting as our guide. However, our way was obstructed by a shaven-headed Russian IDF soldier who ordered us to take a far longer, circuitous route, since the Palestinian boy was banned from walking past the Cave of Machpela. When we eventually got to the raided house, the operation was still in full flow, with heavily-armed soldiers milling around on every floor of the building as the children of the house looked on nervously.

Thanks to the terms of their mandate, TIPH members were unimpeded in their monitoring work, thus the soldiers had to let them photograph the search and interview the commander once he'd declared the building safe. "There were rocks being thrown from the roof," he stated flatly when questioned. "I didn't see anyone in a wheelchair," he went on, looking to his charges for confirmation, "and if there had been, I promise you he'd still be here with us."

"It's a bit fishy that he managed to get out of the house and all the way down the road in a wheelchair in the middle of a raid." He proposed that the man's injuries might instead have been a result of him jumping off the roof and trying to escape arrest, implying that the wheelchair was merely a prop used to garner sympathy from the TIPH team. Once the soldiers had left, we entered the house and interviewed the wounded man's children, who assured us that he had been beaten by the troops.

However, they also admitted that their younger brother had been throwing rocks at the army, and had refused to stop when his older siblings and father remonstrated with him. At the same time, they couldn't give a convincing explanation for how their apparently wheelchair-bound father had made it up the impossibly narrow stairs onto the roof to chastise their brother. This prompted Sibyll to complain that the hardest part of her job was trying to decide who was being honest and who just wanted to apportion all the blame to the other side.

The commander's parting words to us had been "We were just doing our job – no one should have rocks thrown at them, should they?" Whilst entirely right, his concern seemed pretty ironic given the ambivalence the army showed earlier when Mortens and Sibyll tried to report the missile attacks on the Palestinians. And, since the IDF ran the whole show in the city, and since TIPH could do little more than meekly complain from the sidelines, that was the heart of the problem when it comes to fairly policing the area.

Of course, Israel was hardly likely to agree to arming the likes of TIPH, just as they had all but repealed the PA's mandate to be in charge of keeping order in the Palestinian half of the city. However, given that a large part of TIPH's purpose was to try and afford the same level of protection and security to the Palestinians that the settlers enjoy, it was clear that there is no balance whatsoever at present.

Well-meaning, but ultimately impotent, foreigners wielding notebooks and pens were no match for M16-toting soldiers when it came to delivering justice to the city's residents. Therefore it was no surprise that, despite what TIPH was set up to deliver, the Palestinians felt no better looked after now than they did before 1994. And that was no more likely to assuage their frustration and fears than any other half-hearted internationally-led initiative, meaning that their feeling of abandonment was entirely understandable whilst the best they've got is TIPH.

I returned to Hebron a few days later to witness the work of another team of international observers in the city. Ecumenical Accompaniers (EA) – an unofficial body carrying out similar work to TIPH – did their best to bear witness to the settler violence, as well as provide pastoral care to the local Palestinians.

205

Of all the heartbreaking scenes I had witnessed during my time in Israel, an incident on a dusty road in a Hebron valley whilst on patrol with EA stood head and shoulders above the rest. No blood was spilt, no bones broken – but, in the space of a few seconds, I lost all hope that there was any way out of the quicksand. At least, not whilst the vicious sadism of the settlers was allowed to flourish unimpeded and uncontrolled by the Israeli authorities.

Nothing could excuse the cruelty and malice that a gang of five settler youths brazenly displayed in front of us that afternoon. Whilst less constrained by diplomatic rules of engagement than the TIPH team, the EA members were still terrified to intervene when it came to settler crimes, believing that the army would do nothing to protect them from the inevitable savagery which the settlers were notorious for dishing out to international observers.

We had headed over to a Palestinian farmer's field where, for the previous four days, settlers had been illegally constructing a house out of rocks in the middle of his land. Various half-hearted attempts by the army to disperse the invaders had had little effect, as we saw for ourselves when we arrived at the scene. Five teenaged boys and girls were nonchalantly guarding their half-built structure, casually shooting the breeze with one another – until we turned up, that was.

Screaming at me with the husky tones of a voice in the throes of breaking, one of the boys demanded that I put down my camera and "get the hell out of here". Nonplussed by his assumption that he held some kind of authority over me, I ignored his cries and carried on photographing him and his partners-in-crime.

Stalking towards me with what he considered to be a great degree of menace, he again snarled that I should stop taking photos, "or I'll kill you". Given the size of him, I couldn't help but laugh, at which point he demanded to see my ID, "or I'll call the police." "Call them by all means," I replied, as one of the settler girls strutted over to take my photo in an attempt to show that two could play at my game.

Facing off like duellers brandishing pistols at dawn, the ludicrous stand-off only ended when my EA hosts decided that we'd done enough, and that it would be prudent to head off in case the kids' parents showed up on the scene. Decamping to a vantage point on a nearby hill, we kept an eye on the situation – which was when the true horror of the children's superiority complexes came to light.

As a Palestinian man rode slowly up the road to the side of the field, the boys raced towards him with their female counterparts bounding along in their wake, long dresses billowing in the wind. Surrounding the man and forcing him to stop, they furiously demanded that he turn his animal round and ride back from whence he came – and the worst part of it all was that the man, a full ten years older than them, just meekly complied with their orders.

This was the brutal, playground-bully side of the settlers that had become so embedded in their psyches that even their youth thought they ran the town, like some kind of pre-pubescent sheriff's posse. At the same time, this was the cowed and beaten side of the local Palestinians, who had given up trying to retain their dignity or demanding equal treatment at the hands of their oppressors.

And, like I'd seen with TIPH, watching powerlessly from the sidelines were a group of international observers with the best of intentions, yet the weakest of influence when it came to intervening in incidents of this sort. Even I, despite my initial bluster in front of the marauding settler teens, had felt a certain sense of unease as I argued the toss with them in what is essentially bandit country.

The army were, as usual, nowhere to be seen when all this took place, something we took up with a soldier we met a couple of roads away. He was utterly charming as he took the time to explain the situation to us, telling us he was just as sick of the settlers' breaches of the law as us – "but what can we do about it?" He told us that the day before they had rounded up the kids and escorted them back to their homes in Kiryat Arba, but "today they're back. It's just a game of cat and mouse."

Promising to deal with them "in an hour or two", he smiled sympathetically at us before turning back to his fellow guard and carrying on their impromptu kick about with a football. He knew as well as us that he wasn't going to get any orders to take real action against the kids. And why would he, given that the IDF's unofficial brief was to protect the settlers of the town rather than all of Hebron's residents?

One girl I was with mused that perhaps the kids weren't to blame; that they were merely products of parents who educated them to treat the Palestinians with such callous disregard. She might have been right, but it was neither here nor there when they were only a few years off being the adult settlers of tomorrow. When they were old enough to carry guns, then there was no doubt that they would – by which time they'd have moved up a gear.

Whilst there was no one around to take the settlers down a peg or two and show them that they were not lords of all that they surveyed, then their hatred and misanthropy flourished unchecked. At present, no one acted – the army because they didn't care enough; the observers because they weren't confident enough; and the Palestinians because they were not suicidal enough.

As long as the settlers were allowed to run riot, all the empty words of Olmert and Co. about dismantling outposts and appeasing their neighbours aren't worth the time of day. The settlers of Hebron need to be called to heel before anyone will believe that Israel is serious about doing right by the Palestinians.

The sneering, bullying tactics of the settlers are by no means restricted to Hebron; the same disregard is evident all over the West Bank – including in Bil'in, which had been at the centre of the violent protest I attended right at the start of my CIF career.

When I eventually did return to the village, as a volunteer with Rabbis for Human Rights (RHR), I was again assailed with a sense of futility about our mission. This time, however, our tactic was not to antagonise the army, but rather to show solidarity with the local farmers and assure them that they were not alone in their struggle for justice.

RHR had brought us to help plant a few dozen olive trees in the fields next to the settlement of Modi'in Ilit, in response to a recent attempt by the settlers to build a synagogue right in the middle of a Palestinian olive grove. When the farmers tried to block the invasion, the incident had turned violent, with one Palestinian hospitalised after being beaten by the settlers.

A few minutes after we arrived to get the planting underway, a group of ten settlers rolled up in cars and jeeps, apparently to take part in a *sulha* (reconciliation) with the farmers. They sat and drank coffee in the 'peace tent' that had been erected in the field, as they earnestly discussed the situation with their Palestinian counterparts. However, many present were sceptical of the settlers' intentions, suggesting that they'd timed their visit to impress us outsiders rather than out of a real desire to make peace with their neighbours.

Mohammed, the head of the village committee, explained that for his part, "I have to deal with them as humans, even though they're part of the occupation". He insisted that he wasn't against them "because they're Jews, only because their presence here means that our land is stolen from us". He told the settlers that there was a simple way to resolve the conflict between them and the villagers once and for all – "just *leave*" – but, unsurprisingly, his suggestion wasn't warmly received by his visitors.

Whilst they continued thrashing out their differences around the warmth of an open fire, the rest of us headed off to the fields to plant the seedlings. Watching the proceedings, it was clear that the farmers didn't need our amateur tree-planting skills, but rather that it was all about the emotional support provided that made the trip worthwhile. In Judaism, visiting the sick is supposed to alleviate a fortieth of the patients' pain, and so it was here.

The farmers and villagers of Bil'in were, thanks to the occupation and expropriation of their land, suffering constantly at the hands of the Israelis – so every comforting gesture from groups such as RHR was much-needed and warmly received. Of the fifteen-strong group, a third were foreign activists, and the rest native Israelis sympathetic to the Palestinian cause.

According to Mohammed, it was "more important that Israelis come to events such as this, rather than foreigners, since it is the Israelis who can elect the leaders of tomorrow". Rabbi Grenimann, one of RHR's leaders, agreed: "We're trying to show [Israeli Jews] that there is a different religious approach to the conflict; a way to do something positive rather than just create another national ghetto".

However, according to one strident Israeli boy present, "I'm not sure it's worth us doing this at all, since I've seen so many meetings between Arabs and Israelis and it's all just symbolic bullshit." His sentiments echoed those I'd heard in Ramallah from Palestinians fed up of playing nice with their neighbours whilst nothing changed on a political level, but Mohammed disagreed with this approach.

"We *must* work with Israelis who have the ability to act against the occupation, like these people here," he stated. In his opinion, the only way forward was to physically bring together like-minded peace activists on both sides, if only to counter the pervading sense of pessimism that hung over both peoples.

After the trees were planted and we'd returned to the peace tent to break bread with the farmers, Rabbi

210

Grenimann explained why RHR's work was just as vital to Israelis as it was to the Palestinians. "I've had people stop me in the street and say 'you've saved my relationship to Judaism thanks to your work,'" he said proudly. "Whether orthodox, conservative, or reform, we come together to promote a universalist approach to Judaism."

How long the trees we planted would remain in the ground before being uprooted by either army bulldozers or settler hands was anyone's guess. Likewise the fragile truce that appeared to have been agreed on by the farmers and settlers during their brief encounter earlier in the day. But, regardless of how the situation played itself out, it was enough that the farmers knew that there were at least some Israelis who cared sufficiently to brave the cold and rain to give a bit of emotional and practical support.

***

Imagine a London where the day is punctuated by missiles raining down indiscriminately on schools, homes, parks and gardens. A London where the difference between crossing the road or not could be the difference between having your face ripped to shreds by shrapnel from rockets falling from the sky.

For the past seven years, especially in the wake of the Hamas takeover of the Gaza Strip, that had been the fate of Sderot, the beleaguered town on the edge of the Gazan-Israeli border. As Gaza bubbled over with rage, Sderot found itself in the firing line time and again.

When I first visited Sderot, I was struck by the near-deserted streets, the empty malls and cafes, and the air of impending doom that hung over the city like a cloud. My latest journey to Sderot was no different, except that this time the sense of despondency and dejection in the residents I met was far more acute than it had been a couple of months earlier.

The first person I spoke to, a Mizrachi[21] man bedecked in jewellery and scowling behind the counter of an empty shop, grimaced even further when I asked about the effect of the week's events. "Look over there," he muttered sullenly, pointing at a mother hurrying her two children along the high street. "See their suitcases? That's what it's come to now – they're all getting the hell out, and who can blame them?"

In the wake of the escalation of IDF operations in Gaza, and the increased salvo of Kassams fired at Sderot in response, the perennial white knight Arkadi Gaydamak had stepped in to pay for the evacuation of the local children. As he had done many times before – whether for altruistic reasons or for more self-serving ends – the Russian billionaire had filled the void left by the government's inaction, and funded respite care for the embattled city's residents.

However, according to Ruth, the manageress of a local café, his actions only highlighted the utter disregard with which the government treated the citizens of Sderot. "What's going on is a war, isn't it?" she asked plaintively. "Therefore they should evacuate us all until it's over." Only yesterday her sister made headline news after being hit in the head with shrapnel from a rocket, leaving her hospitalised in Beer Sheva and her family praying she would overcome her injuries.

"And just now [when a Kassam landed without the warning siren being sounded], my daughter called me to say it had fallen right in front of her," she continued. Her other daughter was bussed out to a hostel in Jerusalem in the middle of the night, leaving Ruth seething at the chain of events that had wreaked so much upheaval and pain on her family.

"If this was happening in Tel Aviv, it would be dealt with in an instant," she declared, accusing the government of ignoring Sderot's residents simply because they were working class and poor. "Even a third world country wouldn't stand by and take this kind of attack on its people," she said. "We need to go back into Gaza and deal with the terrorists by force. There's no other way – there's no one on either side strong enough to bring peace through talking, so we have to let the army deal with the problem."

Maor, a local man in his twenties eating breakfast in the café, agreed with Ruth's prescription for ending the rocket fire. "We have to kill all the militants [who are launching the Kassams]," he said. "It's the only way to bring quiet back to the town." He maintained that "they had the chance to stop the rockets after we pulled out of Gaza, but they chose to carry on. I know they're suffering in Gaza too, but that doesn't excuse helping the terrorists attack us – they bring it on themselves."

He said that around three thousand of Sderot's residents had left since the rocket attacks began, and that he too would go, given half a chance. "If the government paid us to leave like they did in Gush Katif [during the disengagement], I'd be out of here," he said. He, like many others in the city, didn't want to live on the front line – they were in the line of fire more by accident than out of some kind of ideological desire to live on the final frontier of the country.

These were not the zealous settlers of Hebron who intentionally planted themselves alongside the Palestinians in a drive to strengthen "Greater Israel". Instead these were average Israelis trying to live normal lives in an atmosphere that is anything but. The war had been brought to their doorsteps, and whilst the politicians meandered their way up diplomatic cul-de-sacs in their peacemaking efforts, they were the ones who suffered.

At the same time, their neighbours across the border suffered similarly from the cycle of violence, which was why a military response doesn't seem the best way out of the impasse. Every Israeli incursion brings a heavier rain of Kassams down on Sderot in response, and it might well have been that the only way forward is through negotiations if any long-term truce was to come.

In the meantime, however, the residents of Sderot need to be taken under the wing of a government that, until now, has been reluctant to come to their aid. Evacuating them to safety, whatever the cost, is the least they deserve until the dust settled. Because, as Ruth said sadly, "the worst part of all this isn't the rocket fire – it's the fact that the government just doesn't care". Just as she claimed that no other government in the world would allow attacks from across its borders, similarly no decent government should abandon its neediest citizens.

***

When it was first proved that smoking caused cancer, the reaction of many people was to quit on the spot, to try and salvage what was left of their lungs and health. However, many others went straight on the defensive, looking to blame everyone but themselves and claiming the scientists must have made a mistake in their research.

The second response was almost as understandable as the first, given that the revelation was akin to turning their worlds upside down, countering all the (mis)information they'd been fed throughout their lives that cigarettes don't cause any harm, or even that they may be good for you.

I had a similar problem with Zionism; at least, the brand of Zionism that I was force-fed when growing up in a community where support for Israel 'right or wrong' was a staple commodity.

Whilst at home I was taught that there were flaws with the State of Israel, that teaching was negated by the rhetoric I heard at synagogue, school, and youth group, where Israel was fêted as a Garden of Eden for the exclusive enjoyment of the Jewish people. And the Israel-lionising continued unabated for the first eighteen months that I spent in Israel, thanks to the non-stop indoctrination by my commanders in the IDF.

Thus, when I first began writing about the situation – even though I by now had serious reservations about the way in which the country was run – I still hadn't entirely broken free from the shackles of believing that Israel was a model state beyond reproach. I was like the smoker for whom the penny had started to drop about the side-effects, but who could not quite make the leap to stubbing out the cigarette.

And I still couldn't, to be honest – at least, not at that point in my retreat from my Zionist roots. I was still a Zionist, in the sense that I believed that Israel should be the homeland of the Jewish people (though not necessarily run on a For Us, By Us approach). I still loved *Eretz Yisroel*[22], the Biblical and ancestral home of my people – but that didn't mean I had to love the situation that reigned in the region. The more time I spent seeing the harm that the incumbent brand of Zionism wreaked upon the Palestinians, and – by extension – the Jewish Israelis too, the more disenchanted I became with the politics that had led us to this point.

So it was when I went out on an Israeli Committee against House Demolitions (ICAHD) tour of East Jerusalem and its rash of illegal settlements. I had been on a carbon-copy trip with the same group almost a year ago, and wanted to go again to gauge whether twelve months of opening my eyes to the reality of the conflict would make a difference to how I viewed their work. It had.

Far from falling back on the siege mentality that coloured my view of the group's work last time I wrote about them, this time the blinkers were off. What I saw and heard made me ashamed of my reaction to my original encounter with them. The raw truth was that Israel didn't have a leg to stand on when it came to the flagrant and repeated breaches of international law with which it crushed the Palestinians' aspirations of independence and hopes for freedom.

We toured the woefully underprivileged Palestinian towns to the east of the opulent Jewish side of Jerusalem, witnessing the torn up roads and garbage-strewn streets that the municipality thought nothing of letting slide into disrepair. We saw the fortified settler outposts built right in the middle of Palestinian neighbourhoods, bought with the tacit approval of the authorities.

We stood on the ruins of yet another Palestinian house demolished for breaching building regulations, a phenomenon that was designed simply to intimidate and bully the Palestinian population, given that it rarely occurred in Jewish neighbourhoods, where a vast amount of illegal construction also took place. Finally, we headed to Maaleh Adumim, the settlement city deep in the heart of the West Bank whose mere existence is designed to slash across the heart of any future Palestinian state, bisecting it almost entirely.

As we listened to our guide list crime after crime committed by the Israeli state in the name of its people, I couldn't help think of the readers who – time and again – accused me of washing Israel's dirty laundry in public by airing my views in the *Guardian*. Such accusations were nothing less than an admission that Israel was guilty of many misdeeds, "but God forbid you should talk about it 'outside the family', lest others get wind of what we've done wrong".

Which, as I had said before, was entirely the wrong approach – not least because it made us look dishonest and underhand when addressing our own failings. The same people who wanted to "keep it in the family" were the same who then hammered Arab states for their own repression of dissidents and dissenters, but who had no problem whatsoever with Israel being in the news as long as the country was getting praised rather than condemned.

All the while, groups like ICAHD continued their work in informing the international visitors and activists of Israel's faults, whether the Israel-right-or-wrong crowd liked it or not. Our dirty laundry was going to get aired whether the likes of me were writing or not; the country was effectively a launderette, given the amount of international attention focused on the area. It had to be better that Israelis were seen to be doing the washing too, rather than leaving it solely to outsiders.

216

Equally, it had to be better to wash the clothes than carrying on wearing the same filthy garments behind closed doors, just because we were too ashamed of what others would think if they saw them. One thing Israel had going for it was that it doesn't suppress political dissent. That was something that should have been seized on and capitalised upon by true Zionists, rather than leaving it to the ICAHD and their fellow NGOs to bring the true horror of the occupation to the attention of the outside world.

---

[19] Peace Now is the mainstream Israeli peace movement.
[20] Temporary International Presence in Hebron.
[21] Mizrachi – a Jew of Middle Eastern Background, as opposed to Ashkenazi (East European) or Sephardic (Spanish).
[22] The land of Israel.

Chapter Nine

After the ICAHD tour, I went on a similarly depressing trip run to the refugee camp of Nablus, which – whilst physically close – was light years away from Israel in terms of economic and social standing. According to our guide, Nablus was set between two mountains famed for their role in the Biblical story of Balaam and his donkey. Balaam, a non-Jewish prophet, set out for Israel determined to issue a curse over the land, but – thanks to Divine intervention and revelation – ended up blessing the infant state instead. His change of heart is still cited today, with supporters of the Zionist state claiming that all of Israel's detractors would sing her praises to the high heavens if only they saw the country for themselves.

I had seen the country – yet I didn't have praise pouring forth from my lips. At least, not when faced with the consequences of Israel's "me first" policy that had caused such devastation and heartache to the Palestinian people, as I witnessed yet again in the Balata refugee camp on the outskirts of Nablus. To argue about whether it was a camp or not, as many did, is utterly irrelevant. Yes, the refugees lived in houses rather than tents, but given the atrocious conditions in which they were forced to exist, it was of little comfort to them that their prison cells were made of bricks and mortar instead of canvas.

"The residents aren't allowed to build outside the camp's perimeter, so the only way is up," said our guide – and it showed. Alleyways between houses barely wider than a person; bars on the windows of adjacent houses literally touching across the divide; and raw sewage flowing unchecked down the broken pavement – this was the reality of life behind the barricades.

Pockmarked walls wore the scars of the almost-daily incursions by the IDF, whose stray bullets did more than just damage the facades of the houses, to which the overflowing cemetery bore testament. "The army doesn't give a damn about civilians getting caught in the crossfire," said Muhammad, who led us around his neighbourhood with a grim determination to drill home the horror of life under military rule.

"However," he said, "you can never truly know what it's like till you've lived here yourself. Every family's either had someone killed, wounded or arrested by the IDF; dozens of houses have been smashed apart during raids." He spoke of his childhood friends who had "ended up underground", saying that over twenty of his peer group died "a martyr's death" resisting the occupation.

As we toured the camp and saw the scores of memorials erected in honour of fallen *shaheeds*, it was clear that whatever security reasons were cited for the army's iron-fist approach to Nablus, it was having the opposite effect in terms of crushing the resistance. Children swaggered round in bomber jackets in imitation of the posters of gun-toting fighters which were plastered on every available surface. T-shirts bearing the images of Nasrallah, George Habash and other militant leaders were on sale in the crowded *casbah* in the Old City section of town.

Muhammad told tales of great escapes and assassination survivals by local fighters as though narrating folklore legends of ancient times. The militants' "daring acts of heroism" had turned them into instant idols for the youth of Nablus, who stared wide-eyed at their chiselled features in the posters in the same way that their peers overseas gazed dreamily at pop stars and footballers.

The stallholders in the *souk* begged Muhammad to translate their tales of misery for the benefit of the foreigners in their midst, complaining bitterly of the nightly raids that left their shops destroyed and their produce ruined.

However, for all that I was thoroughly depressed by what I saw in Nablus itself, the worst part of the tour was

219

saved for last. Having decided that the queue at the checkpoint looked too long and foreboding, the leader of our group decided to get us back into Israel via the "back route"; and at the same time taught us a valuable lesson about the true purpose of the security wall.

For ten shekels per head, a minibus driver took us on a convoluted journey through fields and olive groves, eventually delivering us onto the Israeli side of a checkpoint to our astonishment. It was as though witnessing a magician pull a rabbit from a hat; at least, for those of us who believed that the labyrinth of checkpoints and the mile upon mile of security wall were completely impenetrable to intruders.

Of course, the border is almost as porous now as it ever had been; if terrorists wanted to smuggle weapons across in order to attack Israeli civilians, they were not impeded in the slightest, as our clandestine break for the border proved. Instead, as our guide stressed, the checkpoint system was designed first and foremost to crush the Palestinian economy under the guise of security measures, and to remind the Palestinians exactly who was boss.

The authorities had certainly succeeded in getting half the job done, since they'd managed to destroy Nablus's economy and leave its residents in a permanent state of penury. However, given the defiant image of the town – with its concrete homages to fallen fighters on every corner, and air of steely determination in the eyes of those peering down from the martyr posters – it was not at all clear that the locals are ready to roll over and play dead for their Israeli masters, no matter how hard the army hit them.

For those who still cleaved to the notion that the only way to fight fire was with more and more fire from the other side, Nablus should have proved that this was not the answer. No matter how many fighters died at the hands of the army, another generation sprang up to replace them – which, given the desperate situation they found themselves in within the camp, was hardly surprising. Having seen the ease with which they can slip across undetected into Israel should the mood take them, it was a game that the authorities are playing by besieging the city.

Despite the decisions taken by the leaders on both sides of the Israeli-Palestinian conflict, those on ground level still wield a great deal of power when it comes to how they interact with their neighbours. On a daily basis, the choice is theirs whether to do the right thing by those alongside whom they live, or whether to express callous disregard for their fellow man and trample all over them en route to further feathering their own nests.

Over the course of two days, I witnessed both sides of that particular coin, and discovered how precariously balanced the scales of justice were in the minds of those tasked with choosing which path to take. On both occasions the cast was made up of Arab residents of Silwan, an area of East Jerusalem adjacent to the Old City, and their Jewish counterparts living nearby, though the way in which the dramas played themselves out were wildly different.

Having seen for myself the veneer of calm under which the Jewish and Arab residents of French Hill coexisted with one another, I was further buoyed after attending an exhibition in the Jerusalem neighbourhood of Abu Tor. A local community centre was playing host to a display of artworks by students from a children's village in Bethlehem, under the banner of "Conquering Conflict Through Creation", and dozens of guests crowded into the gallery to show their support for the project.

The audience was made up of both Jews and Arabs, none of whom thought twice about socialising with one another, and who were at ease with coming together as one to applaud the young artists for their work. The children had, after protracted negotiations with the authorities, been granted permits to enter Israel to attend the exhibition. For many of them it was their first time across the border.

221

In that context, it was wholly beneficial that they should see Arabs and Jews getting up close and personal with one another, in order to allay any fears they may have had, as well as instilling a positive image that the two sides could get along without violence and hostility.

Also present were a troupe of children from Silwan, who played music and sang under the proud gazes of their parents, many of whom were on first name terms with the Jewish Israelis present and clearly were veterans of such joint-ventures as this. The event lasted long into the night, and belied the image that many people had of the two camps as being divided and polarised, and as never having contact with their peers on the other side.

Which was all well and good – until the dark side of Jewish-Arab interaction reared its head at a demonstration in Silwan a day later. Silwan, which had suffered constantly at the hands of an indifferent municipality which paid scant attention to the basic sanitary and social needs of the village, had salt rubbed into its wound by the ever-growing number of settlers who had set up camp in their midst.

Not content with embedding themselves in buildings all over the town and provocatively draping Israeli flags from the rooftops, they had also been busy conducting archaeological excavations throughout the area, in search of Biblical relics which would reinforce their claims that the district should be recognised as belonging to the Jews. Many ancient tunnels had been uncovered, which – since they were made of stone – hadn't caused any damage to the buildings above, but recently the settlers had begun digging a new series of cruder, flimsier tunnels that had had a serious impact on many homes belonging to Silwan's Arab populace.

Although the locals were bringing a case to the courts demanding a halt to the excavations, the settlers had ploughed on regardless; and, since the authorities had proved reluctant to step in, Silwan's residents decided to take to the streets to garner support for their cause.

Setting up tents on a parking lot on one of the main streets of the town, scores came to protest the settlers' actions and call for intervention by the powers that be.

Huge banners were prominently displayed from lamp posts: "Tunnels are not more important than lives" read one; "No new Nakba" another. "The more they dig out the earth, the more they damage our houses", said Jawad Siyam, a local activist leading the demonstration. "The settlers say they will start work on the tunnels again this week, and we'll be here to stop them – physically, if we have to".

Their numbers were swelled by a dozen or so Jewish Israelis who had come to show solidarity with the Silwan residents, echoing the cooperative spirit at the art gallery the day before. However, the overriding image of the situation in Silwan was of a group of marauding settlers with equal disregard for both the law and their Arab neighbours, whose selfish endeavours threatened to overshadow any efforts made by Jews and Arabs to get along.

At least, that was the view of the cab driver who drove me back to West Jerusalem when the demonstration was over. "Those with the money have the power," he said, referring to the funds made available to the settlers by the US-based Elad organisation to carry out their work. "We have none, so we can do nothing," he continued dejectedly.

"But," he went on, glancing at me in the rear view mirror with a glint in his eye, as he wagged his finger forcefully, "it's all a cycle – one day we'll have the power, and then we'll do to them what they do to us now. As we say, every dog has its day." His reaction to the settlers' actions, and his desire to avenge tomorrow their crimes of today, spoke volumes about what made the most impact on those living in Silwan. He didn't mention the Jewish Israelis who'd stood alongside the Arabs in their struggle, but only had thoughts of those doing his people wrong.

Which was why the actions of the Silwan settlers dragged the process ten steps back for every one tentative step forward made by those trying to bridge the gap between the two sides. Whilst the settlers continued to flout the laws of the land, as well as of decent human behaviour, all the joint art exhibitions in Jerusalem wouldn't be enough to dampen the anger of those who fell victim to their acts of cruelty.

I went to Bethlehem a week later to visit the children's village whose charges had participated in the art project in Jerusalem, before going to see their Israeli counterparts who operated out of the southern city of Arad. One of the teachers in Bethlehem had plans to organise a joint art exhibition between the organisation's Israeli and Palestinian charges, and so I accompanied her to meet with the directors of the Israeli SOS Children's Village.

Both the chief social worker and the head of the home were more than willing to embark on the proposed project, convinced that only good could come from such an endeavour. "Children are children," said Matty, the director. "It's not about politics at all." We were taken on a tour of the village, meeting children just as buoyant and lively as those I encountered in its sister school in Bethlehem. Despite the emotional scars that these youngsters had suffered, they seemed happy in their current environment, free to enjoy their childhood away from the turbulent conditions that had seen them move to the children's home in the first place.

The village had every mod con that the children required – pool table, music studios, petting zoo and sports pitches – and it was clear from looking at the beaming faces all around us that the staff were doing a good job helping the children recuperate from their past traumas. The home did not just cater for Jewish youths; several of the residents were Muslim and grew up in Israeli Arab villages, and a further half dozen came from the Former Soviet Union (FSU) countries and had Russian Orthodox parents.

This was an important feature of the home, Matty told me, since "it sets a good example of collaboration to the other SOS villages." When he made the decision to bring Arab children to live in the home six years ago, "things were much worse. The other kids used to run around chanting 'Death to the Arabs', but we persevered and now things are working out very well." The Arab boys I met seemed utterly at home alongside their Jewish friends, and clearly the experiment had worked out for the best, despite the initial resistance.

As for taking the coexistence model a step further and bringing the Israeli children together with their Palestinian peers, Matty was positive that it would reap benefits for both sides, but at the same time was realistic about the chances of the project actually getting off the ground. "Two years ago we decided to run a joint summer camp along with SOS Bethlehem," he said, "but then Hamas got elected, and it was the wrong climate to continue with our plans. It will happen, though," he assured me, "but these things take a long time to push through."

In the meantime, Sarah – the teacher from Bethlehem – spent the afternoon encouraging the young artists in Arad to paint pictures relating to children's rights, just as she had done with her Palestinian students. Their paintings were remarkably similar to those done in Bethlehem, but when it came to filling out questionnaires about the children's hopes and fears for the future, the imbalance of the conflict shone through.

The Arad students, who had suffered just as much familial strife as their Bethlehem counterparts, chose to focus on themselves when it came to discussing their aspirations and dreams. They wrote of their desire to become footballers, actors, models and singers, with several of them expressing their wish that their parents would come into money and be able to raise themselves out of destitution.

The Palestinian children, on the other hand, eschewed their own personal dreams in place of writing how desperately they wished for their country to be freed from the yoke of occupation. They spoke of their desire to return to their ancestral villages and their wish to see their families' expropriated fields and olive groves handed back to their rightful owners.

Whilst there were huge similarities between the two groups of children that made Sarah's project seem entirely worthwhile and valuable, what was clear from reading both groups' responses was that the conflict had taken a far greater toll on the Palestinian youth. This fact shouldn't have stood in the way of the planned collaboration between the two sets of children, but anyone looking to draw equivalences between the suffering on both sides need only look at the disparity in the dreams and desires of children on either side of the divide.

Of course, during the height of the Intifada when Israeli buses were being blown up on an almost daily basis, many Israelis did go through hell, the scars of which still haven't faded. But, save for the unfortunate residents of Sderot who were still besieged by Kassam fire from Gaza, life within Israel is by and large calm and serene once more; at least, in comparison with Gaza and the West Bank.

Which was why the SOS children gave such wildly differing answers to the same set of questions about their burning desires for the future. Their hopes and dreams reflected the conditions in which they lived, as well as the atmosphere amongst the adults with whom they resided. That the Israeli children felt confident enough about their surroundings to focus on their individual aspirations was very encouraging, in the context of producing a new generation of Israelis who weren't wracked with fear of war or annihilation.

But that their Palestinian peers were still so caught up in their national struggle for independence that they cared more about liberating their people than their own personal futures, means that the omens don't look good. These were children who, when they grew up, would be just as desperate to resist the occupation as the generations who had tried, and failed, before them – which spelled just as much trouble for the security of the Israelis as it did for the Palestinians who take up arms for the cause. Anyone who failed to understand the children's responses to the questionnaire would only have themselves to blame when it all came back to haunt them ten or fifteen years down the line.

The next morning I made my way to the Western Wall to say the traveller's prayer, as I always do before leaving Israel for any length of time. The sun was blazing down in a cloudless sky, the azure blue of the heavens complementing the rough hewn yellow stones of which every house in Jerusalem is built. The deeper into the Old City I strolled, the more I again marvelled at being able to walk down the same cobbled streets and alleyways as my ancestors did two millennia ago.

As I approached the Kotel Plaza in front of the Wall, the feelings grew even stronger, and by the time I found myself at the Wall itself, I was completely at one with my identity as a proud, God-fearing Jew, able to offer my supplications in the same spirit as my antecedents. Upon finishing my prayer and heading back to West Jerusalem, I paused momentarily to gaze down into the valley where Silwan was located – and in so doing learned the essential difference between me and those of my detractors who refused to hear a bad word said against the state of Israel.

In the film *New Jack City*, there is a scene towards the beginning where Ice-T is watching a group of inner-city children chant anti-drugs slogans in a local playground. He watches them with a benevolent smile on his face, before catching a glimpse of used syringes strewn near the swings, and his beaming features quickly switch to a grimace of despair. Upon leaving the otherworldly cocoon of the Kotel and glancing down at Silwan on my way home, I felt exactly the same way.

There is a huge difference between loving the land of Israel and loving the way in which the country's rulers go about imposing their will on those living within its borders. Those who accuse me of being anything from a fifth

227

columnist to a self-hating Jew because I didn't take the crimes of the government lying down would have done well to consider the Catholic mantra: love the sinner, hate the sin. The ironic part of this was that many of the right wing, settler crowd in Israel despise the incumbent government just as much as those on the left, but refuse to see their own dissidence as being borne out of malice towards Israel; quite the opposite, in fact.

They asserted that they, and only they, were the true *Ahavei Yisroel* (lovers of Israel), and that they were not to be challenged by anyone when it came to knowing the ideal path for the future of the state. No matter how much their opponents remonstrated with them, there was no headway to be made whatsoever, since they convinced themselves long ago that they were the only ones with Israel's best interests at heart. Their opponents, they believed, were either blinded by self-loathing, or had been duped by Islamist, anti-Zionist tricks, and were beyond salvation, so they decided that the only way to deal with them was to knock the wind out of their sails.

It was as true on the threads of CIF as it was in real life. The same hectoring condescension I had come up against in face-to-face meetings with settlers and their supporters were repeated in electronic form all over the threads beneath my articles. There was no acknowledgement that a left-wing viewpoint on Israel could carry the same weight as a right-wing version, hence the conservative Zionists spent their time avoiding proper debate, preferring to stamp on any dissenting views as though putting out a fire on their living room carpet.

But, despite their vehement assertions of being the sole owners of the truth, the facts that emerged from ground level upwards aren't easily suppressed. The sadistic acts of the settlers in Silwan; the equally vicious behaviour of the residents of Modi'in Ilit; the complicity of the army in the various settler outrages across the West Bank: none of these issues could be casually dismissed, as the settlers are finding out to their dismay.

The world is watching, and exerting more pressure on the Israeli authorities the more evidence they find of wrongdoing against the Palestinians. Witness the recent acquiescence of the government to American demands for a freeze in settlement construction; a long overdue step, of course, but a massive indicator that even the usually tolerant US regime is getting fed up with the status quo.

So, regardless of what my detractors say, I love Israel just as much as those to the right of me; it was just that in my eyes, love doesn't have to be blind. The passion I felt when I walked through the Old City was not to be mistaken with a passion for the current Israeli government, nor for the types of Zionist who run roughshod over justice and in the process do incalculable harm to Israel's reputation and legitimacy. It is a love for the land I have chosen to call home, and until it is run by people of whom I was proud, I will continue to separate sinner from sin, no matter how hard that concept was for the diehard cynics to comprehend.

***

Jewish Book Week in 2007 culminated with a stormy session in central London, in which Alan Rusbridger and David Landau took to the stage in front of a largely hostile crowd, several hundred-strong, to discuss reporting from the Middle East. Winning over an audience made up in the main of conservative Jews was never going to be easy for the editors of the *Guardian* and *Haaretz*, given the reputations of both their papers in Anglo-Jewish circles.

Against a backdrop of renewed hostilities in Gaza, and outrage at the *Guardian*'s handling of recent Israel-related stories, the two men were required to answer some serious criticism from the floor. Thanks to his position as *kipa*-wearing Israeli Jew and left-wing newspaper editor, David Landau was able to act as middleman between the audience and Alan Rusbridger, and he stood his ground firmly when making his defence.

He launched an impassioned tirade against the "misguided" Diaspora Zionists who "invest an inordinate amount of time bashing the *Guardian*, the BBC, and others, rather than helping Israel solve its existential dilemma". He castigated the "pro-Israel community [around the world]" for its "nascent McCarthyism" when it comes to their witch-hunt against media outlets and individual journalists, describing their actions as both "dangerous and anti-democratic".

Instead of spending so much effort demonising those reporting on the conflict, he said, true supporters of Israel ought to be trying to cure the cause of the problems in the region, not wasting time focusing on the symptoms, such as how the papers reported on the troubles. Ignoring the hecklers, he ploughed on with his message, citing his own moral journey as reason for others to face up to reality, rather than claiming that the world is irredeemably biased against Israel.

He spoke of his initial outrage when he read Chris McGreal's famous piece in the *Guardian* comparing Israel to Apartheid South Africa. On re-reading the article recently, he found that his outrage had all but disappeared. "Now I think he does have a point," Landau explained to a hushed room. "Israel is heading towards a South Africa style dilemma," he continued, and – whether those in the audience agreed with him or not – they could hardly dispute his authority when it came to the subject of the Zionist state's policies.

He then pointed out that the Israeli press was full of stridently critical articles towards the incumbent government, and exposés of their crimes, yet their publication caused barely a ripple amongst Diaspora Jews. However, when organisations like the BBC or the *Guardian* reported exactly the same stories everyone was up in arms. "But it doesn't register with them that they can see the same thing on Israeli TV, since they are obsessed with *Guardian*-bashing [rather than the story itself]," he said dejectedly.

Alan Rusbridger made it quite plain that his worm was not for turning, no matter how much mud was thrown at either him or his paper, asserting that "our editorial position is quite clear: we support the two state solution, and we see Israel as a moral necessity". As far as he was concerned, the *Guardian* did not have "an obsession" with Israel, nor did his correspondents research their stories "carelessly" when covering the conflict. He stated that of "593 pieces about Israel on CIF, 200 are pro-Israel"; at the same time heralding CIF and the internet news medium in general as being "as important a revolution as Gutenberg" in terms of pushing the media forward.

Rusbridger also made an explicit apology for the *Guardian's* notorious Jenin editorial, which prompted applause from the more open-minded members of the crowd, who acknowledged the significance of making such a gesture to his critics. Both he and Landau had to contend with not only an unfriendly audience but also the shockingly partisan Alex Brummer, ostensibly on stage merely to chair the proceedings, but who instead harangued the two editors non stop from his perch alongside them.

Brummer displayed all the hallmarks of the type of Zionist of whom David Landau so despaired. He constantly made digs at the way the media "delegitimises" the Jewish state, upbraiding papers for "making Israel out to be the oppressor, which is obviously nonsense...". David Landau's withering retorts to his remarks more than dealt with his weak and insubstantial allegations.

But, despite their successful rebuttal of the charges levelled against them, I couldn't help wonder how long their words would remain in the minds of their critics. Only a day later, and the outraged emails were flowing once more, one castigating the *Independent* for its "anti-Israel bias" under the heading "Enablers of murder"; another accusing them of "promoting Palestinian propaganda" and "publishing [pro-Palestinian] photographs without checking their veracity".

Another day, another incensed burst of wagon-circling and wild allegations aimed at anyone daring to take a stance different to that of the hard-line Zionists in their Diaspora armchairs. Despite David Landau's plea to "help us [Israel] think what to do [to solve the conflict] rather than parsing the Sunday headlines," it seemed that his words went in one ear and straight out the other.

And, for all that Alan Rusbridger firmly made his case as being not only no enemy of Israel, but in fact on Israel's side, it would only be a matter of time before the bell rang and the next round of "*Guardian*-bashing" got underway in earnest. Because for some, as David Landau said, it was far easier to pin the blame on everyone else than to admit that – at the core of the issue – Israel bore no small share of responsibility for the state it found itself in at present.

***

Upon my return to Israel, I headed straight back into the thick of the protests and demonstrations that were a staple part of life in and around the West Bank. My first port of call was a town bordering Bethlehem, where locals and internationals gathered every week to call for the dismantling of the security wall being built nearby.

All the elements were in place for a Bil'in-style brawl. Dozens of Palestinians sporting keffiyehs and flying their national colours; an equal number of tooled-up, olive-clad soldiers in gas masks; and the press pack waiting in the wings for the fun to start. The weekly demonstrations often resulted in violent clashes with the IDF; that week, however, the protest was over before it had barely begun.

The Muslim faithful spread out their prayer mats in front of the phalanx of soldiers, made their supplications, then retreated fifty yards down the road, away from the coils of barbed wire that blocked their path. As they milled about and considered their options, a few of their number broke off and began hurling rocks in the direction of the troops, but their tame efforts elicited no response

232

from the bored-looking soldiers.

A gaggle of teens began setting light to tyres, then placing them at intervals along the deserted strip of tarmac between the protesters and the APCs, but again they were ignored by the onlooking forces. No one seemed willing to make the first move; both sides aware that the stakes had been raised in the wake of the IDF's shooting of four militants in Bethlehem earlier in the week, and neither side wanting to test the other's capacity for violent response if it all kicked off in El Khader.

At that point, several of the international activists who had come to take part in the protest decided they'd had enough, and that it was time to decamp to a local restaurant for lunch. I was invited to join them – and, in doing so, found that the real story of the day was far away from the bitumen-coated battleground that this time had hosted no more than a couple of half-hearted attempts to goad the army into retaliation.

Almost a year ago, I had written a highly-inflammatory and highly-regrettable piece about the influx of foreign activists who flock to the region, in which I displayed the kind of hostility normally dished out by the *Daily Mail* to Polish migrant workers. As with several of my early articles, I had since seen the light; in this case, as a result of actually talking to the individuals involved rather than speculating from afar.

Sitting around a table in the courtyard of an opulent Bethlehem hotel, I quizzed my fellow diners as to what motivated them to drop everything and make it their mission in life to defend those who cannot defend themselves in this conflict.

Three of our group were American Christians – two of them volunteers for the Christian Peacemaker Team; the other a veteran activist who now resided in Ramallah and continued to campaign against the occupation. All three were practising Anglicans, and invoked the doctrines of their faith as reason enough to persevere in their quest to bring justice to the Palestinian people.

233

I asked them whether, with so many activists flocking to the region, there was justification for the claim that the world focused disproportionately on Israel. "No, quite the opposite," one woman replied: "There aren't enough activists." She complained of her church's ambivalence towards the conflict, "I want my church to take a stance on the issue, [rather than sitting on the fence and refusing to take a position]."

As far as she was concerned, there was a reticence amongst the world's Christians to intervene on the Palestinians' behalf. "The people living Christ-risen lives are the anarchists, communists, Muslims, and the Israelis [who show solidarity at the protests]. Where were the Christians of El Khader at the demonstration? Why was it only the local Muslims who came?"

Her friends agreed with her view that there was nothing sinister about foreigners coming to show support with the Palestinians', denying any link between their actions and an obsession with Israel and/or the Jews. "We – along with many Jews, by the way – supported the people of El Salvador in their struggle, and were active in the American Civil Rights movement as well, and there's nothing different about our getting involved here," said one of the CPT volunteers.

Listening to them as they discussed their hopes for the region's future, as well as their reflections on all they'd witnessed so far, it was clear that – for this trio at least – they were motivated by a clear sense of right and wrong. For all that many Zionists (my former self included) railed against the way Israel was continually put under the microscope, the fact was that it was not just *our* conflict. Just as Israel's supporters raised no objections to hard-line Christian Zionists in America donating funds to the state and wielding domestic influence over Congressmen, similarly they should have understood that critical overseas intervention in the conflict was likely.

The Palestinians require both emotional and financial support in their struggle, just as the Jewish state was founded on similar benevolence from quarters of Diaspora Jewry, and many others besides, who supported the idea of re-establishing a Jewish homeland. And – in the case of the weekly protests at El Khader, the similar demonstrations at Bil'in, and elsewhere – it was no bad thing at all that the likes of the CPT volunteers were self-less enough to provide what assistance they could. To dismiss it out of hand as being malevolently-intentioned did their work no justice.

Providing palliative and pastoral care, as the American volunteers did, was the theme of my next article, which centred around the several hundred refugees from Sudan who had ended up in Israel.

***

"Even though we're Muslim, the Islamic world has done nothing to protect us," said Yassin, whose tortured flight from Darfur finally brought him to Israel three years in 2005. He was one of the first Darfuris to make it into Israel across the border from Egypt, and had dedicated his life to helping hundreds of his fellow countrymen who had made the same perilous journey.

Yassin, a genial thirty year old former architect, was now director of Bnei Darfur [Sons of Darfur], an organ-isation which assisted Sudanese refugees in integrating into Israeli society, and which that week had finally been granted non-profit status by the Israeli government. Sitting in his office in downtown Tel Aviv, Yassin painted a harrowing picture of the way in which Darfuri refugees were mistreated by the authorities in Egypt, which was the first port of call of many fleeing the violence in Sudan.

Darfuri children were scared to set foot outside in Egypt for fear of attack, Yassin said, citing the slaying of dozens of refugees after a protest outside the UNHCR headquarters in 2005. "It's not that Egypt doesn't look after refugees in general," he said, "after all, they treat the Somalians very well. However, when it comes to us, they are different. It's racism."

It didn't help that the Darfuris were accusing fellow Muslims of genocide, said Yassin, noting that the Muslim states who supported the Sudanese government in turn claimed that the refugees were collaborating with enemy states in the West. "All of the Arab countries support the government of Sudan – our problem is with the Arab League," Yassin stated with a shake of his head at his people's plight. Having watched most of his family slaughtered in a militia attack on his village, he fled the region hoping to find shelter in Egypt, but was soon forced to move on.

After the cold and often violent reception the refugees received at the hands of the Egyptians, Yassin decided that things couldn't possibly be worse on the Israeli side of the border, despite the anti-Israeli indoctrination he'd been spoon-fed when growing up in Sudan. "The government controlled all of the media back home," he said. "The television stations, the radio, the newspapers... and all of them were very hostile towards Israel. They described it as an enemy state full of killers, and the cause of all of the world's problems."

He smiled at the irony of Israel turning out to be the first country where he and his fellow refugees could finally find sanctuary, although it was hardly plain sailing at first. "When the army picked me up, I spent five days on their base in a tiny room with five Egyptian men. The conditions were awful, and one of the judges was very cruel, threatening to deport me back to Egypt. She told me that I wasn't welcome in Israel because I was from an 'enemy country' – but in the end I was transferred to a larger prison in the south."

He spent fourteen months in jail, where he banded together with other Darfuri refugees and founded an informal support group to assist one another; teaching English, Arabic and Hebrew to those who required educating. After a few months, the Israeli press started picking up the story of the refugee crisis, and soon several NGOs and welfare organisations began campaigning for their release. The UN got involved, and eventually many of the refugees were let out of jail and sent to work on local kibbutzim.

However, once free they faced large-scale exploitation by employers who took advantage of their lack of proper permits and rights, forcing them to work for a pittance and in dreadful conditions. Again, intervention from the UN and local NGOs caused a change of heart on the part of the government, who granted 600 of the 750 refugees with 'A5' temporary residency status, with the remainder receiving protection as asylum seekers.

The rest was recent history. Yassin and his friends formed Bnei Darfur, and have been successful in their mission to create a self-sufficient community "that isn't a drain on Israeli society". Every one of the refugees had a job, a house, and access to medical care; "the only ones without jobs are the ones who've just arrived, and we soon take care of them," he said. The children had been found places at Israeli schools, where they learn Hebrew and befriend their locally-born peers. The future appeared bright for those who had managed to make it into Israel.

Many Israelis took up the Darfuris' cause on the basis that Jews have been denied refuge by indifferent countries throughout history, and that Israeli Jews should remember their own troubled past when dealing with the victims of today. However, whilst the way in which Israel (eventually) received the refugees was to be admired, there was of course the accusation of double standards to be dealt with regarding Palestinian refugees being denied the chance to relocate to the Promised Land.

But the unresolved issue of the Palestinian right of return was not something on which Yassin wished to be drawn. As far as he was concerned, Israel has provided for his people in a way that no Arab country would, and for that he was eternally grateful. In terms of Israel's image in the eyes of the refugees as well as the outside world, accepting the unwanted Darfuris was an astute move to make.

You could take the boy out of Palestine, but not Palestine out of the boy, and the Leeds University student I had lunch with later in the month was no exception. I had first met Akram the year before in his father's jewellery shop in Jerusalem's Old City, where I'd ended up by chance as I strolled through the heaving *souk*. We got talking about our mutual love of Jerusalem – and, by extension, Israel/Palestine – and he told me of the struggles he was having engaging with the various I/P activist groups amongst the Leeds student body.

A sporadic email correspondence followed in which we discussed his difficulty in feeling positive about the Shalom Salaam dialogue initiative which he helped found at the university. The key impediment appeared to be his inability to overcome the deep antipathy with which he viewed Israel's cheerleaders:

> *"How can I possibly understand, for instance, how a Jew feels about Israel? How can I ever feel that Zionism is a good thing? How can my views and my Jewish friends' views converge on the issues when our frame of reference is so completely different? The answer is depressingly simple. They cannot."*

He went on to explain why he felt unable to be anything more than coolly civil to those students on the other side of the I/P divide:

> *"It is far too easy to slip back into viewing the Jewish Society as 'the enemy' and to shout about Palestinian rights, which I feel is more productive than trying as hard as I can to view the conflict from a viewpoint which I fundamentally disagree with."*

In reply, I pointed out that by merely founding Shalom Salaam in the first place, he'd expressed a willingness to engage with the other side which was worth capitalising on, rather than allowing to be swallowed up in a fog of dejection and disheartenment. When we met again, Akram still appeared unsure as to the best path to go down, and, after hearing him speak about his dilemma, it was wholly understandable that he continued to feel this way after almost a year immersed in student politics.

The scenario he painted of entrenchment and deep division amongst the opposing camps in the university I/P scene was, depressingly, reminiscent of the similar standoff that occurred on a national scale between the Israeli and Palestinian authorities. The innocence of youth wore off long before teenagers set up home in university towns, and campus Middle East politics bubbles over just as furiously as in any other arena.

We were joined at lunch by David, an active member of a prominent university Jewish Society, who had come along to meet Akram and see if there was any common ground with which the two could work to reach across the impasse and lay the groundwork for future joint projects. Despite the obvious differences between them – David as a Jewish Zionist from London, Akram a Jerusalem-born Palestinian nationalist – they didn't allow the disparity to get in the way of their overriding mutual goal, namely promoting better understanding of "the other" in their respective circles.

Over a leisurely lunch in a Lebanese restaurant behind the imposing masonry of Jaffa Gate, the three of us discussed ways in which to avoid the minefields that awaited anyone trying to reach out of their comfort zone and deal head-on with their political opponents. Both David and Akram railed against the tired, hysterical accusations of anti-Semitism regularly hurled by pro-Zionists at those who dared speak out against the crimes of the Jewish state. At the same time, both had harsh words for those in the pro-Palestinian camp who dragged the debate into the realms of Nazi-comparisons, recognising the futility as well as the unnecessary offensiveness of such incendiary analogies.

239

They spoke at length of their own experiences of taking part in the I/P debate at their respective universities. David decried the ostrich-like mentality of the Israel-right-or-wrong crowd who seemed to believe that better PR alone will hoodwink the world into ignoring Israel's misdeeds and force them to believe that the country was nothing but a beacon of virtue cast adrift in a sea of barbarity. Whilst Akram broadly supported the underlying politics of those in the pro-Palestinian societies, he still took issue with some of the tactics employed in getting their message across.

Plans were made to meet when they returned to England, with David offering to arrange speaking engagements amongst Jewish youth groups for Akram, who was keen to take him up on the suggestion. Whilst realising they wouldn't be solving all the region's ills overnight, there was a mutual recognition that things had to begin somewhere: little acorns, mighty oaks, and so on.

However, despite the positive signs that emanated from our three-strong gathering, the momentum appeared to be against such ventures, both in the Middle East and on campuses around the world. In the vacuum left by decades of unfulfilled promises to bring peace to the region, dogmatism had filled the void and left the moderates struggling to make their voices heard.

Which is why the likes of Akram and David have a vital role to play, and why every effort ought to have been made to encourage their cooperation. Because otherwise, as Akram said, it becomes all "too easy to slip back into viewing the [other side] as the enemy", and when that happens, universities found themselves becoming battle-grounds every bit as hostile as Israel and the Occupied Territories themselves.

***

"You do know this is the bus for Ein Rafah, don't you?" inquired the puzzled driver as fifteen Jewish gap year students clambered aboard, confused as to why any Jewish group would be making their way to the rural Israeli Arab village way out in the Jerusalem hills.

After explaining the purpose of our trip – to take part in a *mifgash* (meeting) between Jewish and Arab teenagers – he turned his attention back to the road, although similar bewilderment was etched on the faces of all the other Arab passengers who boarded after us and caught sight of our incongruous troupe. The bus wound its way through the lush countryside, passing through the hamlet of Ein Naqub before depositing us outside the mosque in the centre of Ein Rafah, where we were met by the town's imam.

He took us on a tour of the mosque, patiently explaining the central tenets of Islam and answering the dozens of questions from inquisitive students. As he spoke, several local teens drifted into the carpeted hall, peering at the strangers in their midst from behind the safety of the pillars propping up the domed roof. Once the imam's talk ended, we headed outside and the two groups began tentatively chatting to one another in broken Hebrew and rudimentary English.

The similarities between the kids was clear: they sported the same piercings, the same brash, branded trainers and the same shy, nervous smiles as their opposite numbers, despite the Jewish group all hailing from South Africa and Australia and the Arab youth from no further afield than the roads adjoining the town square. By the time we headed into a classroom in the local primary school to hold the formal *mifgash* it was clear there was much both sides wanted to know about the other.

Sitting in a circle on undersized plastic chairs, everyone introduced themselves in turn, and then began the process of quizzing one another on their respective lives. The gap year students explained that they were part of a Zionist youth movement, but that they were interested in learning about more than just the standard, saccharine Israel-friendly propaganda that most year-off courses were fed by the Jewish Agency.

241

Therefore, they said, they didn't want their Arab counterparts to feel embarrassed if they were critical of Israel in any way, since the point of the exercise on their part was to hear the reality of life for all of Israel's citizens, no matter how hard the truth.

The Arab youngsters spoke candidly about life as "second class citizens", describing the deep suspicion and mistrust with which they are treated whenever they venture outside their village and into Jewish areas. "As soon as people hear us speak Arabic on the street, we're stopped by the police and ID'd," said one boy flatly. "Whilst I understand that they have security fears, when it happens again and again and again, in all areas of our lives, it can drive you crazy," he went on.

"Even though we live here as full citizens, we're constantly made to feel different, which doesn't create the possibility of feeling part of the whole," added Ada, a middle-aged woman who headed up the Arab group. She said that even though she could get on with Jewish Israelis on an individual basis, there was widespread discrimination both on a government level and in the job market, which was something she and her charges found very difficult to take.

"I don't care if it's an Arab or a Jew in charge of the government," said Shiriann, a recently-married girl from the village, "so long as I get my full rights and am treated like a human being here." The Jewish students were clearly uncomfortable with what they were hearing: "Which is no bad thing," according to Nic, their leader and educator, who intended the *mifgash* to challenge the preconceptions many of the students had about the situation on the ground before they came to Israel.

Ahmed, one of the more vocal of the speakers on the Arab side, made the most poignant statement so far, saying: "Given the racism the Jews have faced throughout their history, they have a duty to learn from that and not discriminate against non-Jews here now that they're in charge of the country." In response, however, some of the students asked whether it wouldn't be better for the Arabs to escape the discrimination and move elsewhere.

"Why should we?" retorted Hani, as the atmosphere in the room grew palpably tense. "It's our land – it's where our fathers, grandfathers and great-grandfathers came from; someone else took over and now you ask why *we* don't leave?" His words provoked a flurry of responses which – whilst no one left fully satisfied with the other sides' replies – at least opened the eyes of both groups to how the other side felt about the situation, on both an intellectual and emotional level.

In the main, the experience was a positive one for all involved, with the discussions continuing long after the meeting broke up, phone numbers being exchanged, and positive noises made by the Jewish students on the bus journey back to Jerusalem. As the man chairing the session told them, "since you're all your movement's youth leaders of tomorrow, it's your duty to deal with the complications that come from Jews being given a homeland here."

Despite the uneasiness caused by hearing what life under Israeli rule was like for those physically on the inside but in all other regards out in the cold, the issues raised in the space of one morning shone more light on the conflict than any amount of sanitised museum visits and trips to the Dead Sea could have done. At the same time, showing their faces in a village all but bereft of interested Jewish visitors showed the local youth that their plight was by no means overlooked or ignored by groups such as this. And since these children would more than likely make *aliyah* themselves in the future, it was essential that they got to see the country warts and all, rather than be conned into believing it's all milk and honey in the Holy Land.

***

Though my detractors often claimed otherwise, I saw myself as anything but a "self-hating Jew", and the more vocal I was in my criticism of the Israeli government's crimes, the more credence I gave that claim. I passionately loved my religion, and just as fervently defend its teachings in terms of how to treat our fellow human beings. That Zionism had come along, hijacked Jewish doctrines, and twisted them to form part of an all-out supremacist movement was not something I could swallow if I want to stay loyal to the true values of Judaism.

Unfortunately, by demanding that the world saw Zionism as a philosophy essentially based on Jewish principles, Zionists had managed to unforgivably drag the religion's name through the mud for over sixty years. However, I drew some comfort from an unlikely source, after talking to a boy my age in the Deheisha refugee camp in Bethlehem.

I was there as part of a marathon tour that took in Hebron, the village of Al-Nueman, the Machpela Mosque, the Church of the Nativity and various other stops along the way, including the pitiful, crumbling buildings of Deheisha. Halfway through the trip, my eyes began to glaze over, as I sought to put a barrier between myself and the relentless barrage of proof we were shown of how cruelly the authorities deal with the Palestinians.

Sneering soldiers manning checkpoints, freshly-demolished family homes, welded-shut shop fronts, bloodthirsty settler graffiti crudely daubed on Palestinian houses... the list was endless, the evidence was overwhelming. Whilst it was clearly an invaluable experience for those on the tour who'd never faced the occupation up close and personal, I'd seen it all before – not that it got any easier to take, however many times I was exposed to the reality.

But that was before I met Jihad, a young man charged with showing us round the garbage-strewn streets and decrepit homes of Deheisha. The first thing I noticed about him was his eyes, which were as dead as any I'd seen in all my four years living here. As he sat on a chair facing our ten-man semicircle, his face was devoid of emotion, and he

244

simply went through the motions as he reeled out his clearly well-polished introduction to life in the camp.

I could hardly begrudge him his lack of enthusiasm; we were probably the hundredth group he'd spoken to about his community's plight, and what difference had all this made to their situation? He and his people were still here, still caged in their concrete prison, still at the mercy of the Israelis, and still no nearer to achieving their dreams of independence and freedom.

"I just want to be like you," he said tiredly as he gazed into the middle distance. "I've got two arms, two hands... why am I any different from other people?" he went on, and – of course – the answer was staring us in the face from the gun turrets of the guard towers overlooking the camp.

As we wended our way up the narrow alleys where skinny children clad in ill-fitting clothes played amongst the refuse, I asked Jihad to elaborate on how he could be "like us". His answer was simple, and – he said – representative of the views of the majority of Palestine's millions of refugees. "We want to go home," he said flatly. "There is no other way [that will suffice]. A two state solution will not bring peace – the fight will go on". He told me that although he'd chosen to use pen rather than sword to get his message across, he had no truck with those who chose to join the armed resistance.

He was vicious in his condemnation of the Israeli government, castigating tit for the decades spent keeping his people down and subjugating them with brute force and bloodshed – however, he was adamant that he did not view their actions as emanating from Jewish sources. "Zionism is far, far removed from the Jewish religion," he assured me. "I have no issue with Jews – just as I have no problem with Christians or Buddhists. I don't mind Jews living here, just so long as they do it peacefully."

He echoed the words of another local I'd met earlier, who'd asked why Zionists had felt the only way to emigrate to the region was via conquest and control, rather than "the way my brother moved to the United States. He went there not to kill, not to occupy, but just to live there in peace and be a citizen like anyone else." Both his and Jihad's ability to clearly distinguish between Zionism and Judaism has to be capitalised on by those with an interest in bringing this sixty-year-old conflict to an end.

The window of opportunity won't stay open forever. Islamic radicals and fundamentalists are highly adept at conflating the Zionist philosophy with the Jewish faith, and Israel's hiding behind a façade of acting on behalf of World Jewry only plays into their hands. Which is why it is essential that those Jews who recoil at the criminal actions of the Israeli government make it quite clear that this is not being done in their names.

The dominant form of Zionism might have been a racist, supremacist ideology, but Judaism was most definitely not. The more Jews who made this distinction, the better: both for the security of their fellow Jews, as well as to prove to the Israeli authorities that they most definitely do not have carte blanche to crush the Palestinians forevermore under the guise of religious values.

In many ways, my secondary school experience had been the perfect precursor to living in Israel and understanding the paranoia that envelops the country's citizens like a dense fog. Seven years at JFS, a Jewish school in the heart of Kentish Town, gave me first hand experience of what happens when you fence in a group of people behind a wall and convince them that everyone on the other side is out to get them, and that they will go on the attack the minute they are given the opportunity.

Admittedly, I believed the hype as much as the next blue blazer-clad boy or girl. The dark forces of Holloway Boys, Richard of Chichester, and all the other schools that surrounded us in every direction were, in my eyes, as frightening a prospect as the Syrians, Iranians et al were to today's terrified Israeli public. The walk from the school gates to Kentish Town station every afternoon was approached with trepidation by us all, fevered

246

imaginations running wild as to where and when the next assault would come.

On one famous occasion, two infiltrators scaled the fence between the school and the skateboard park and jumped down into the playground. Five hundred startled JFS pupils stampeded for the sanctuary of the dining hall. No one stopped to weigh up the odds; it could have been two hundred and fifty on one, had a fight broken out. Instead, the pre-instilled terror proved too weighty for logic to even get a look-in.

Of course, the tales of hate and harassment weren't entirely apocryphal; there were plenty of occasions when JFS pupils bore the brunt of the violent tendencies of the local thugs and carried the scars into school the next day. However, as saner elements pointed out, there was every reason to believe that the internecine fighting was born of plain, inter-school rivalry, rather than some deep-rooted anti-Semitic streak common to every uncircumcised male within a five mile radius.

The net result of all of the tension and paranoia was that, bit by bit, our school was transformed into a fortress, replete with twenty-foot high metal fences, CCTV cameras, and a full-time security team headed up by a thuggish skinhead who was as close to a modern day Golem as it got. Our lot was to be shepherded to and from the tube station by our protectors, who spent the rest of their time patrolling the school's borders with a zeal all too familiar to anyone who has spent time in the Holy Land.

The grown-up version of JFS which I now inhabit was just that – secondary school all over again. Same fear, same heavily fortified perimeter, same collective mentality: afraid that all who inhabited the surrounding area were after our blood. However, in the case of Israel, the crucial distinction was that our 'school' was built on the ruins of a former school, whose dispossessed pupils had every reason to avenge their loss. But that point is completely ignored by those running the show, who preferred

247

to peddle the canard that the reason for their resentment and rage was the old anti-Semitic gene that can be found in every soul outside the flock.

One of CIF's I/P heavyweight commentators often made the point that had it been Catholics rather than Jews who established a state in Israel in 1948, the Palestinians would have responded just as viciously to the injustice which they were dealt. Anyone with an ounce of sense would reach the same conclusion, provided they are not under the spell that there is an inherent lust for Jewish blood in every Arab. As I argued in a comment to another reader, belief in such a preposterous theory was as stereotyping and racist as a belief that all Jews were leeches and cosmopolitan anarchists.

Of course there were extremists amongst the Palestinians who wanted to maim and kill Israeli civilians for no reason other than they are Israeli civilians. Those true terrorists had to not be given the freedom to operate. However, perpetually occupying an entire people and keeping them in prison and in penury played into the hands of radical elements. Collective punishment bred collective rage, and Israel has to recognise this before there was any chance of a cessation of violence.

But beyond the extremists there exists a majority of Palestinians who couldn't give a damn about the ethnicity of those oppressing them; they just cared about the oppression itself. If Israel unlocks its vice-like grip they would breathe again, and with each breath more oxygen would rush to their heads and they'd be able to think straight once more. Then the Israelis would realise that the Palestinians are no more or less human than the Israelis themselves, and the sixty-year fear would begin to recede.

Just as it did for we JFS pupils once we reached the sixth form and were allowed out into the bandit country of Kentish Town during our free periods. Unchecked, we wandered the streets amongst our supposedly mortal enemies, wondering how we'd been worked into such a state of suspicion for so long, when the truth was far removed from the urban legends that swirled around our penned-in playground.

Even though I look forward a time when Israelis and Palestinians could reside together in peace, it was foolish to suggest the conditions were sufficiently clement for this to occur today. Clearly, the rogue elements who do wish genuine harm on the country's inhabitants have to be neutralised before any kind of integration can begin in earnest. But that doesn't mean neutralisation by force, since that route only generated more fundamentalists.

Instead, the Israelis have to begin by rebuilding the Palestinians' lives step by step – economically, socially, emotionally – and demonstrating a clear wish for rapprochement. The Israeli public has to be treated like sixth-formers and allowed back into the West Bank (as they had been in pre-Intifada days), to see for themselves that not all Palestinians were masked gunmen with only murder on their minds. Once that happens, the hysteria will dissipate as it did for we JFS kids. Only then would it truly be possible to move forward to a future of harmonious coexistence.

Chapter Ten

One group committed to laying the groundwork for such a climate of mutual trust was Centre for Creativity in Education and Cultural Heritage (CCECH), which I'd first written about a year earlier. I spent another day in their company, witnessing the work they carried out in the interests of bringing peace a little bit closer.

"These are simple things – it's not about building a home together; it's just learning to see the person behind the nationality," said Sagi, one of CCECH's staff, as she explained why bringing Israeli and Palestinian school-children together was essential to forging a better relationship between the two communities.

The pre-teen children visited their counterparts at their schools for organised activities, which include trips to each other's places of worship and learning the culture and traditions of their contemporaries. I joined them on their latest meeting in the village of Ein Rafah, where they went on a tour of the local mosque, guided by the community's imam. I'd been there a week earlier, in the company of a group of Zionist gap-year students, but whilst that had been a one-off visit, this session was part of a far longer, far deeper relationship being fostered between Jewish and Arab youth.

This was the sixth time that the children had met one another, and it was clear that they were more than at ease with one another, mingling freely and chatting away happily to their peers. For their last meeting, the group visited a synagogue in West Jerusalem to learn about Jewish prayer and ritual, and this time round it was the turn of the Muslim students to show their own traditions and beliefs.

They had been asked to bring examples of traditional Muslim dress to show to their Jewish friends, as well as any objects with a religious connection that their families kept at home. Several of the children stood proudly at the front of the mosque displaying finely-embroidered carpets that relatives had bought for them during their Haj pilgrimages to Mecca. The Jewish students were keen to question their Muslim counterparts on various aspects of their religion, and listened attentively to the imam as he gave them a detailed overview of Islam and its core values.

The imam finished the presentation by asking several of the Muslim boys to join him in prayer, and they bowed and supplicated in the nave of the mosque, giving the Jewish children the chance to see first-hand how a Muslim service compared with their own form of worship. Once copies of the Koran had been handed round and perused by the children, they decamped to the Ein Naquba Community Centre up the road for a more light-hearted session of traditional childhood games.

The students were encouraged to suggest games that they'd played when growing up, which was a key part of the CCECH ideology. "[This way] we're bringing the two worlds together," explained Sagi. "The children get to see a new culture, whilst also getting in touch with their own, and dealing with their own roots." The boys gathered in one room of the centre, whilst the girls formed a circle in the other and enthusiastically played boisterous games for close to an hour. Laughter filled the air, and if there had been any trepidation at the beginning of the day, it had totally dissipated by this point.

Dr. Simon Lichman, who headed CCECH, expressed admiration for the teachers involved in bringing their students together in this way. "They are standing up against a trend, which is very brave," he said. "The principals of these schools realise that it is important to build relationships between Israeli Jews and Palestinians, and an understanding of each other as well."

Sherihan, a girl from Ein Rafa who graduated the programme almost ten years earlier and now worked with the CCECH team, said that the scheme had given her the opportunity "to see [the Jewish community] for myself, rather than just get the media perspective". Her words were echoed by several of the Jewish children, one of whom declared "how close Islam is to Judaism in so many respects", a lesson central to both sets of students' understanding of their contemporaries.

Although there was often public opposition to collaborative projects between Israeli and Palestinian children, most of the parents CCECH came across had no problem with their children participating, according to Lichman. "Occasionally we'll find a student who doesn't want to take part, so we don't force them to come", he said, "But usually it's because they're scared – and once they see their friends come back [and tell them how much they enjoyed the experience], then more often than not they join in the next time." Visits to their respective schools in Bayit Ve'gan and Bet Hanina also helped demystify the neighbourhoods for children who might have otherwise never set foot in such places, and thus played an important part in their education about their city.

Bringing the children into one another's realities involved more than simply sitting in a classroom and talking to each other, which is why CCECH put such an emphasis on hands-on activities which involved sharing cultural experiences. "That's why it works," said Sagi – "it's less talking, and more doing". They were due to meet once more before they headed their separate ways to high school, and though their paths may not have crossed again in such a carefree setting, their shared experiences would bind them that bit closer than had they never been allowed a window into each other's worlds.

Watching the children at play was a massively instructive experience for anyone who had any doubt that people from the two sides can put aside their differences and seek common ground between them. The children might not have had the reins of power in their hands, but they were the potential voters, soldiers and militants of tomor-

252

row, and childhood memories like these could be critical when it came to choosing which path to take in the future.

***

Supporters of the Israeli authorities love to blame the country's poor reputation as being a result of woeful PR, believing that all that was required to redress the balance was a slick *hasbara* campaign. However, given the reality of the occupation, to suggest that a superficial gloss job would do the trick is fantasy.

I found as much when I went to Hebron as a guest of the Christian Peacemaker Team (CPT), who were desperate to highlight the plight of a Palestinian orphanage threatened with closure by the IDF. For nearly a month, the scores of children had been living with the threat of closure after the army issued an eviction order, claiming that the Islamic Charitable Society (ICS) – which runs the orphanage – was a front organisation for Hamas.

According to an army spokesman, ICS "masquerades as a charity organisation in order to cover its activities of increasing support of the Hamas terror network", and as such any property connected to the charity had to be seized in order to maintain the "general order... and security of the area". To that end, the IDF ordered several facilities on the site to be evacuated, setting the 28th of April as the final deadline before they began the closure.

Despite a legal challenge being brought to the Israeli high court, "our chances of stopping the eviction are nil," said Rasheed Rasheed, who taught English at the ICS boys' orphanage up the road. Since the case was terror-related, in the eyes of the IDF, the army lawyers weren't required to let the defence see their classified 'evidence', so there was no way for the ICS legal team to defend themselves against the charges.

He noted that this was the first time an entire organisation had been targeted in such a way by the IDF: "It's a new trend – they used to arrest individuals; now they're taking on the institutions themselves", he said, surmising that "maybe it's their way of trying to break the bones of Hamas".

As we toured the orphanage, we were mobbed by dozens of bright-eyed students, all eager to greet their visitors and beaming as they ran excitedly round the playground. They were all local children, who either lost their parents or, due to financial crises, couldn't live at home, and the ICS had stepped into the breach to rebuild their lives and offer them a better future by way of education and employment.

To support the orphanage's work in the community, the ICS ran several small businesses to raise funds, such as a bakery, sewing workshop and a warehouse where donated goods from foreign donors were stored. I was taken to see the results of the army's heavy-handed treatment of these facilities, and the results weren't pretty.

The bakery looked as though it had been on the receiving end of a D9 bulldozer: huge chunks missing from the masonry, debris everywhere, and the *coup de grace* being the torched skeleton of the industrial-sized oven, which the soldiers poured petrol over and set alight in order to destroy the bakery's ability to function. Similar treatment was meted out to the nearby warehouse, where around $300,000 worth of donations were commandeered and confiscated by the army, who smashed up the storeroom's interior and left it ruined.

Next up was the sewing workshop, which was still in operation when I visited it, with several local women hunched over their machines turning out intricately-embroidered dresses. The army had warned that the workshop was due to suffer the same fate as the bakery and warehouse, and had ordered that every piece of equipment and fabric be left in its place so that it can be sequestered by their troops when they decided to pounce. (Two days after our visit, the army came in the night and came good on their threat, confiscating everything within the workshop's four walls, despite the staff's pleas).

Ghassan Mohammed, one of the orphanage's supervisors, told me in desperate tones that "the organisation [ICS] has no connection whatsoever with Hamas", and that the army clearly knew that, "otherwise they'd have brought the world's media to see the evidence they'd uncovered". As far as Mary Anne, one of the CPT team, was concerned, the IDF's motivation was simply "sociocide – they want to chip way at the Palestinian infrastructure in order to take over the whole area".

She said that any time the Palestinians found a way to stand on their own two feet – such as supporting the weaker elements of their society, educating their children and building up their economy – the Israeli authorities sought to find a way to crush their efforts. "This area is meant to be under Palestinian control according to the Oslo Accords," she said, "but the Israelis are still here; still asserting their authority."

Rasheed agreed: "Most of us have got over what happened in 1948," he remarked, "and we are ready for a state based on the '67 borders. The question is, do the Israelis even want to give us that? I don't think so." Just as he was resigned to justice not being done by the Israeli courts, similarly he had little hope in the Israeli government standing by their promises to give the Palestinians independence.

And his scepticism was now being recreated amongst the next generation, namely the orphans whose lives were being turned upside down by the army's actions. "Our kids are terrified when the soldiers come," said Rasheed, "and all they ask is 'why?'" One thirteen year old student in the nearby boys' orphanage told us "This is my home – if they come to shut us down, I won't leave." His predicament, as well as his youthful defiance, should have served as a warning to the Israeli authorities as to what really causes animosity towards Israel from the Palestinian population.

255

As I was sitting down to write an article a few weeks later, I was forced back on my feet as the siren for *Yom Hazikaron* pierced the Jerusalem night in memory of Israel's fallen soldiers. Regardless of where one stood on the political spectrum, the memory of those who were lost in battle was sacrosanct, and paying tribute to the dead united all Israelis in their grief.

Earlier in the day, I had been in Ramle to pay my respects to another IDF soldier, though in a somewhat happier framework. Alex Stein, CIF regular and one of my closest friends, had just finished his twelve month spell in the Home Front division of the army, and we celebrated his demobbing in a restaurant near his base in Ramle.

If a week was a long time in politics, a year was an eternity for anyone serving in the IDF, as Alex's experience proved. In the days before he joined up, he wrote a piece explaining his decision to serve, and spent the best part of a thousand words seeking to justify himself to his readers. Now, however, he felt "no need to justify myself whatsoever. Israel needs an army, plain and simple, which is why [it was incumbent on me] to serve".

The by-line of his article a year earlier summed up perfectly the main reason for his unforced enlisting: "I am joining the IDF because I want to make a difference instead of screaming from the sidelines". I agreed with his sentiment, and – regardless of my reservations about certain parts of my own time in uniform – was absolutely convinced that I was far better equipped to face my critics precisely because I served.

Unfortunately, in order to be taken seriously in Israel, right- and left-wingers alike have to jump through certain hoops to prove they not only know what they were talking about, but also that they were prepared to do their bit for the society in which they lived. But that didn't mean having to don jackboots and maraud across the West Bank making the Palestinians' lives a misery: "it can mean any type of national service", according to

256

Alex. "Every citizen – Jew, Arab, gay, straight – should do some form of service for the country. Nation-building is as important as defending the borders".

Alex was spared the dilemma of whether to serve in the Occupied Territories by virtue of his being posted in a *jobnik* (non-combat) division, although he partly wished he'd ended up as a *kravi* (combat) soldier, if only to have helped counter the prevailing atmosphere in fighting units. "I see the type of immigrant soldiers who do *kravi*, and they're often raving right-wingers," he said. "There is also a real problem that combat officers increasingly come from settlement backgrounds," a trend that had alarmed many political commentators of late.

The rite of passage that was service in the IDF was something that Alex refused to forego in order to placate those who demand an internal boycott of the Israeli military machine. "There was a time I used to call myself primarily a Jew; then I called myself a Zionist – and now, having served, I am an Israeli," he said proudly, as he looked over to the next table where a group of rookie soldiers ate lunch decked out in their olive green fatigues.

However, he expressed remorse that the army still played such a leading role on the Israeli stage. "Israel *has* to emancipate itself from the army and become less militaristic. I describe the [status quo] as the poet that produces his best work on the heroin that kills him", he said. He stated that he hoped the country would "take all the positive things that the army has done and channel them into civilian life."

We discussed where such adulation for the IDF left him politically. "Even *you* are proud that you served," he declared, pointing his finger at me like Lord Kitchener, "despite your political transition." He was both right and wrong; whilst I still believed I had done the right thing in terms of proving my commitment to my adopted country, I was not comfortable at all with having served across the Green Line. Like Alex, I agreed that Israel needed an army, given the eternal conflict in which it was caught

257

up, but I did not accept that breaking international law was somehow permissible just because it was the Israeli army doing it.

As for Alex, he had lost none of his drive to change Israel for the better, nor any of his belief that Zionism and the pursuit of social justice are compatible. Twelve months in uniform had taught him that he was right to believe that his acceptance into Israeli society depended on his agreeing to serve – sad as that truth may be – and trying to effect change from the inside was a far easier task than the option of "screaming from the sidelines".

However, despite his desire to get stuck into civilian life again in Israel, first he was following the example of thousands of demobbed IDF troops and heading to India for the summer. "I need to detox," he said, citing the experience of spending an entire year as a cog in the army system as reason enough to take time off to devote to his own pursuits.

Just as each soldier who fell in battle deserved the honour of being mourned as an individual, and not just part of a war machine, similarly those – like Alex – who came to the end of their service deserve being judged on their own merits rather than those of the IDF as a whole. I trusted Alex's motives, just as I trusted my own when I signed up, and to deny him that right simply because he did what his country expected of him was not an acceptable way to treat his decision.

As well as heralding the end of Alex's military service, May also marked the 20th anniversary of the founding of Noam, a British Zionist youth movement of which Alex and I were members from its inception. Under the umbrella of the Assembly of Masorti Synagogues, Noam had flourished over the years to become one of the largest Jewish youth organisations, and had taken a markedly different path from the more traditional Zionist youth movements.

Whilst promoting Zionism was high on its agenda, it also put much emphasis on the concept of *tikun olam* (literally, "repairing the world"), which had led to some extraordinary offshoot projects undertaken by its alumni. One such scheme was the Tibetan Jewish Youth Exchange (TJYE), set up to forge links between Jewish and Tibetan youth groups and to provide support to each other in their respective endeavours.

Since 2000, there had been a steady stream of Noam volunteers heading off to the Indian town of Dharamsala, to work with the exiled Tibetan youths and help empower them in their struggle to achieve independence for their people. Noam graduates were also instrumental in founding an Aids educations programme for street children in Nairobi, applying the values inculcated in them by their Noam leaders back home to a situation that cried out for experienced youth workers.

Over the previous few years, there had been a mass influx of ex-Noam members to Israel, myself included, which was testament to the power of the Zionist message we were taught during our formative years in the movement. However, rather than ignore our responsibilities to fulfilling *tikun olam*, we felt a collective responsibility to continue promoting the core Noam principles with which we grew up.

One recent immigrant, Naomi Magnus, had been working with the Darfuri refugees living in Tel Aviv, whom I had written about earlier in the year. Less than two months since I met them, their economic and social situation had deteriorated markedly, and many were now struggling even to pay the rent for the meagre shelters in which they lived. Naomi, along with three other Noam *olim*, decided to take action on their behalf and organise a fundraising event which would draw on all the resources to which the Noam network had access.

To that end, they established an NGO, Israel Activists, which would undertake to assist worthy causes across the country, such as the Darfuri refugees. Their inaugural event was a two-day hike in the north of Israel at the end of May. Dozens of participants had already signed up, each committed to raising a minimum of $200, which would provide a massive boost for the refugees and their families, and which would go a long way to preventing eviction from their homes.

At the same time, Israel Activists hoped to use the hike as the launching pad for a far wider series of activities, including three-month activism programmes for British students spending their gap year in Israel. Whilst most year-course participants were only exposed to a saccharine, Jewish-focused side of Israel and its society, there was a need to open the students eyes to the darker side of life in the Holy Land, according to Nic, one of the founders of Israel Activists.

"We want to work with any sector of Israeli society that is in need, be they Jewish, Arab, Druze, Bedouin or anyone else. It is imperative to provide the students with the necessary skills, motivation and experiences to help them continue their activism after their year in Israel – whether back home at British universities, here in Israel if they make *aliyah*, or anywhere else around the world. We believe in bringing contemporary Israeli societal issues to the awareness of young people, in order to create activists who are eager to effect change. Our mission is therefore twofold; firstly to raise awareness, and secondly to provide opportunities to make an impact."

Momentum was building behind the scheme, mirroring a sea change which had come over British Jewish philanthropy in recent years regarding the projects in Israel they viewed as most worthy of their support. The Pears Foundation – a prominent charitable organisation established by the Pears brothers, three British-Jewish property tycoons – had poured large amounts of money into causes assisting Israeli-Arab communities and fostering Jewish-Arab relations.

Similarly, the first Magen David Adom-funded medical station in an Arab village opened in 2007, with the bulk of the donations coming from a group of Jewish philanthropists from England. *Tikun olam* was increasingly

260

being recognised by donors as not only a practical way to apply the values of Judaism in general, but more specifically a means of demonstrating to the non-Jewish citizens of Israel that they were supported in their struggles by Jews and Zionists alike, regardless of what they, the recipients, might otherwise have believed.

So it was with Israel Activists which, by taking on the cause of the Muslim refugees from Darfur, was following one of the central tenets of Judaism: "Love thy neighbour as thyself". All who were taking part in the hike, as well as all who supported it financially from the Jewish community back home, were helping to redress the image of Zionists as caring merely about themselves and their own people's situation.

Once the activism programmes began in earnest over the following year, the potential for building bridges and establishing links between groups of young Jewish and Arab students would increase exponentially. The larger the group got, and the more financial support it received from the Jewish community in Britain, the more efforts could be devoted to breaking down the walls of silence that exist between the various sectors of society in Israel. When that happened, it would prove that Noam's joint principles of Zionism and *tikun olam* were by no means mutually exclusive, and that its members were applying those principles in a way which could only enhance the prospects of peace in the region.

***

An attempt in May at deflecting criticism away from the actions of the Israeli authorities came in the form of a broadside launched at UNRWA[23] by a group of US congressmen. According to the "bi-partisan, pro-Israel" congressional Israel Allies Caucus, it was the UN agency responsible for providing pastoral care to the Palestinian refugees which was the real culprit responsible for "perpetuat[ing] political hatred against Israel".

261

Eliot Engel, who chaired the Caucus, declared that UNRWA was at fault because "instead of resettling them, they keep them in refugee camps". He was backed up by Israeli MK Benny Elon, who proclaimed that "without the rehabilitation of the Palestinian refugees, no peace will come". Both men could have been mistaken for people who actually cared about the plight of the refugees, based on their apparent concern for the limbo and squalor in which the Palestinians were forced to dwell. However – unsurprisingly – that wasn't the case at all.

At least, their concern for the refugees came a distant second to their blind belief that Israel had to remain an exclusively Jewish state from now until eternity, regardless of how many people were displaced and dispersed as a result. To them, the refugees were just unavoidable collateral damage; their trauma a necessary evil that had to occur in order for the Zionist dream to be realised in full.

"The Palestinians are in the refugee camps because the Arab nations want them in refugee camps in order to perpetuate political hatred against Israel," Engel complained, apparently comfortable with attacking the symptoms rather than the cause of the refugee "disease". The refugee camps only existed in the first place because the Palestinians were forced into exile when Israel came into being, which was the crux of the matter, whatever Engel and his fellow "Israel Allies" would have had the world believe.

Similarly, Elon's assertion that "it has been a big mistake not to deal with the issue of the Palestinian refugees" was correct; except that in his mind it was the responsibility of everyone other than Israel to "deal" with the refugees. Every statement that he and Engel came out with could, and should, have been turned on its head, so that the true guilty party was forced to pay the price for the crime that was committed against the Palestinians who were forced into exile.

But, of course, to do so would have been to strike a blow against the concept of a Jewish state, and we all knew what that meant. The horror and fear with which certain elements of society treated the idea of an Israel without a Jewish majority overrode any rational thought or sense of justice towards those dealt a hammer blow by the state's creation. According to their way of thinking, allowing the refugees to return to their homeland would spell disaster for the Jews, who would apparently be set upon by the incoming bloodthirsty hordes and murdered in their thousands.

Why this would happen was not immediately obvious; at least, not to anyone who refused to believe that all Palestinians hate all Jews. While there was no doubt that there were murderous and malevolent elements of Palestinian society, the extrapolation to tarring all Palestinians with the same brush was as unconscionable and unacceptable as that used by those who meted out the same treatment to Jews throughout history. The grotesque cartoons of the hook-nosed, obese Jew with his talons clutching the globe in a vice-like grip were evidence of what happens when madness takes over and it becomes standard practice to portray an entire people as one, evil caricature.

But when the tables are turned, and it was the Jews' turn to demonise another demographic group, then the phenomenon became acceptable. Centuries of being kicked when we were down had done more than physical damage; it had cemented the belief in our minds that the only way to prevent it happening again was to dole out an almighty beating to whoever was nearest, in order to show the world how tough we had become.

Nadia Matar, the firebrand leader of Women in Green, told me as much when I met her the previous summer. "No one respects a person who crawls," she thundered. "The only time the world looked up to us was after the six-day war, when we crushed the Arabs decisively. It's a psychological thing. People respect those who respect themselves."

That "it's a psychological thing" was not in doubt, especially in her case, but where the screws were loose

263

was not in the heads of UNRWA officials, nor those of the refugees themselves. The problem lay in the minds of those who had been duped into believing that the only way the Jewish people could feel safe was to ape Harriet Harman's flak-jacket performance[24] on a national scale. They believed that there really were monsters under their beds, and that the only way to keep them from pouncing was to forever sleep with the lights on.

But the facts just didn't add up. If all Arabs really hated all Jews, then why was the same level of murderous intent – as witnessed by Islamic Jihad in Gaza – not playing itself out across the world? Why was it that the supposedly safest place to be a Jew had turned out to be the most dangerous? And why were the lessons of our own history not being learned, just because the tables had now turned and we were in the position of power?

There was no excuse for the wanton murder of Israeli civilians, yet to pretend that the reasons behind the attacks were anti-Semitic in essence, rather than anti-occupation and anti-colonialism, was a wilful distortion of reality. You create what you fear; Richard Barnbrook's "Blame the immigrants" article in the *Daily Telegraph* that week was a perfect example of such a fabrication. If our leaders wanted us to believe that we were hated for being Jewish, rather than for what had been perpetrated in the name of the Jewish people, then of course the facts could be tailored to suit their way of thinking.

In England, if a government minister had advocated the mass expulsion of all Muslims on the back of the 7/7 bombings, he'd have been drummed out of parliament, and rightly so. But that was because England was the quintessential "one-state", and its citizens had come to terms with differentiating between extremist elements of certain communities and the rest of their co-religionists or co-nationals. In Israel, however, such a way of thinking was anathema to the perpetuation of the myth that it's "us or them".

So when Engel and Elon talked about resolving the refugee issue, they really meant they wanted the world to hold its hands up in defeat and accept the unacceptable; namely, that it was entirely fair and just to expel a population in the interests of another. Instead of demanding everyone else clean up after us, it was we who had to face up to our responsibilities to the refugees and rehabilitate them ourselves.

Instead, not only were the Israeli authorities making no such overtures towards the beleaguered refugees; they were further compounding the agony by encroaching onto more and more Palestinian land and crushing everything in their wake. A village not far from Bil'in was the latest victim of this cruel, expansionist policy, and the locals had taken to violent protests to try to prevent the inevitable loss of land and livelihood. I visited the town at the start of June 2007, and the experience left an indelible impression that was both thoroughly depressing and all too familiar.

Scrambling up the rock-strewn hillside in the baking midday sun, we stumbled across two middle aged men taking shade under an olive tree. As they bade my guide "Salaam Aleikum", their eyes scanned my face for a hint of recognition. Finding none, one of the men ventured a tentative greeting in English and, when I responded in kind, proffered two items in my direction.

One was a surgeon's mask; the other a strip of alcohol saturated prep-pads: "You'll need them for where you're going," he assured me. As we edged closer to our destination, it was clear we had been well advised. Plumes of tear gas criss-crossed the air, trailing the canisters fired by the border police towards the scores of demonstrators. The pungent, acrid fumes filled our nostrils and mouths, while our ears resonated to the sporadic bursts of rubber bullets being shot in our direction.

From our vantage point atop the hill, we had a perfect view of the operating table that lay beneath us, and our surgical accessories added to the sense of theatre that we were witnessing. As we looked on, we watched the obligatory rocks flung at the troops from youths wielding slingshots; the equally standard opening of fire by the police in response and the familiar sight of wounded protesters being rushed by stretcher to waiting ambulances.

There was nothing we onlookers and reporters could do but record the events in our notebooks and cameras; our roles no different to that of medical staff witnessing the slow deaths of terminally ill patients. In this case, the patients were the villagers of Nilin, and the disease they were vainly fighting was the ever-spreading cancer of Israeli settlements across their ancestral land.

In 1948, the first symptoms of Nilin's impending malaise took the form of an expropriation of forty thousand dunams of land by the newly formed Israeli army. Whilst crushed by the weight this blow dealt to their livelihoods, the townspeople believed the tumour had gone into remission, only for a second attack to strike during the Six Day War, when several thousand more dunams were invaded.

Since then, they had realised that the malignant growth was spreading further: yet more of their land had been sequestered by the Israeli authorities and the detested security wall erected in the midst of their olive groves.

Attempts to halt the cancer's progress had failed; the Israeli government appearing resistant to any of the balm which the villagers had sought to apply, whether in the form of legal action, international pressure, or the intervention of local peace activists. Faced with what could well prove a fatal blow to the entire town, the residents had been forced to take drastic measures. Now, on an almost daily basis, dozens of youths take to the hills to impede the wall's construction; their medieval arsenal of sticks and stones no match for the heavily-armed troops who surround them on every side.

Talking to the locals was akin to visiting the terminally ill in a hospice; all one could do was offer words of comfort and try to placate them as the decline continued. "In the end, they will win – and we know it," said Khaled Mesleh, a fifty-eight year old grandfather whose family had lived in Nilin for over eight hundred years. "We might succeed in holding up the building of the wall for a matter of days or weeks, but ultimately they will achieve their aims."

Those aims, according to Mesleh, were to crush the villagers into submission once and for all. "The Israelis take our land, refuse us permission to expand the village, prevent us being able to work inside Israel... so that eventually we will simply say 'we've had enough' and leave. There are six thousand residents of Nilin, and none of them are happy; it's impossible to be happy in such conditions."

As the border police continued to pick off protesters with rubber bullets and live ammunition, we returned to his modest house to continue our discussion out of the line of fire. Children and grandchildren swarmed round the living room and kitchen; "They all live with me," said Mesleh. "Where else can they go?" With the town's borders continually narrowing, those of his offspring who had married and had children of their own were forced to continue living in the familial home, or else to leave the village for good.

In the meantime, Hindi, one of his sons, had taken it upon himself to help organise the protests against the wall's erection. Breathless and bathed in sweat, he returned to the house enraged by what he'd seen; a freelance photographer and cameraman by trade, he had plenty of evidence of the scale of the injustices being dealt to his fellow villagers. He showed us footage of border policemen letting off rapid-fire bursts of rubber bullets in random directions, as well as clips of the wounded being rushed away from the scene by panicked medics.

Hindi was just as resigned to the reality as his father: "At least by protesting we can try to prevent them taking even more of our land, but we [are in no doubt] that the wall will still be built." All that the locals could do was

267

keep placing themselves in the firing line, in the hope that their actions would do more good in the long run than the harm caused by the tear gas and rubber-coated missiles fired into their bodies.

In Nilin specifically, as well as in the West Bank as a whole, one thing was certain: the drugs didn't work. The idea of international intervention was laughed at sorrowfully, by Khaled and his peers; similarly the aid of the Israeli courts: "An Israeli judge banned them from continuing to build the wall here," said Khaled, "But they [the army] couldn't care less. They're still here – and if the courts can't stop them, who can?"

The answer – as he, his son, and the rest of the villagers know all too well – was that no one could. The eyes of the world looked on either benevolently (in the case of Israel's backers in the US and elsewhere); or impotently, too cowed to act, too diplomatic to intervene. Time was not on the Palestinians' side. Just as Nilin appeared in its death throes that day, so too would another village the next, then another, then another. As the life of the Palestinian nation ebbed away, the best treatment on offer was merely palliative.

***

Back in Jerusalem, life was no easier for the Palestinians living in the so-called 'reunified' city – especially on the day of *Yom Yerushalayim*, the annual celebration of the Israeli conquest of the eastern half of the capital. Slumped on a cheap plastic chair in the protest tent that had become his second home, Jawad's eyes blazed momentarily as he vented his rage. "Just because we're Palestinian, does that mean we have to believe their lies?" he spat, when asked how he felt about the claim that Jerusalem was now a united city.

"Everything's become worse [since the occupation]," he continued. "We pay almost fifty percent of the municipality's budget, and get less than two percent of the services

268

in return. Our families are scared to visit us in Silwan ever since the settlers set up home here; the settlers have stolen all of our trade by encouraging the tourists to only buy from them; they're trying to turn the whole of our village Jewish – and there's every likelihood that they'll succeed."

Jawad, a veteran activist who had been taking on the settlers in his home town for years, was in no mood to join in the celebrations of the Jewish population of Jerusalem. Yards from where he was sitting, hundreds of jubilant partygoers had swarmed in to the grounds of Ir David [the City of David], where a free concert was in full flow to mark the 41st anniversary of Jerusalem's unification.

"I call it 'Occupation Day,'" muttered Jawad bitterly. "I am very pessimistic about the future; I don't see a peaceful solution whilst the settlers have all the power". Those same settlers were making their presence fully felt with the sound and light show they had put on in the middle of the predominantly-Arab district of Silwan. Sponsored by right-wing millionaire Irving Moskowitz, the event had attracted an enormous audience, including Women in Green head Nadia Matar.

"What does unification mean to me? [Ultimately], from the Nile to the Euphrates," she declared, when asked by my friend. Her sentiments were shared by almost everyone we met inside the venue, many of whom were unconcerned with the side-effects of their fervent nationalism.

"I don't feel guilty at all about capturing their territory," said a wiry man sprawled on the grass listening intently to the music blaring out from the sound system. "If they don't like it, they can leave."

"Life's tough," shrugged Rabbi Pesach Lerner, an associate of Moskowitz who had flown in from New York for the show. "They kicked us out of here first, so now we're taking back what's ours," he boomed, warming to his theme and brushing away any dissenting opinion espoused by my friends and me.

269

We then fell into conversation with a young religious man who had been tasked with interviewing members of the audience for a promotional film commissioned by the organisers. He quickly realised his mistake in seeking our opinion and, once he turned off his camera, it was our turn to quiz him on his reasons for celebrating the event in such a brazen and provocative fashion in the midst of a Palestinian village.

Pointing at the scores of Arab houses with a front row view of the open air concert, my friend asked him "Is this event a hand reaching out in peace to our fellow residents of Jerusalem?" "I'm not sure," came the man's hesitant reply. "You have to understand, this is an event for Zionism; not an event for world peace..."

That much was clear; as Jawad and his peers sat listlessly in their protest tent over the road, listening to the jubilation and joy with which their neighbours celebrated the conquest of the Arab half of the city, his anger was matched only by his sad air of defeat. The sheer number of celebrants he watched stream in and out of Ir David only served to convince him how futile his struggle was to bring justice to the village of Silwan, as well as to the Palestinian people at large.

"There are the ideological settlers, of course," he said. "But [compounding the problem] is the majority of the Israeli population. Either they are naïve and have no idea what is being carried out in their name, or they simply don't care about the Palestinians' suffering. We try our best to educate the Israeli public about what is going on, but we have less than one percent of the funds that the settler groups have with which to publicise the reality".

The contrast between the unrestrained delight on one side of the street and the despair and resignation on the other was stark: the Jewish joy was the Palestinians' pain. The streets were filled with buoyant, buccaneering gangs of Jewish youths proudly waving outsized Israeli flags as they marched round the Old City, as well as the occasional Palestinian walking past with head bowed,

270

hoping to avoid bearing witness to the carnival of conquest.

If this was the unity that the authorities spoke of when
promoting Yom Yerushalayim, then clearly they were
lacking in either etymological prowess, tact or simple
understanding of the reality of life for the non-Jewish
half of Jerusalem which had been forced to become part
of the 'unified' city.

For Jawad and his peers in Silwan, there was no question that the event was just another chance for the
Zionist nationalists to kick them while they were down;
and, it seemed, those doing the kicking weren't denying it
either. "Life's tough"; "I don't feel guilty..."; "From the
Nile to the Euphrates"; phrases that rang out far louder
than the music emanating from the stage, and sentiments that showed the true colours of those championing
the cause of conquest and capture for another year.

---

[23] United Nations Relief and Works Agency.
[24] Harman famously wore a flak jacket when visiting Peckham,
in her own constituency.

Postscript

This morning, I was invited to speak to a group of senior aid workers who were keen to approach both the Israeli and Diaspora Jewish communities with their latest campaign. They were, understandably, apprehensive about the best way to proceed, given the minefield that exists under the feet of anyone seeking to criticise elements of Israel's policies.

We talked about the most effective way to open people's eyes to the reality of the occupation, in order to bring home the truth of what is being perpetrated in the name of Israel's security. Given the about turn which I'd performed since moving to Israel four years ago, I was asked to describe my most influential experience thus far, in terms of providing a catalyst to the political journey upon which I've embarked.

Without hesitation, I replied that it had been my illicit trip to Bethlehem during a weekend furlough from the army. Our unit was serving in the city at the time, and – until then – I had been conditioned to see the residents as potential terrorists, who had to be dealt with accordingly in order to avert a deadly threat to our safety.

With no M16 by my side, nor grenade in my pack, I passed through the checkpoint and took my first tentative steps on so-called enemy terrain. In jeans and a t-shirt, I walked the same streets of the Aida refugee camp that a day earlier I'd been patrolling armed to the teeth, and with five other soldiers backing me up.

I gazed casually at the same windows and doors at which I'd previously had to stare, hawk-like, in case a gunman or bomber should burst out and attack our squad. I looked calmly at the same gangs of youths who, when in uniform, I'd had to decide in an instant whether were benignly intentioned or baying for my blood.

The fear instilled in me by the army all but dissipated once I was simply a tourist strolling through the town. Conversely, the more weaponry and protective gear I carried, the more terrifying the place became – which, it dawned on me, was a distillation of Israel's core and eternal paradox; one which has dogged it since the moment the state was created.

For there to be a justification for Israel's existence, there first has to exist an existential threat to the Jewish people. Granted, history has handed us that fear of annihilation on a plate, but just because the fear exists, it doesn't necessarily follow that what is feared does too.

A prominent narrative of the Jewish tradition is that, in every generation, a manifestation of Amalek will attempt to wipe out the Jewish people, just as the original marauding Amalekites did during the Jews' exodus from Egypt. The Romans, Babylonians, Greeks, Soviets, and Nazis have all, understandably, been described as modern-day Amalekites – and now Iran is being touted as the most recent member of the millennia-old dynasty.

Fear of extermination is the ace in the Jewish pack of emotions, and has been capitalised on by the nationalism encapsulated in today's Zionism. Occupy an entire people and crush their hopes and dreams for forty years? A necessary evil; if we don't then we're done for. Fly in the face of international law, basic morality, and even the central tenets of our own compassionate, religion? Sorry, but you have to understand that 'they' all want us dead; it's us or them, from now until eternity.

It's almost irrelevant who 'they' are. One day it's the Palestinians for daring to try to shake off the yoke of oppression; the next it's the European left for having the nerve to intercede on behalf of justice and decency. 'They' can be a lone man, such as Norman Finkelstein[25], or 'they' can be a billion people, such as the world's entire

273

Muslim population, conveniently repackaged as one homogenous group based on spurious racial profiling.

Concrete walls are built between 'us' and 'them'; orders are given banning Israelis from crossing the divide into PA territory – all under the banner of protecting the security of Israelis. However they are merely an insidious attempt to hermetically seal ourselves off from the outside world and convince ourselves that it's an unavoidable measure to take.

Those of us who've come, seen, and conquered our preconceptions of the Palestinian street know full well that the canards being propagated are simply preposterous. Of course, there are some very angry, very violent militants amongst the Palestinian people, but so too are there similarly dangerous elements in Israeli society, as well as in every ethnic group around the world.

The reaction amongst my Israeli friends when they hear of my trips to Jenin, Ramallah or Bethlehem is usually one of horror that I had even set foot inside the cities, let alone met the locals and visited them in their homes. "They'd kill you if they knew you were Jewish," they cry, convinced that a Palestinian wolf lies behind every refugee camp door. The truth is far different, of course; almost everyone I meet knows I am both Jewish and Israeli, and – thus far – I've been neither beaten, beheaded nor bludgeoned to death.

It's understandable why the mythology and misconceptions flourish amongst the Israeli man and woman in the street, or in the Diaspora Jewish community. In the vacuum left by enforced separation between Jews and Palestinians, fabrication runs riot, and fiction becomes truth in the minds of the masses. It's also understandable that the government encourages and promotes such fairy tales, in order to garner support for their never-ending policies of irredentism and subjugation.

But by continuing to provoke and bully the Palestinians, we create what we fear. Another generation branded Amalekites: another reason for us to circle the wagons, batten down the hatches, and convince ourselves that it is simply our lot to be eternally hated and reviled. And no amount of well-intentioned pressure can ever be sufficient to penetrate the calcified layer of mistrust between us and the outside world.

***

For all that I have rejected the rose-tinted Zionist vision, which was painted for me by various educators during my youth, I am still passionately in love with the place I now call home. My attachment to the land of Israel, as opposed to the State of Israel, has never been in question; it is my ancestral and religious homeland, and I would forever fight for the right of Jews to dwell here. What has changed, however, is my belief that the country must be governed by the Jewish people run along ethnic lines. To advocate such a regime goes against all the morals and principles inculcated in me by my parents, not to mention my religion's central tenets, by which I strive to live my life. Namely, in the words of Hillel, that "the entire Torah can be distilled into one phrase: 'Love thy neighbour as thyself'; and all the rest is commentary."

I previously described my emergence from my Zionist cocoon as 'Now the blinkers are off...", but such phraseology does not do the transition justice. Rather than merely shedding the blinkers that so impeded my vision, my journey was instead equivalent to having a lengthy course of laser surgery, in which my entire optical system was reprogrammed and tuned into the proper and correct frequency. No more can I fall back on the ethical blind spot which ails so many supporters of Zionism. No more can I pretend that the standards that I wish to be applied to nations and peoples around the world can be suspended when it comes to Israel and the plight of the Palestinian refugees. And no more can I pretend that what is being perpetrated in the name of my people is in any way to our benefit. Israel has become the most dangerous place on the planet to be a Jew; the reputation of world Jewry has, rightly or wrongly, become tarnished by the continuing crimes carried out by the Jewish state. We've reaped what we've sown.

***

It is worth ending on a positive note, one that appeared unlikely when I sat down to write the article, but which dawned on me as I decoded the message in the words of the Israeli girl I had interviewed.

Jerusalem is permanently festooned with thousands of Israeli flags; they hang from lampposts, apartment windows, shop-fronts and any other setting where their nationalistic message can best be delivered to those passing by. It's a case of thinking those that flaunt them do protest too much, as though they are so uncertain in their identity that they drown any doubt under a sea of blue and white cloth.

Drive out into the countryside, and the locals are far more restrained in their patriotism. Not for them the urge to drape their national colours from every available surface; rather they are either self-assured enough to not require such flamboyant gestures or – as with the girl I met on the weekend – their nationality comes a long way down the list of what makes them who they are.

Carmel, who spent many of her formative years ensconced in Kibbutz Merhavia, a Shomer Hatzair bastion of socialist ideology, has now reached a point where she "couldn't care less" about the make-up of the State of Israel. "I'm not Zionist," she explained, "but at the same time I'm not anti-Zionist either. It is acceptable to be neither," she continued. "It's the death of idealism; and it's the same with a huge number of my generation across the country."

Despite being encouraged to play an active role in left-wing campaigning during her youth, Carmel freely admits that she was inspired more by her peers than by any burning desire to effect change in her homeland, hence her reluctance to continue her activism upon leaving the kibbutz. "It's not 'cool' to be leftwing anymore,", she said. "It used to be about being macho, being in the best army units, and working the land."

Now, however, "people want out of the army, and if you are a farmer on a kibbutz, everyone calls you a sucker and says 'go and work in the stock market.'" Despite being born and raised in the kibbutz movement, her parents left Merhavia "at the first opportunity, and never looked back". The kibbutz movement, which has died a slow death over recent years, "failed because it ate itself", according to Carmel.

"It's an inhuman ideology; human nature is to want more, and to never be satisfied with what you have," she explained. "Which is why we have phrases like 'the sky's the limit' and 'the grass is always greener on the other side'. If you live on a kibbutz near to a city and you see someone your age driving a new Audi, you get frustrated and think 'why shouldn't I have that too?'"

After serving as a commander in the IDF, Carmel entered the business world: "capitalism is much easier to identify with [than socialism and leftwing politics]," she said. Her pulling away from her childhood encoding has left her cynical about the Israeli left's future prospects. "The leftwing here are finished, especially after the kibbutz movement collapsed; whereas the rightwing continue to thrive on hatred and religious indoctrination."

Religion is to blame for much of the region's woes, according to Carmel, who feels no spiritual connection whatsoever to the land of Israel. "The religious rightwing dwell on the past, [to the point that] they're willing to sacrifice their future to preserve a two thousand year old tradition," she commented. "I understand why we don't give up the Golan Heights , as they're strategically important and necessary for our security, but the Wailing Wall in Jerusalem? If it gives us trouble, then fighting for it is a stupid idea."

She can't see things changing for the better in the near future either. "It'll be exactly the same in twenty years: the occupation will continue, there'll still be terror attacks, and people will still be scared of each other." She has reached a point where "I don't talk about politics anymore with my friends; we've become cynical and numb like no other country has.".

Instead of a passionate political movement emerging from within Israeli society, Carmel expects the political climate to continue being dictated by American policy.

"We just do what the U.S. says," she said. "They're our mum and dad, and we're not stupid – we don't want our inheritance cut off. If their government goes to the right, so will we; if they go left, we'll follow also. It's got nothing to do with what Israelis think."

On the face of it, her assessment of the state of play seems pretty pessimistic, at least in terms of rallying support for change from within. However, Israelis' apathy and their desire to embrace capitalism like their peers in the West could well prove fertile ground for a rejection of ultra-nationalism and continued conflict with the Palestinians.

After all, as Carmel put it, "the idea of a Jewish state [exclusively] for Jewish people is the exact opposite of capitalism. In the rest of the world, people care about the price of goods, not who made them. Here, some people are happy to pay extra, just because the products were made in the settlements and they want to support their ideology."

As more and more young Israelis reject the continued expense of propping up the settlement enterprise – with all of the embedded security expense, the state subsidies provided to the settlers, and so on – the more difficult it will be to justify their continued existence.

The only way out of the impasse is to sideline those for whom religious and nationalist fervour has replaced all other emotions and principles, and quick. If socialism's death allows capitalism to flourish in its stead, then – whilst it may appear unpalatable to the old guard of Israeli politics – at least it might bear unexpected fruit in terms of bringing peace with the Palestinians.

The best remedy for the region's ills is to encourage Carmel's (and my) generation of Israelis and *olim* to realise that there is an alternative to never-ending hostilities and conflict with our neighbours. Her experience shows that there is another way; that nationalism and imperialism only thrives where there is a dearth of other options – capitalism being just one of the possible substitutes. In order for both Israelis and Palestinians to reject the lure of extremism and fundamentalism, they need to be shown that their lives – and the lives of their children – can be greatly enriched by taking a different path.

That different path can take many forms; for some it may mean the pursuit of material wealth, for others the acquisition of academic learning or scientific expertise. However, the common strand between all of these myriad possibilities is that they can best be achieved in a climate free from war and hate, and it is in the interests of all citizens on both sides of the Green Line to herald in such a new dawn.

Zionism achieved one of its primary goals, that of bringing the Jewish people back to dwell in the land of their forefathers, and for that I am grateful. But those at the helm of the Zionist ship went too far, and Israeli and Palestinian society has been paying the price ever since the moment Zionism's leaders began exploiting and expelling the non-Jewish populace under their control. In an era when many of Israel's own children describe themselves as "neither Zionist nor anti-Zionist", surely now is the time to chart a new course for the next sixty years. If we don't, then all the signs point to another sixty years of hatred and fear, and the decline of the region into even deeper cycles of violence and war. But if we do, then we will have made far more than just the desert bloom; we will have removed one of the major thorns in the side of global coexistence, by providing the ultimate model for reconciliation and resolution for all the world to admire.

Jerusalem and London
November, 2008

---

[25] A pro-Palestinian advocate of "two states", son of Holocaust survivors, and loathed by the Zionist right.